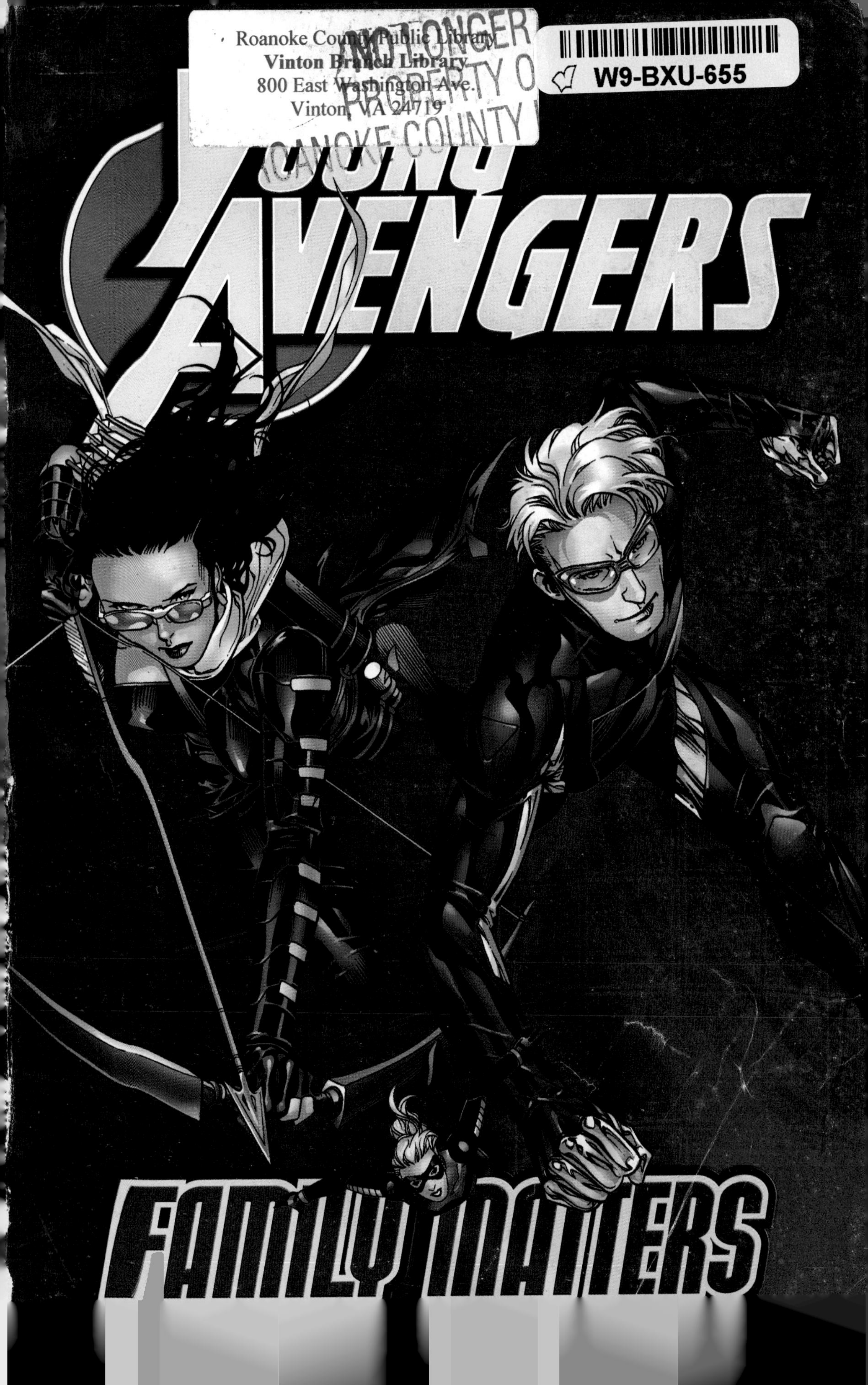
YOUNG AVENGERS
FAMILY MATTERS

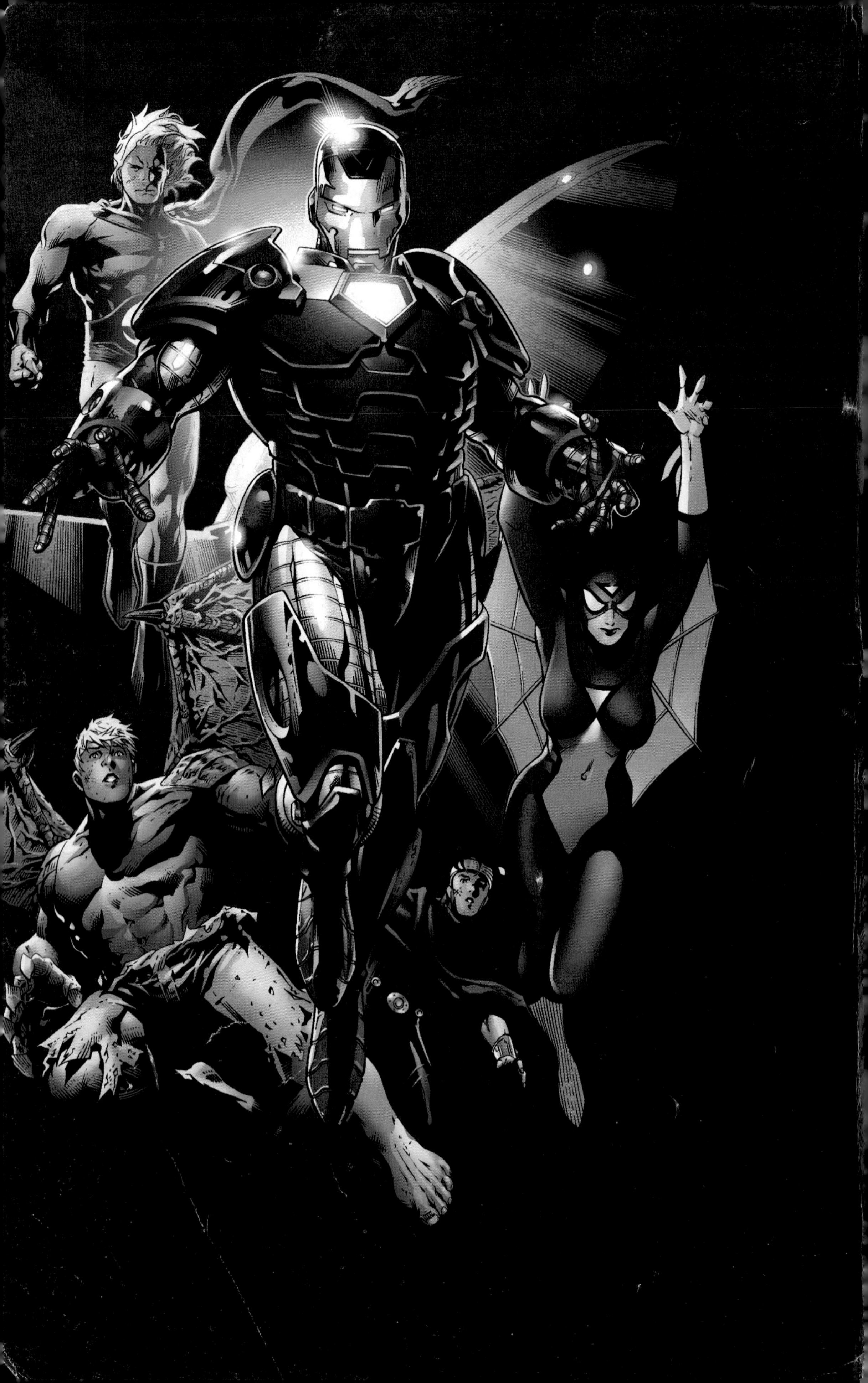

# YOUNG AVENGERS
## FAMILY MATTERS

WRITER: **ALLAN HEINBERG**

PENCILERS: **ANDREA DIVITO (ISSUES #7-8) & JIM CHEUNG**

INKERS: **DREW HENNESSY (ISSUES #7-8), DAVE MEIKIS, JOHN DELL, ROB STULL, DEXTER VINES, LIVESAV, JAY LEISTEN, MATT RYAN, JAIME MENDOZA, MARK MORALES & JIM CHEUNG**

COLORIST: **JUSTIN PONSOR**

LETTERER: **VIRTUAL CALLIGRAPHY'S CORY PETIT**
COVER ART: **JIM CHEUNG, JOHN DELL & JUSTIN PONSOR**
ASSISTANT EDITORS: **MOLLY LAZER & AUBREY SITTERSON**
ASSOCIATE EDITOR: **ANDY SCHMIDT**
EDITOR: **TOM BREVOORT**

YOUNG AVENGERS CREATED BY ALLAN HEINBERG & JIM CHEUNG

YOUNG AVENGERS SPECIAL #1
PAGES 1, 2, 8, 9, 20, 21, 25, 26 & 34-36:
ARTIST: **MICHAEL GAYDOS**
COLORIST: **JOSE VILLARRUBIA**
PAGES 3-7:
ARTIST: **NEAL ADAMS**
COLORIST: **JUSTIN PONSOR**
PAGES 10-14:
ARTIST: **GENE HA**
COLORIST: **ART LYON**
PAGES: 15-19:
ARTIST: **JAE LEE**
COLORIST: **JUNE CHUNG**
PAGES 22-24:
ARTIST: **BILL SIENKIEWICZ**
COLORIST: **JUSTIN PONSOR**
PAGES: 27-33:
ARTIST: **PASQUAL FERRY**
COLORIST: **DAVE MCCAIG**

COLLECTION EDITOR: **JENNIFER GRÜNWALD**
ASSISTANT EDITOR: **MICHAEL SHORT**
ASSOCIATE EDITOR: **MARK D. BEAZLEY**
SENIOR EDITOR, SPECIAL PROJECTS: **JEFF YOUNGQUIST**
VICE PRESIDENT OF SALES: **DAWN GABRIEL**

PRODUCTION: **JERRON QUALITY COLOR**
VICE PRESIDENT OF CREATIVE: **TOM MARVELLI**

EDITOR IN CHIEF: **JOE QUESADA**
PUBLISHER: **DAN BUCKLEY**

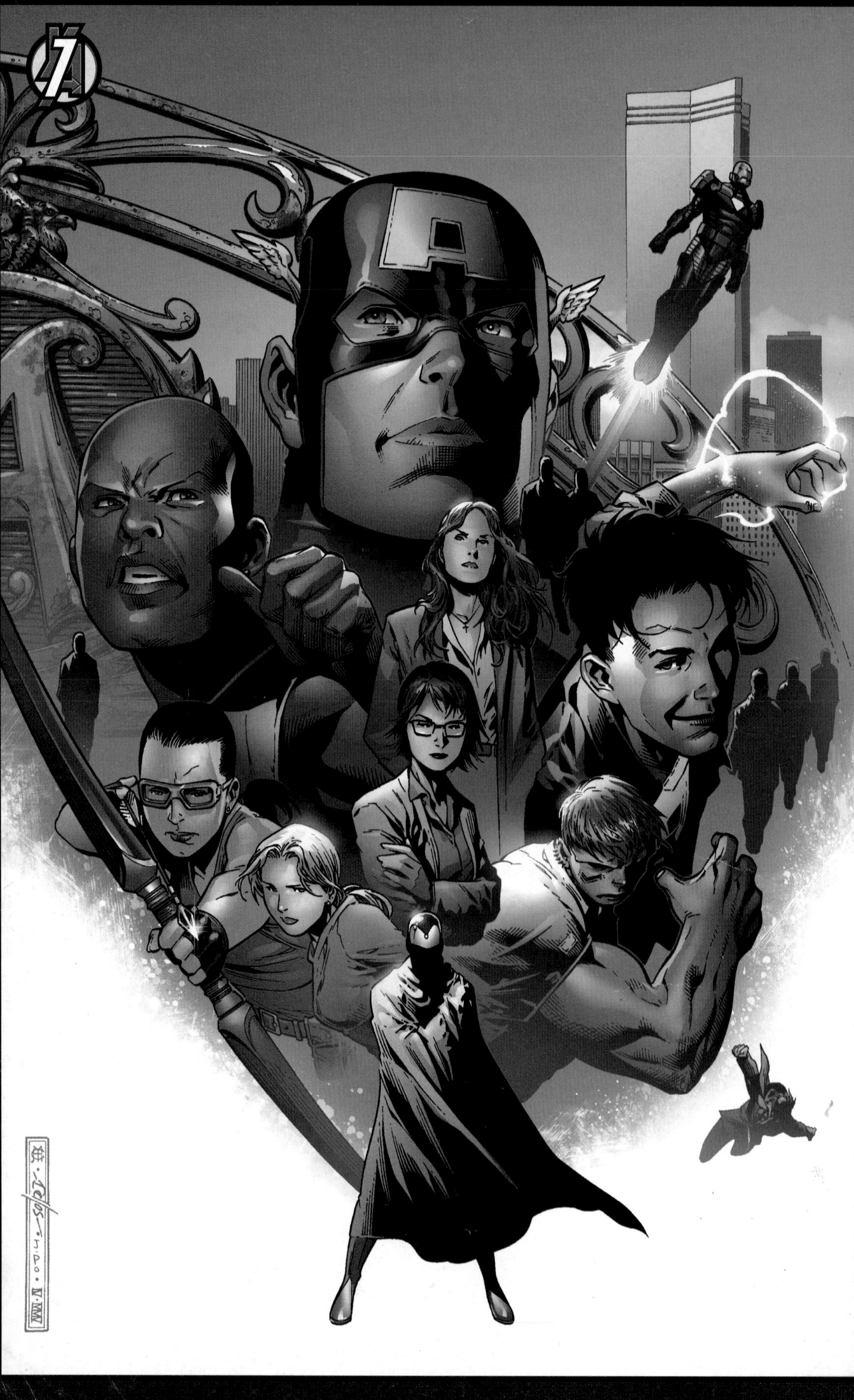

# DAILY BUGLE

# THE NEW YOUNG AVENGERS?

WHAT THE HELL DO THESE KIDS THINK THEY'RE DOING?

-Photo by Todd Casey

The reinvented supergroup brings a "shocking" end to attempt... ...st. The Young Avengers proudly display their quarry, The Shocker, amid the fluttering evidence of his failure. One hundred percent of the... ...was recovered. The Shocker is currently in custody.

By Bugle Reporter Kat Farrell
Staff Writer

Dolor sit amet, consectetuer adipiscing elit, sed diam nonummy nibh euismod tincidunt ut laoreet dolore magna on aliquam erat volutpat. Ut wisi enim ad twe minim veniam, quis nostrud exerci tatio ullamcorper suscipit lobortis nisl ut ang.

Eliquip ex ea commodo consequat. Duis ... vel eum iriure dolor a hendrerit in

cumsan ... usto odio dignissim qui blandit praese... ...ptatum zzril delenit augue duis dolore ... feugait nulla facilisi.

Ut w... enim ad minim veniam, quis nostrud ...erci tation ullamcorper suscipit lobort... nisl ut aliquip ex ea commodo conseq... t. Duis autem vel eum iriure dolor in he... rerit in vulputate velit esse molestie co... sequat, vel illum dolore eu feugiat n... la facilisis at vero eros et accumsan et i... sto odio dignissim qui blandit praesent ... ptatum zzril delenit augue duis dolore te ... insum dolor

drerit in vulputate velit esse molestie consequat, vel illum dolore eu feugiat nulla facilisis at vero eros et accumsan et iusto odio dignissim qui blandit praesent lupta tum zzril delenit augue duis dolore te wh feugait nulla facilisi.

Bolfang iktum dolor sit amet, fanstaticv adipiscing elit, sed diam nonummy nibl euismod tincidunt ut laoreet dolore ma aliquam erat volutpat.

Duis autem vel eum iriure dolor in her drerit in vulputate velit esse molestie ... nostrud exerci tation ulla

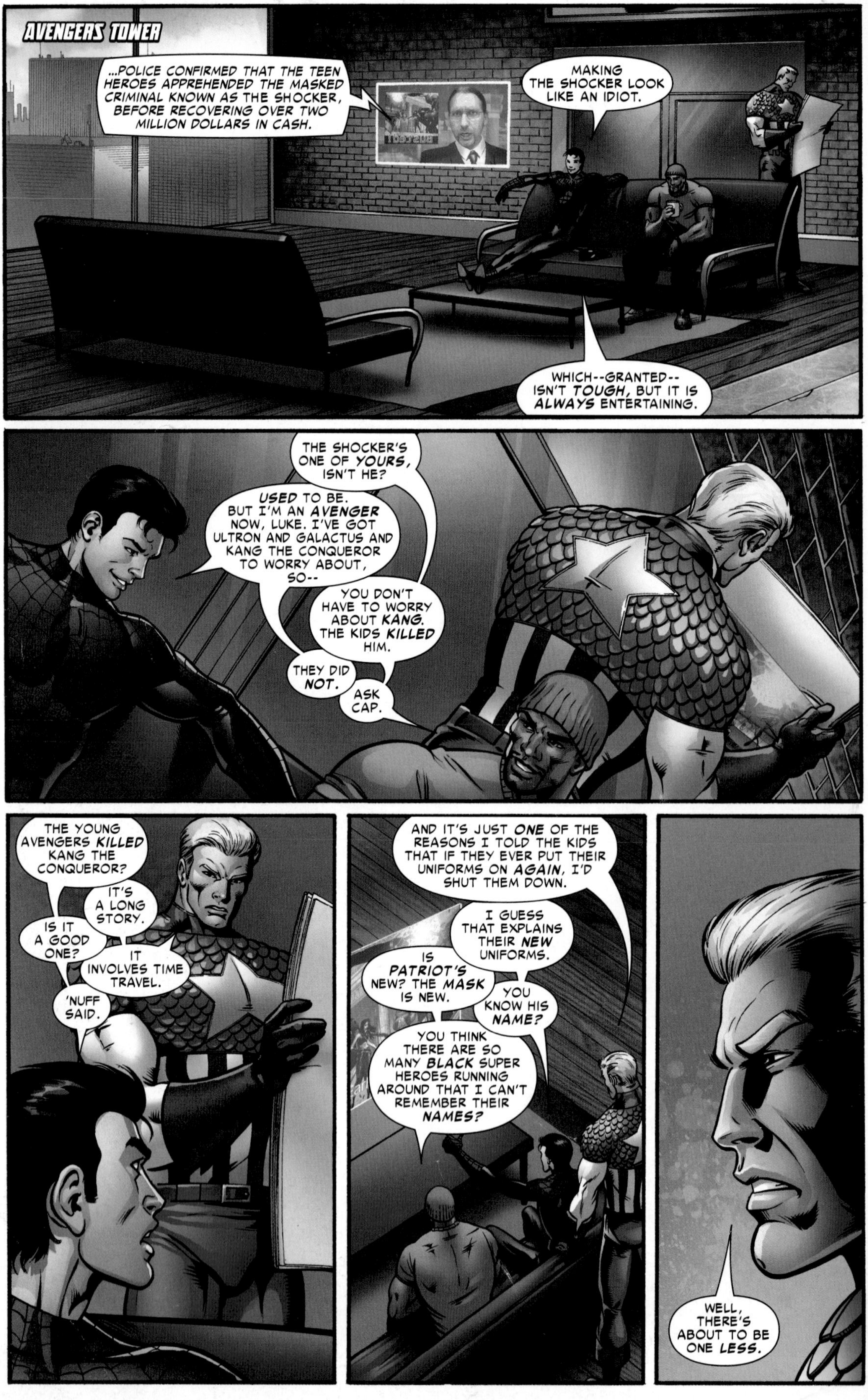
AVENGERS TOWER
...POLICE CONFIRMED THAT THE TEEN HEROES APPREHENDED THE MASKED CRIMINAL KNOWN AS THE SHOCKER, BEFORE RECOVERING OVER TWO MILLION DOLLARS IN CASH.
MAKING THE SHOCKER LOOK LIKE AN IDIOT.
WHICH--GRANTED--ISN'T TOUGH, BUT IT IS ALWAYS ENTERTAINING.
THE SHOCKER'S ONE OF YOURS, ISN'T HE?
USED TO BE. BUT I'M AN AVENGER NOW, LUKE. I'VE GOT ULTRON AND GALACTUS AND KANG THE CONQUEROR TO WORRY ABOUT, SO--
YOU DON'T HAVE TO WORRY ABOUT KANG. THE KIDS KILLED HIM.
THEY DID NOT.
ASK CAP.
THE YOUNG AVENGERS KILLED KANG THE CONQUEROR?
IT'S A LONG STORY.
IS IT A GOOD ONE?
IT INVOLVES TIME TRAVEL.
'NUFF SAID.
AND IT'S JUST ONE OF THE REASONS I TOLD THE KIDS THAT IF THEY EVER PUT THEIR UNIFORMS ON AGAIN, I'D SHUT THEM DOWN.
I GUESS THAT EXPLAINS THEIR NEW UNIFORMS.
IS PATRIOT'S NEW? THE MASK IS NEW.
YOU KNOW HIS NAME?
YOU THINK THERE ARE SO MANY BLACK SUPER HEROES RUNNING AROUND THAT I CAN'T REMEMBER THEIR NAMES?
WELL, THERE'S ABOUT TO BE ONE LESS.

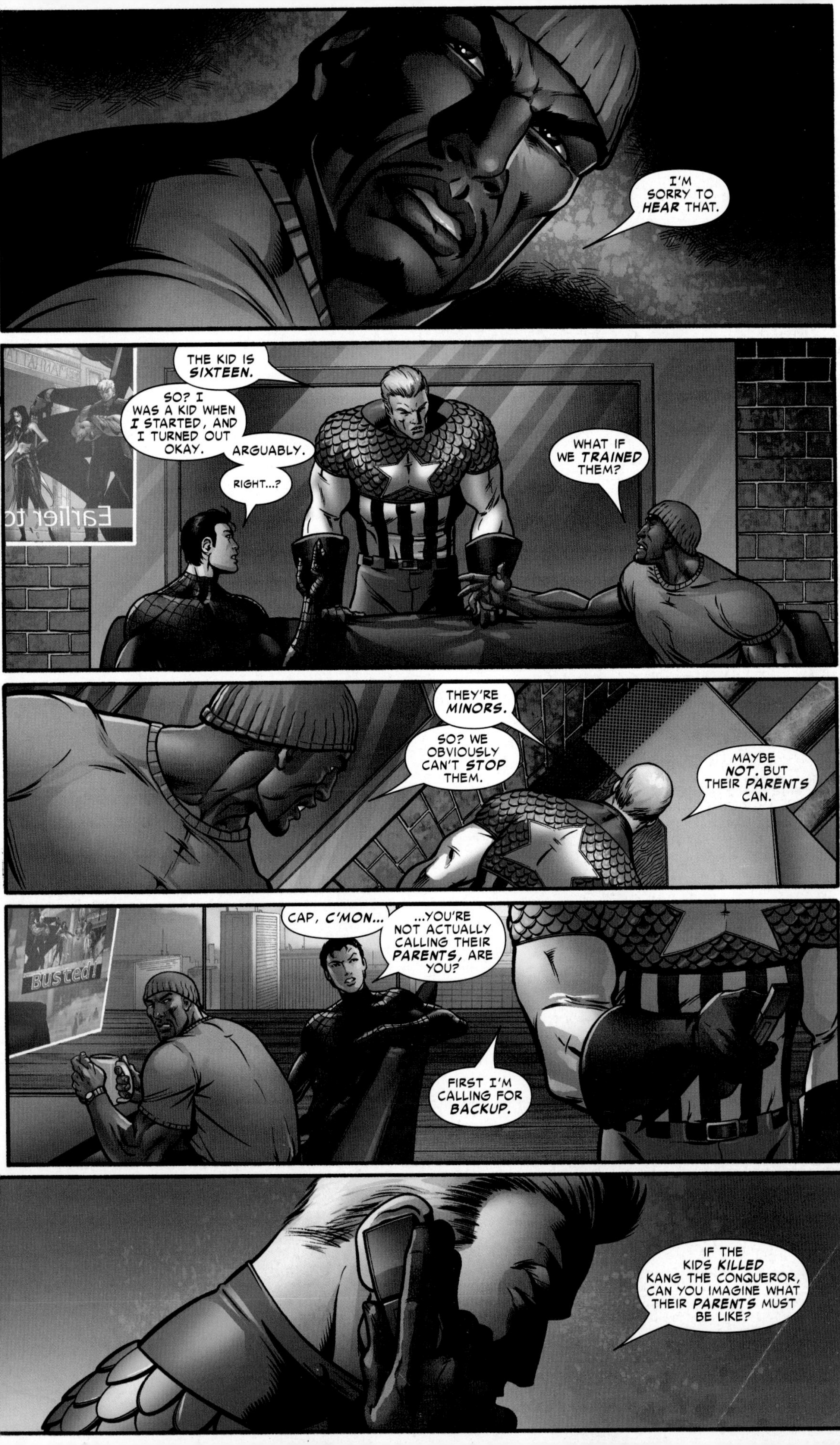
I'M SORRY TO HEAR THAT.
THE KID IS SIXTEEN.
SO? I WAS A KID WHEN I STARTED, AND I TURNED OUT OKAY.
ARGUABLY.
RIGHT...?
WHAT IF WE TRAINED THEM?
Earlier to
THEY'RE MINORS.
SO? WE OBVIOUSLY CAN'T STOP THEM.
MAYBE NOT. BUT THEIR PARENTS CAN.
Busted!
CAP, C'MON...
...YOU'RE NOT ACTUALLY CALLING THEIR PARENTS, ARE YOU?
FIRST I'M CALLING FOR BACKUP.
IF THE KIDS KILLED KANG THE CONQUEROR, CAN YOU IMAGINE WHAT THEIR PARENTS MUST BE LIKE?

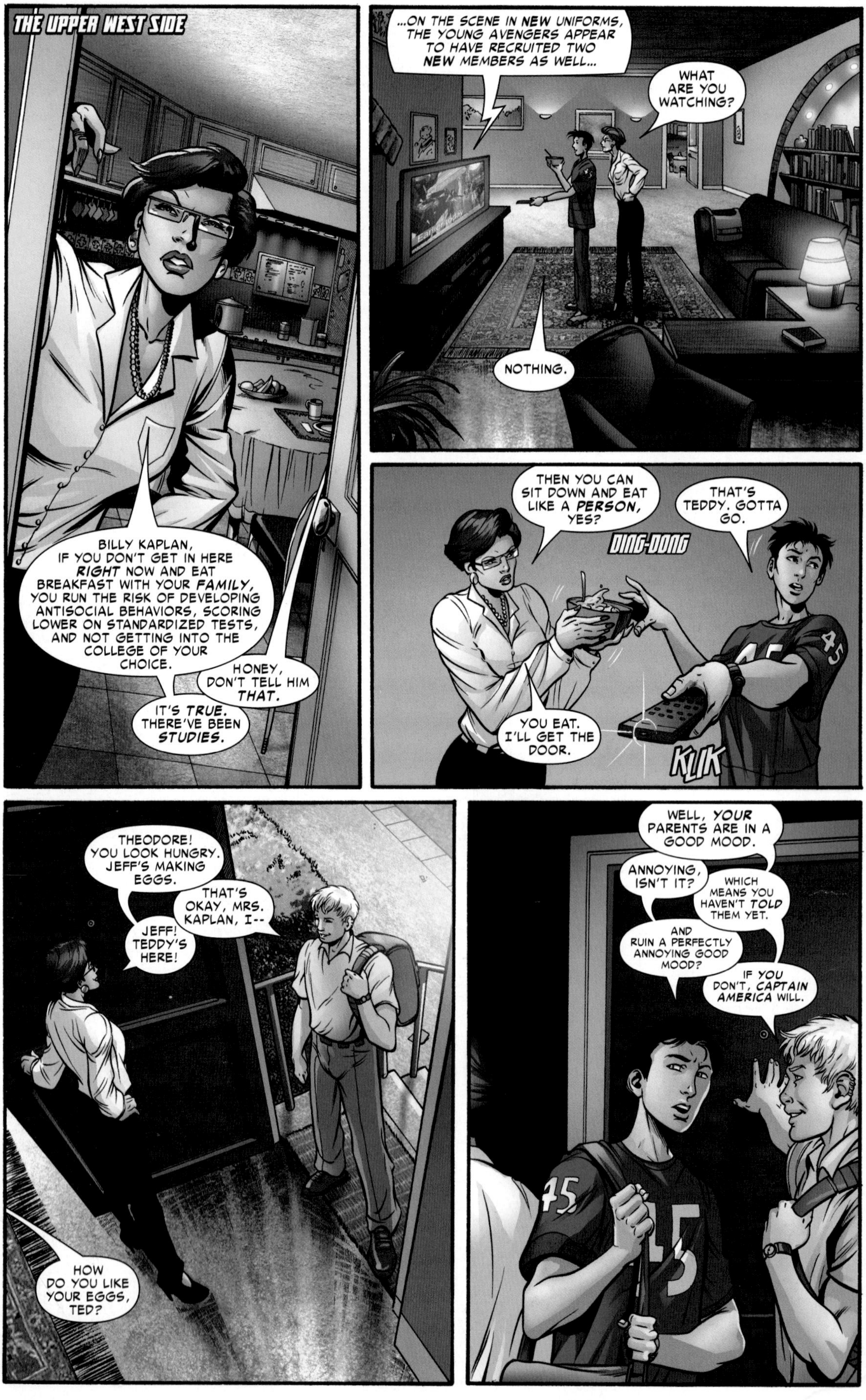
THE UPPER WEST SIDE
BILLY KAPLAN, IF YOU DON'T GET IN HERE RIGHT NOW AND EAT BREAKFAST WITH YOUR FAMILY, YOU RUN THE RISK OF DEVELOPING ANTISOCIAL BEHAVIORS, SCORING LOWER ON STANDARDIZED TESTS, AND NOT GETTING INTO THE COLLEGE OF YOUR CHOICE.
HONEY, DON'T TELL HIM THAT.
IT'S TRUE. THERE'VE BEEN STUDIES.
...ON THE SCENE IN NEW UNIFORMS, THE YOUNG AVENGERS APPEAR TO HAVE RECRUITED TWO NEW MEMBERS AS WELL...
WHAT ARE YOU WATCHING?
NOTHING.
THEN YOU CAN SIT DOWN AND EAT LIKE A PERSON, YES?
DING-DONG
THAT'S TEDDY. GOTTA GO.
YOU EAT. I'LL GET THE DOOR.
KLIK
THEODORE! YOU LOOK HUNGRY. JEFF'S MAKING EGGS.
THAT'S OKAY, MRS. KAPLAN, I--
JEFF! TEDDY'S HERE!
HOW DO YOU LIKE YOUR EGGS, TED?
WELL, YOUR PARENTS ARE IN A GOOD MOOD.
ANNOYING, ISN'T IT?
WHICH MEANS YOU HAVEN'T TOLD THEM YET.
AND RUIN A PERFECTLY ANNOYING GOOD MOOD?
IF YOU DON'T, CAPTAIN AMERICA WILL.

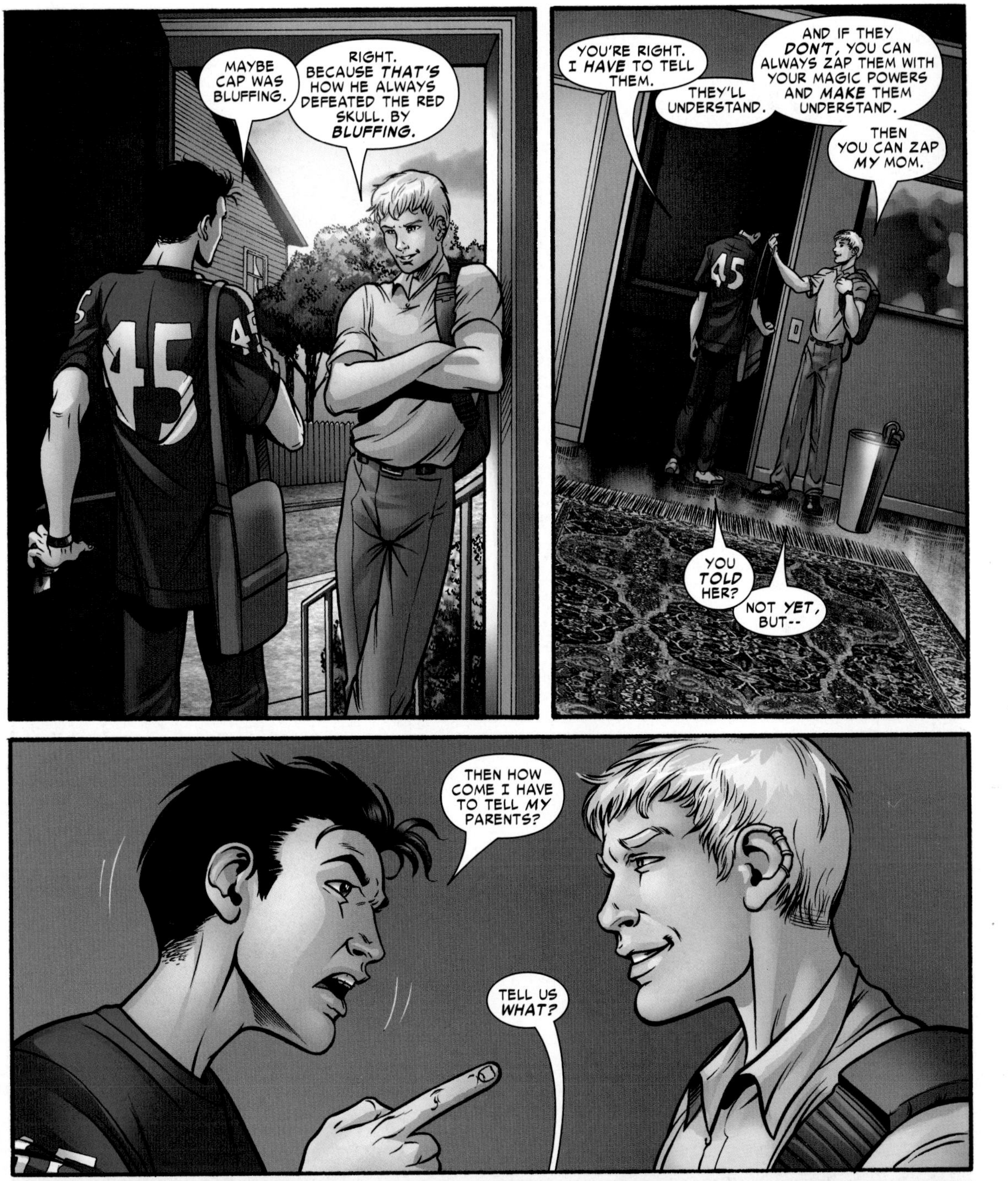
MAYBE CAP WAS BLUFFING.
RIGHT. BECAUSE THAT'S HOW HE ALWAYS DEFEATED THE RED SKULL. BY BLUFFING.
YOU'RE RIGHT. I HAVE TO TELL THEM.
THEY'LL UNDERSTAND.
AND IF THEY DON'T, YOU CAN ALWAYS ZAP THEM WITH YOUR MAGIC POWERS AND MAKE THEM UNDERSTAND.
THEN YOU CAN ZAP MY MOM.
YOU TOLD HER?
NOT YET, BUT--
THEN HOW COME I HAVE TO TELL MY PARENTS?
TELL US WHAT?
WHAT IS IT, SON?

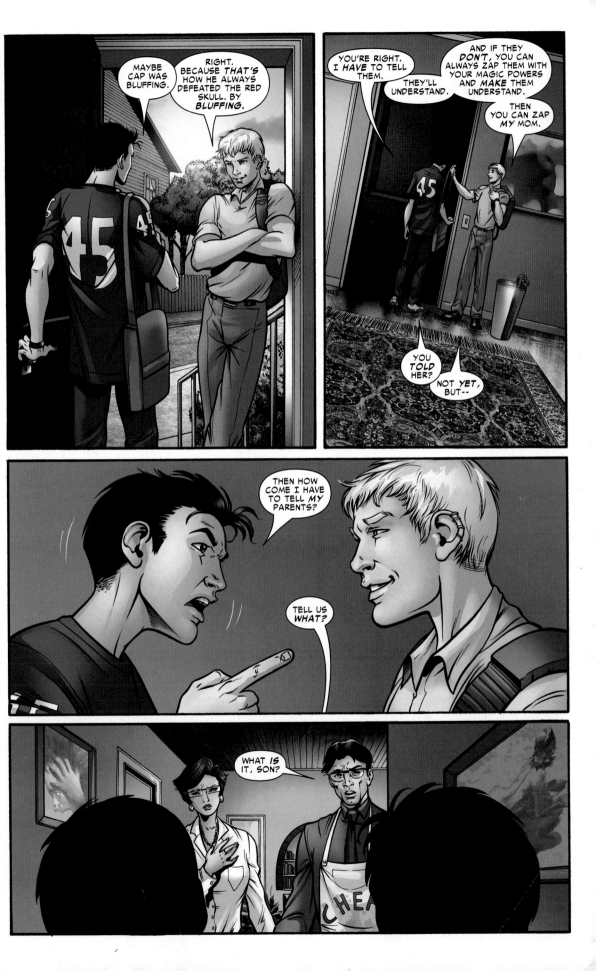

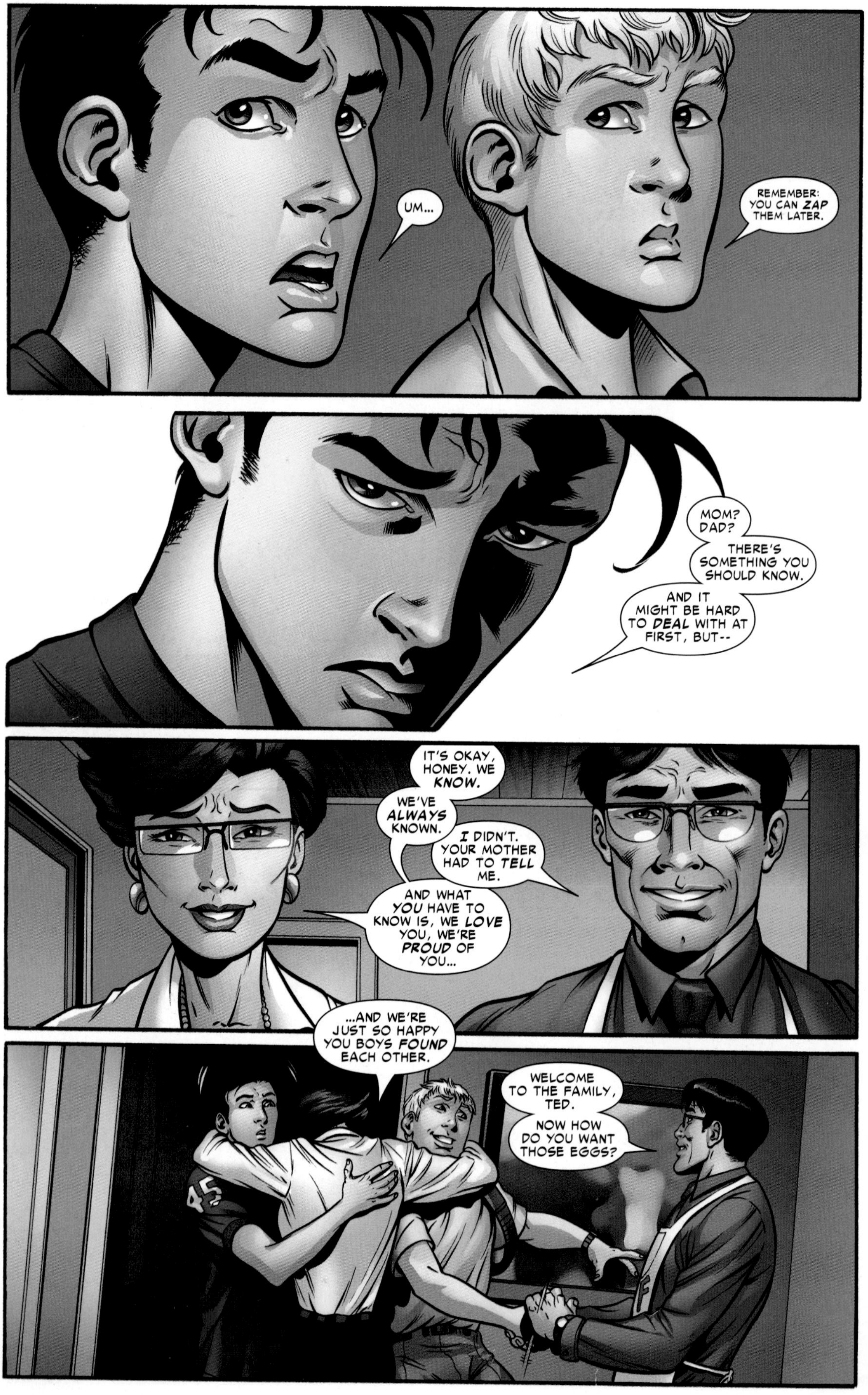
UM...
REMEMBER: YOU CAN ZAP THEM LATER.
MOM? DAD?
THERE'S SOMETHING YOU SHOULD KNOW.
AND IT MIGHT BE HARD TO DEAL WITH AT FIRST, BUT--
IT'S OKAY, HONEY. WE KNOW.
WE'VE ALWAYS KNOWN.
I DIDN'T. YOUR MOTHER HAD TO TELL ME.
AND WHAT YOU HAVE TO KNOW IS, WE LOVE YOU, WE'RE PROUD OF YOU...
...AND WE'RE JUST SO HAPPY YOU BOYS FOUND EACH OTHER.
WELCOME TO THE FAMILY, TED.
NOW HOW DO YOU WANT THOSE EGGS?

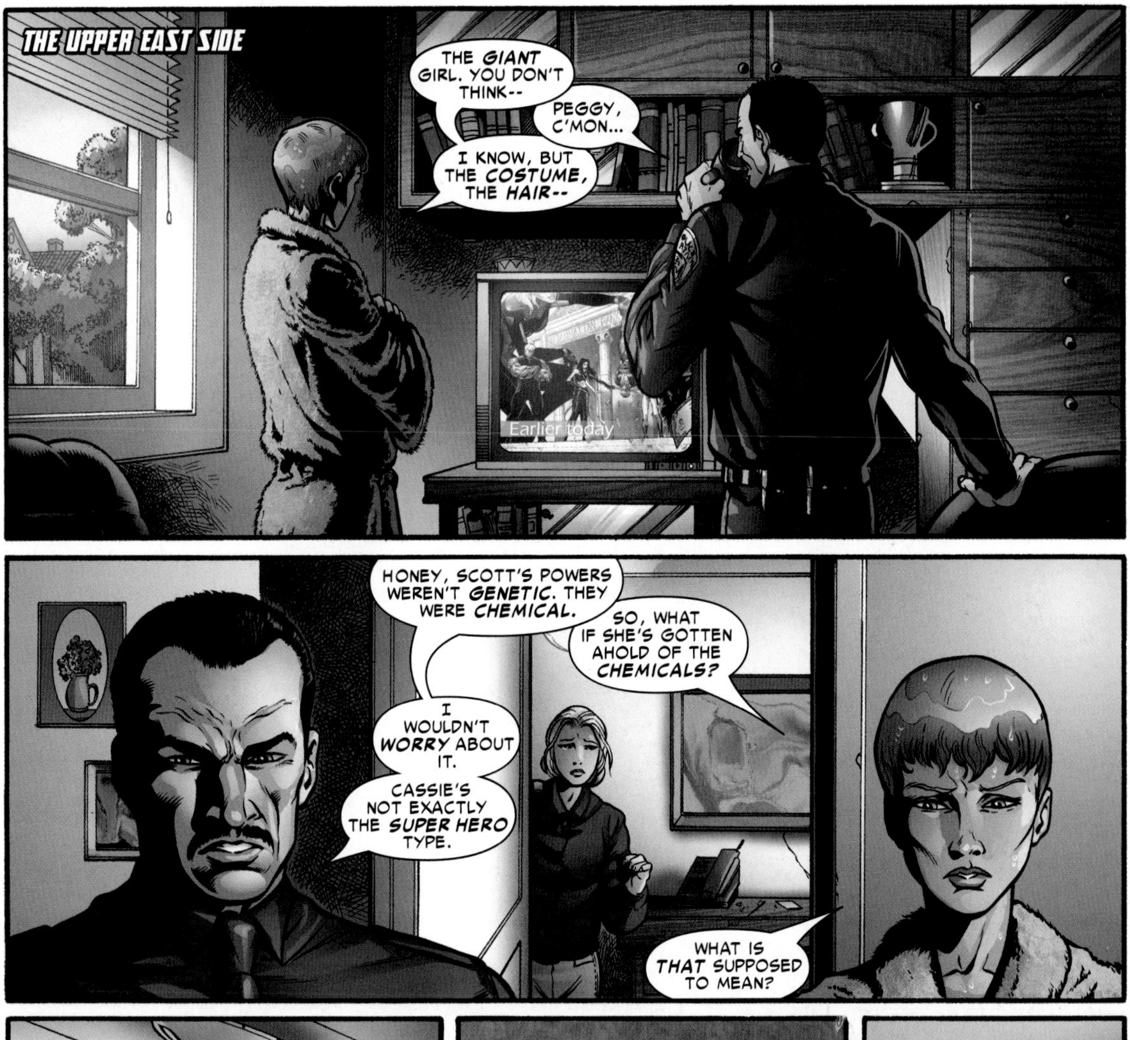
THE UPPER EAST SIDE
THE GIANT GIRL. YOU DON'T THINK--
PEGGY, C'MON...
I KNOW, BUT THE COSTUME, THE HAIR--
Earlier today
HONEY, SCOTT'S POWERS WEREN'T GENETIC. THEY WERE CHEMICAL.
SO, WHAT IF SHE'S GOTTEN AHOLD OF THE CHEMICALS?
I WOULDN'T WORRY ABOUT IT.
CASSIE'S NOT EXACTLY THE SUPER HERO TYPE.
WHAT IS THAT SUPPOSED TO MEAN?
IT MEANS SHE CAN BARELY FOCUS LONG ENOUGH TO DO HER HOMEWORK, LET ALONE CAPTURE THE SHOCKER.
BESIDES, CASSIE KNOWS HOW YOU FELT ABOUT HER DAD BEING ANT-MAN.
THERE'S NO WAY SHE'D PUT YOU THROUGH THAT AGAIN.
SHE LOVES YOU TOO MUCH.

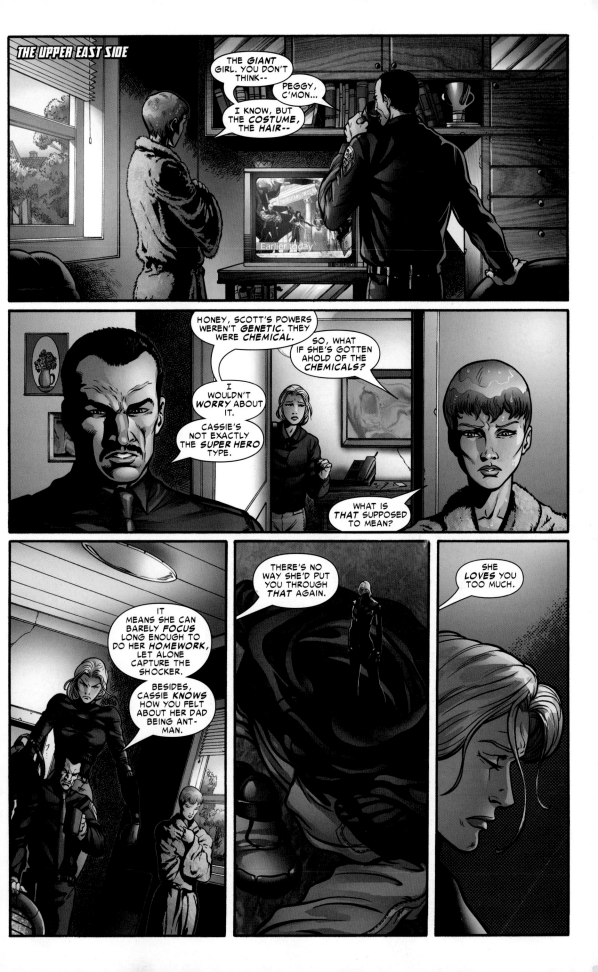

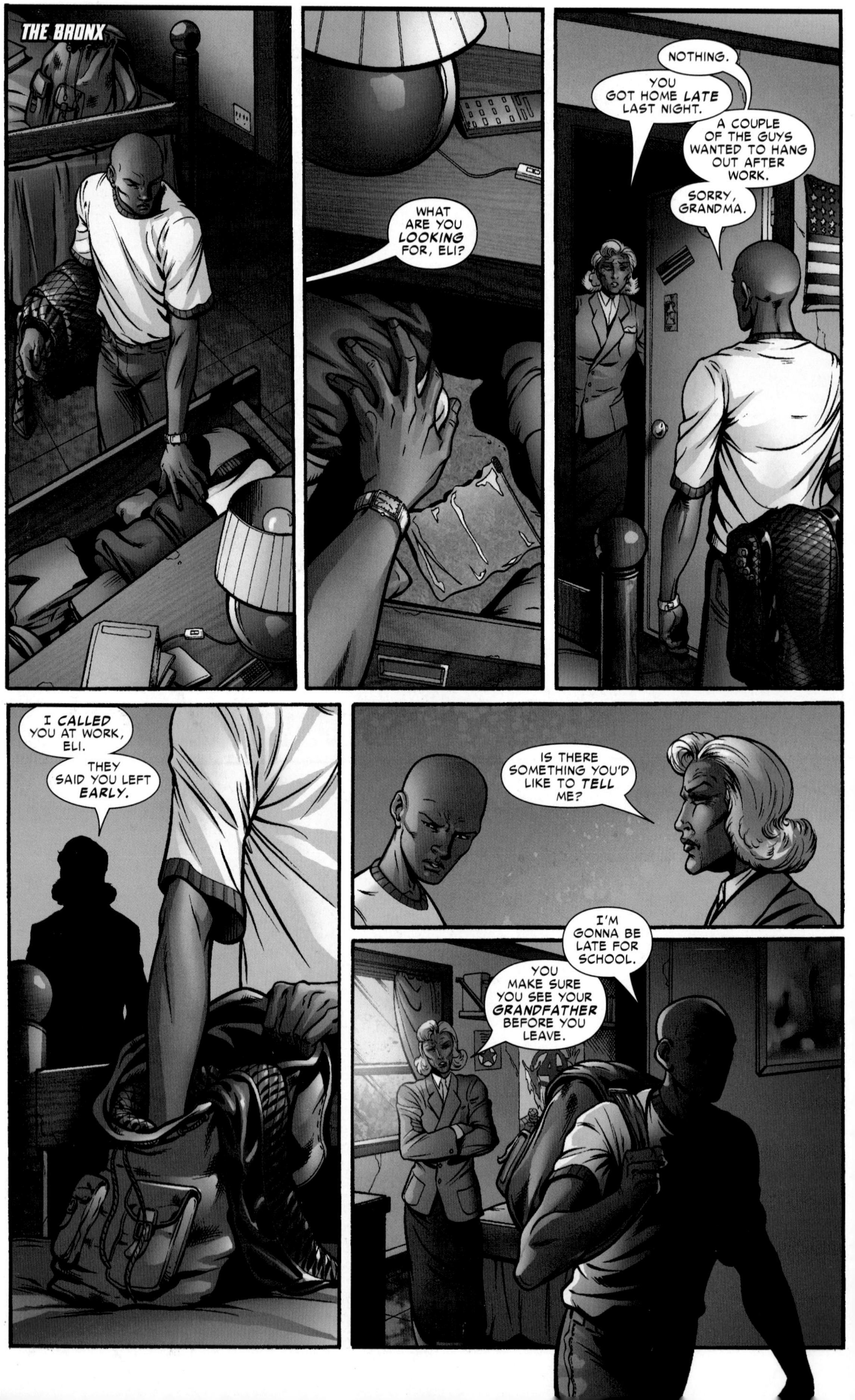

THE BRONX
WHAT ARE YOU LOOKING FOR, ELI?
NOTHING.
YOU GOT HOME LATE LAST NIGHT.
A COUPLE OF THE GUYS WANTED TO HANG OUT AFTER WORK.
SORRY, GRANDMA.
I CALLED YOU AT WORK, ELI.
THEY SAID YOU LEFT EARLY.
IS THERE SOMETHING YOU'D LIKE TO TELL ME?
I'M GONNA BE LATE FOR SCHOOL.
YOU MAKE SURE YOU SEE YOUR GRANDFATHER BEFORE YOU LEAVE.

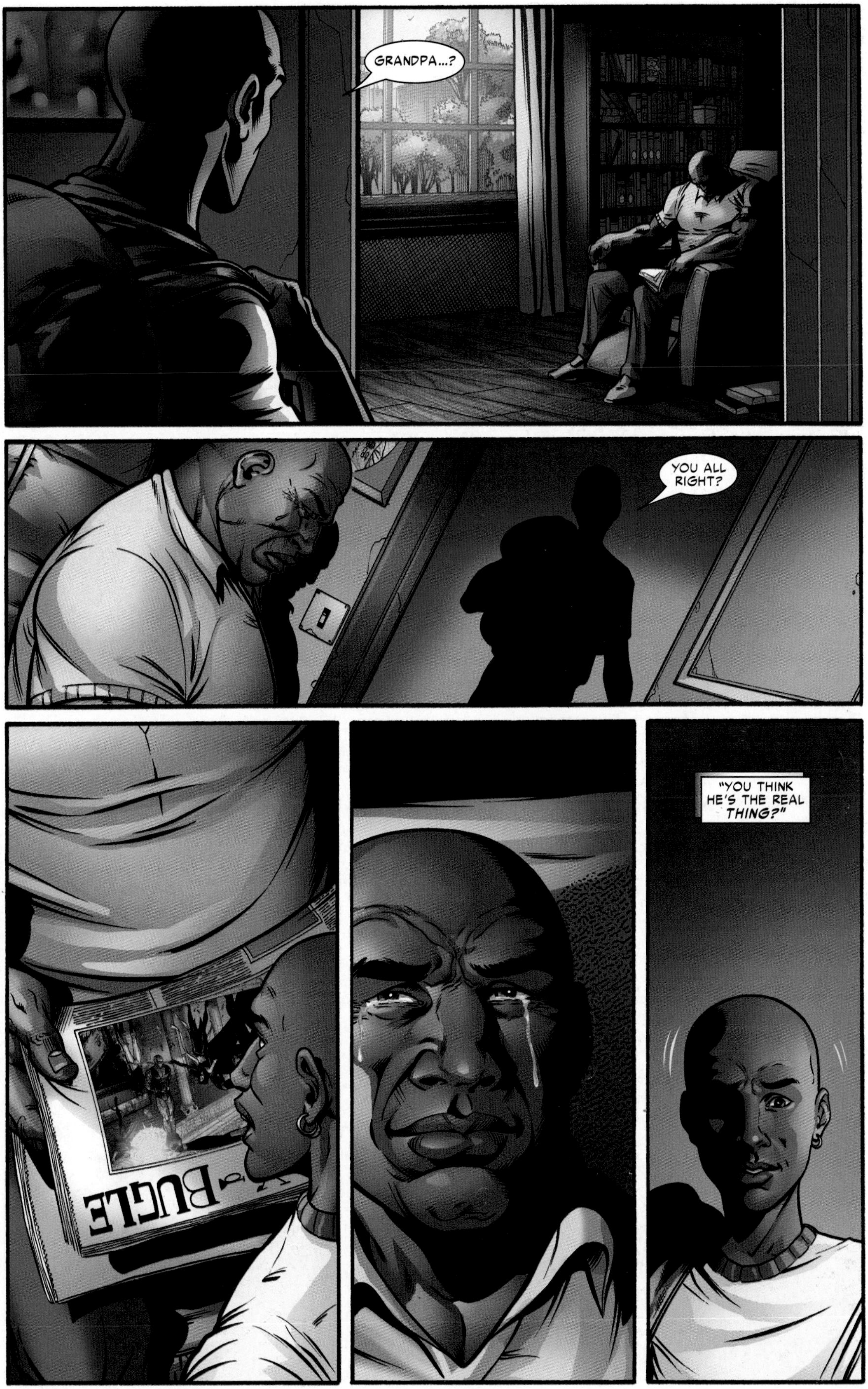
GRANDPA...?
YOU ALL RIGHT?
BUGLE
"YOU THINK HE'S THE REAL THING?"

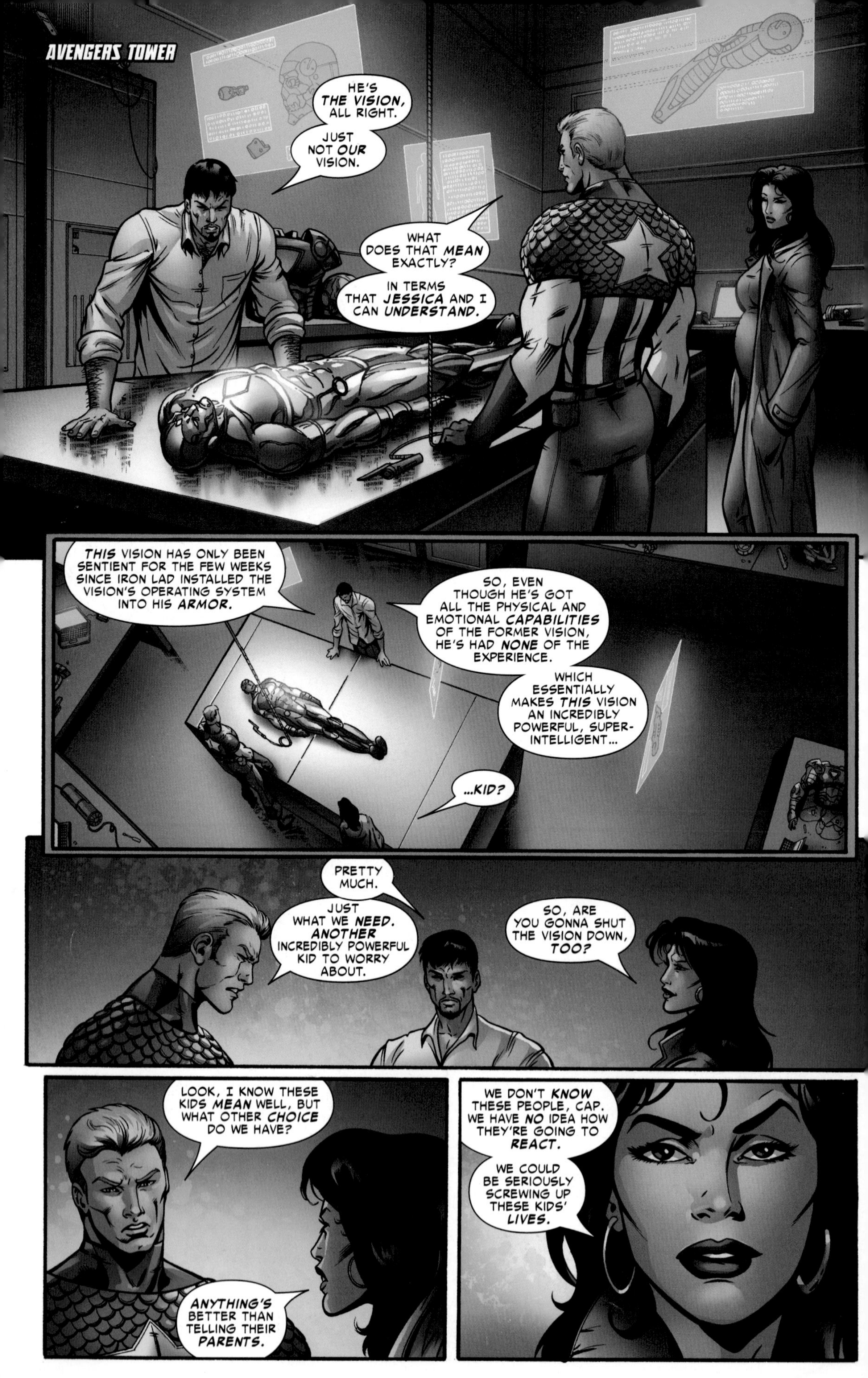
AVENGERS TOWER
HE'S THE VISION, ALL RIGHT.
JUST NOT OUR VISION.
WHAT DOES THAT MEAN EXACTLY?
IN TERMS THAT JESSICA AND I CAN UNDERSTAND.
THIS VISION HAS ONLY BEEN SENTIENT FOR THE FEW WEEKS SINCE IRON LAD INSTALLED THE VISION'S OPERATING SYSTEM INTO HIS ARMOR.
SO, EVEN THOUGH HE'S GOT ALL THE PHYSICAL AND EMOTIONAL CAPABILITIES OF THE FORMER VISION, HE'S HAD NONE OF THE EXPERIENCE.
WHICH ESSENTIALLY MAKES THIS VISION AN INCREDIBLY POWERFUL, SUPER-INTELLIGENT...
...KID?
PRETTY MUCH.
JUST WHAT WE NEED. ANOTHER INCREDIBLY POWERFUL KID TO WORRY ABOUT.
SO, ARE YOU GONNA SHUT THE VISION DOWN, TOO?
LOOK, I KNOW THESE KIDS MEAN WELL, BUT WHAT OTHER CHOICE DO WE HAVE?
ANYTHING'S BETTER THAN TELLING THEIR PARENTS.
WE DON'T KNOW THESE PEOPLE, CAP. WE HAVE NO IDEA HOW THEY'RE GOING TO REACT.
WE COULD BE SERIOUSLY SCREWING UP THESE KIDS' LIVES.

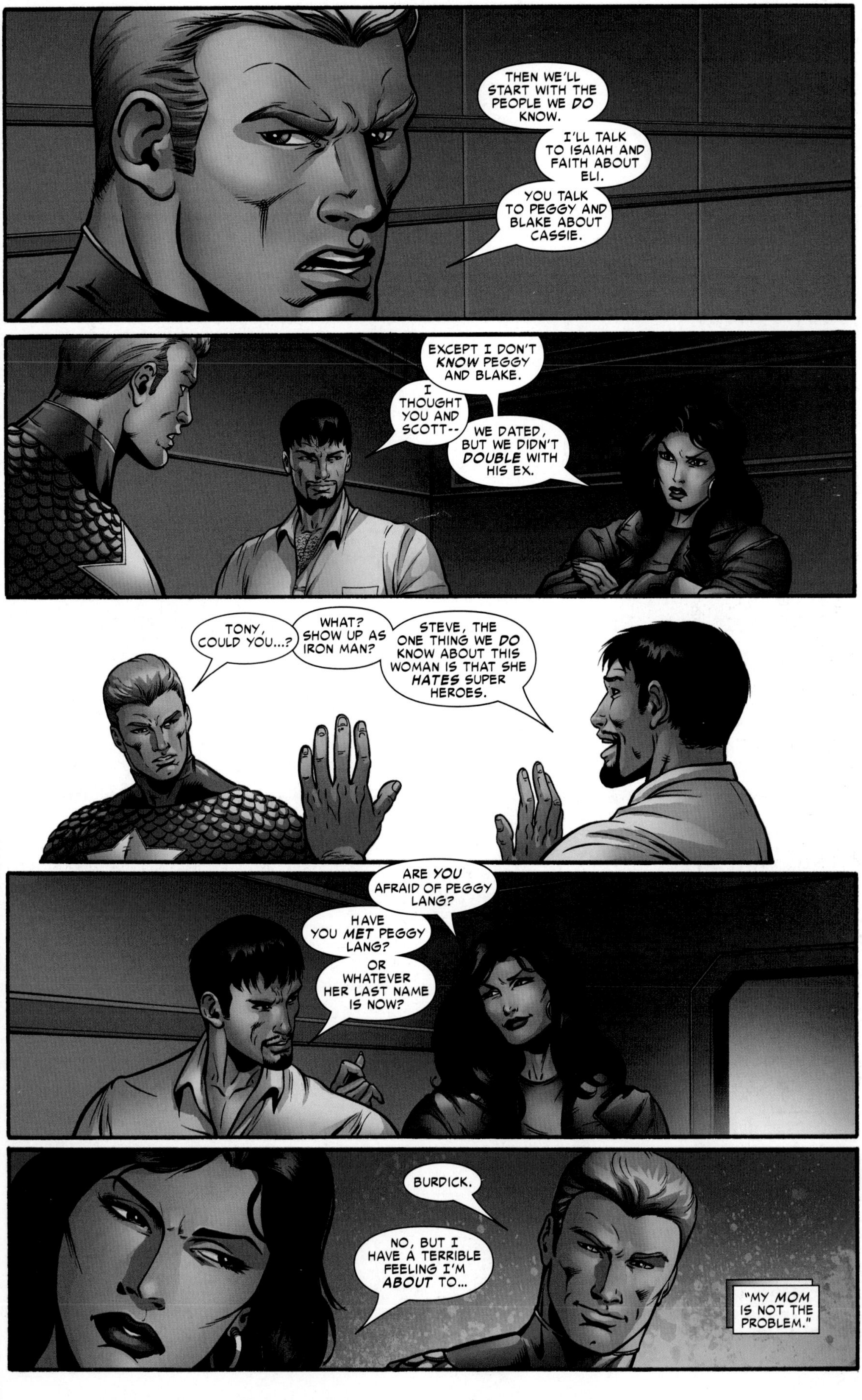
THEN WE'LL START WITH THE PEOPLE WE *DO* KNOW.
I'LL TALK TO ISAIAH AND FAITH ABOUT ELI.
YOU TALK TO PEGGY AND BLAKE ABOUT CASSIE.
EXCEPT I DON'T *KNOW* PEGGY AND BLAKE.
I THOUGHT YOU AND SCOTT--
WE DATED, BUT WE DIDN'T *DOUBLE* WITH HIS EX.
TONY, COULD YOU...?
WHAT? SHOW UP AS IRON MAN?
STEVE, THE ONE THING WE *DO* KNOW ABOUT THIS WOMAN IS THAT SHE *HATES* SUPER HEROES.
ARE *YOU* AFRAID OF PEGGY LANG?
HAVE YOU *MET* PEGGY LANG?
OR WHATEVER HER LAST NAME IS NOW?
BURDICK.
NO, BUT I HAVE A TERRIBLE FEELING I'M *ABOUT* TO...
"MY *MOM* IS NOT THE PROBLEM."

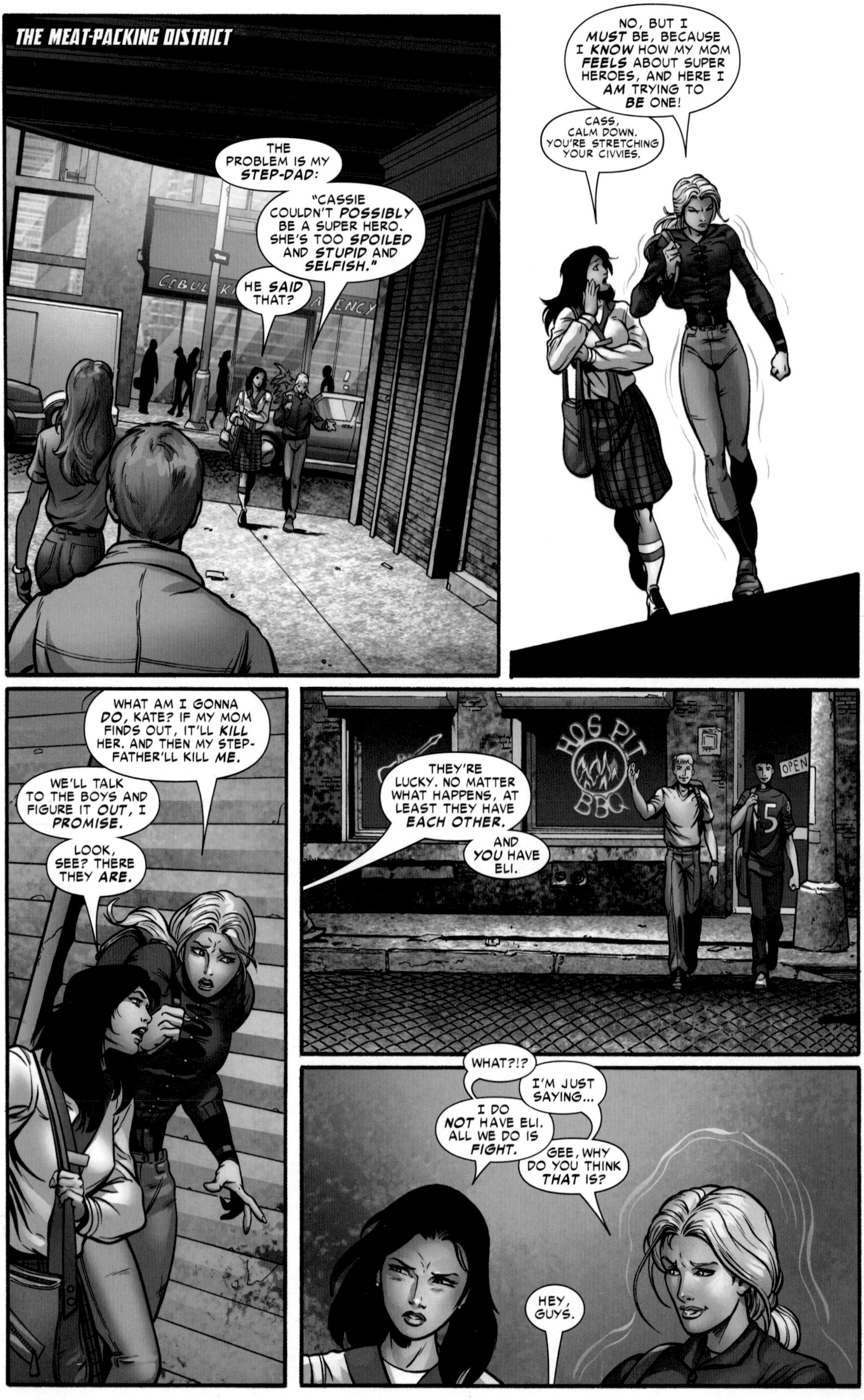
THE MEAT-PACKING DISTRICT
THE PROBLEM IS MY STEP-DAD:
"CASSIE COULDN'T POSSIBLY BE A SUPER HERO. SHE'S TOO SPOILED AND STUPID AND SELFISH."
HE SAID THAT?
NO, BUT I MUST BE, BECAUSE I KNOW HOW MY MOM FEELS ABOUT SUPER HEROES, AND HERE I AM TRYING TO BE ONE!
CASS, CALM DOWN. YOU'RE STRETCHING YOUR CIVVIES.
WHAT AM I GONNA DO, KATE? IF MY MOM FINDS OUT, IT'LL KILL HER. AND THEN MY STEP-FATHER'LL KILL ME.
WE'LL TALK TO THE BOYS AND FIGURE IT OUT, I PROMISE.
LOOK, SEE? THERE THEY ARE.
HOG PIT BBQ
OPEN
THEY'RE LUCKY. NO MATTER WHAT HAPPENS, AT LEAST THEY HAVE EACH OTHER.
AND YOU HAVE ELI.
WHAT?!?
I'M JUST SAYING...
I DO NOT HAVE ELI. ALL WE DO IS FIGHT.
GEE, WHY DO YOU THINK THAT IS?
HEY, GUYS.

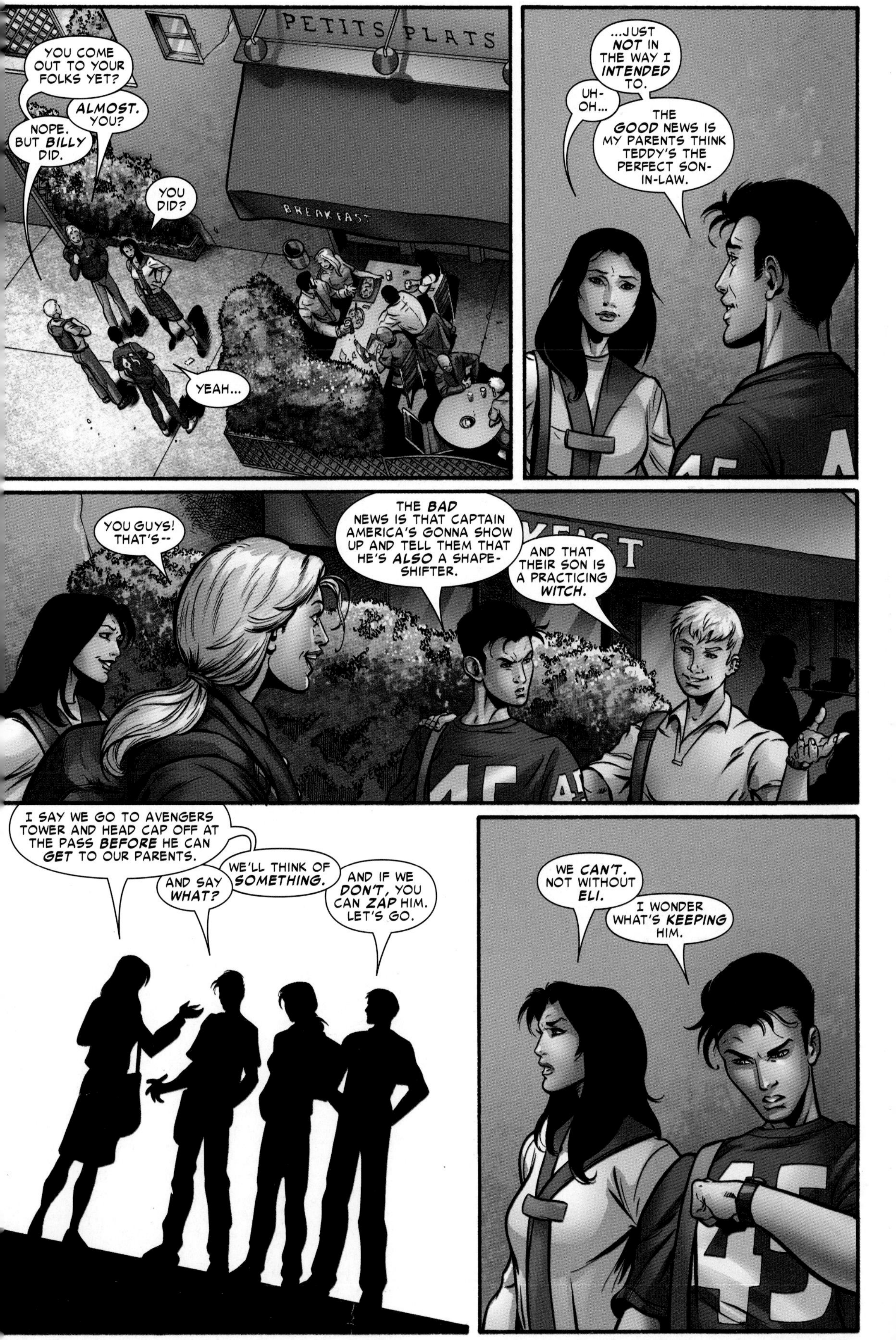
PETITS PLATS
YOU COME OUT TO YOUR FOLKS YET?
NOPE. BUT BILLY DID.
ALMOST. YOU?
YOU DID?
YEAH...
BREAKFAST
...JUST NOT IN THE WAY I INTENDED TO.
UH-OH...
THE GOOD NEWS IS MY PARENTS THINK TEDDY'S THE PERFECT SON-IN-LAW.
YOU GUYS! THAT'S--
THE BAD NEWS IS THAT CAPTAIN AMERICA'S GONNA SHOW UP AND TELL THEM THAT HE'S ALSO A SHAPE-SHIFTER.
AND THAT THEIR SON IS A PRACTICING WITCH.
I SAY WE GO TO AVENGERS TOWER AND HEAD CAP OFF AT THE PASS BEFORE HE CAN GET TO OUR PARENTS.
AND SAY WHAT?
WE'LL THINK OF SOMETHING.
AND IF WE DON'T, YOU CAN ZAP HIM. LET'S GO.
WE CAN'T. NOT WITHOUT ELI.
I WONDER WHAT'S KEEPING HIM.

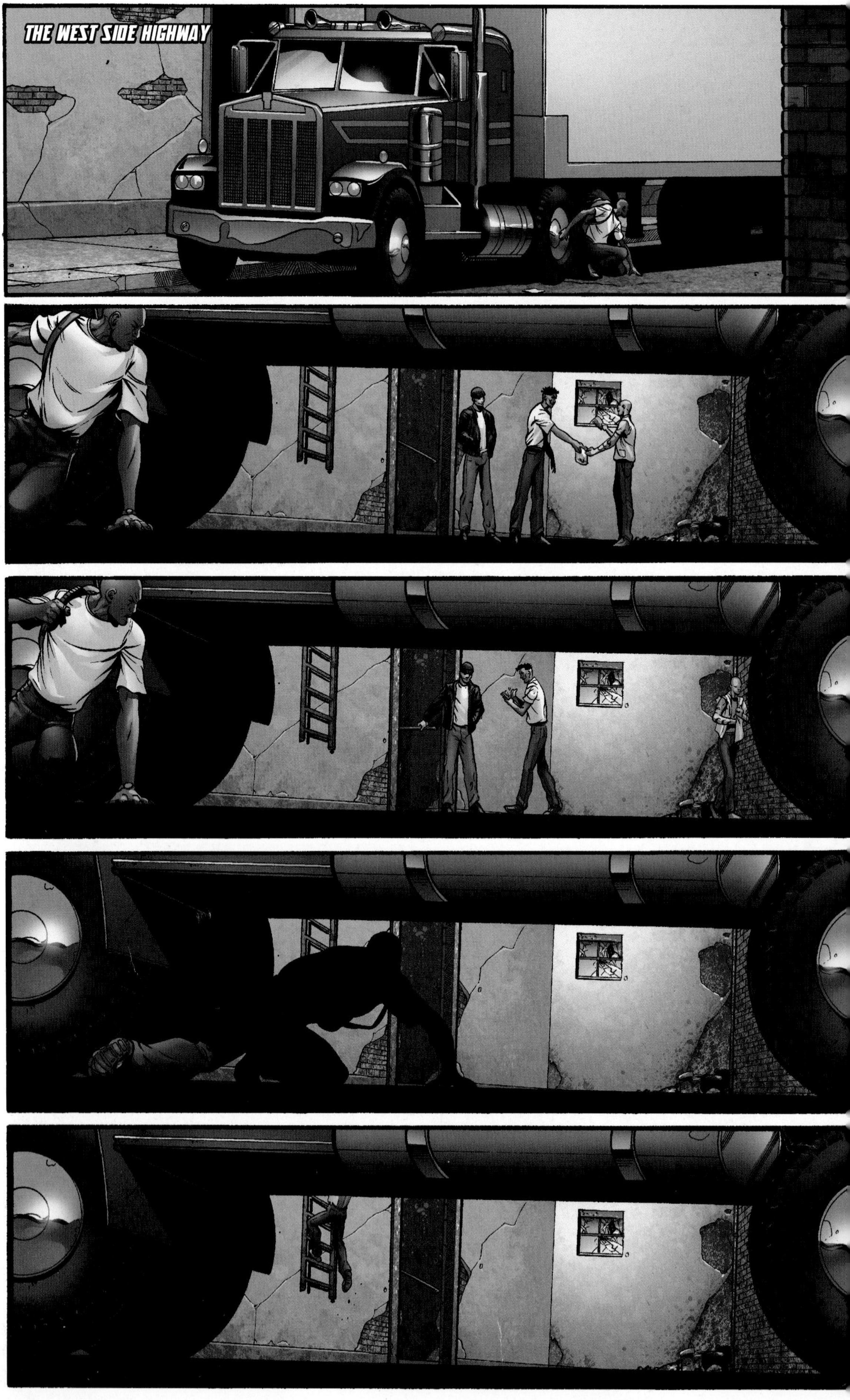
THE WEST SIDE HIGHWAY

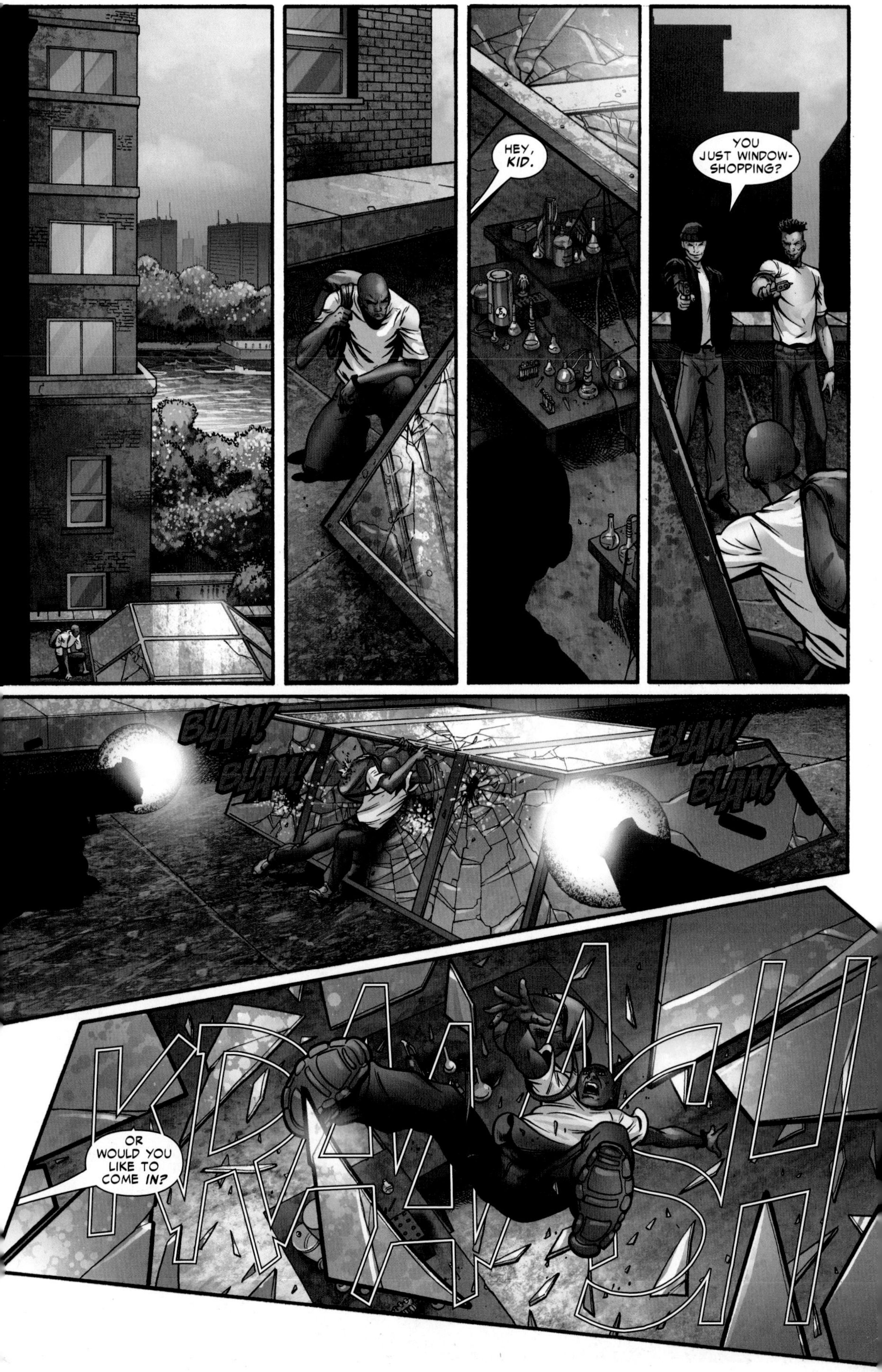
HEY, KID.
YOU JUST WINDOW-SHOPPING?
BLAM! BLAM!
BLAM! BLAM!
OR WOULD YOU LIKE TO COME IN?
KRAAASSH

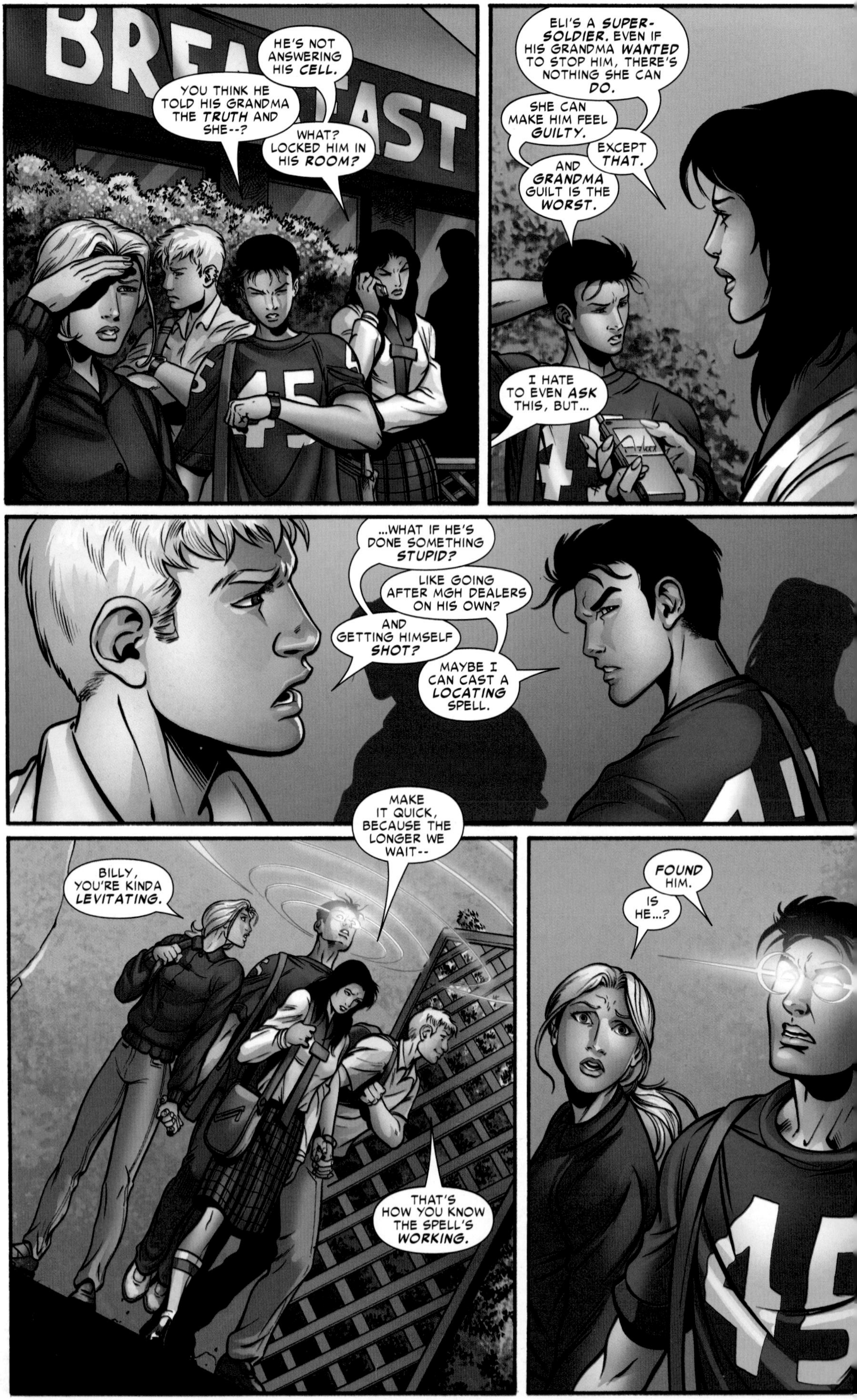
BREAKFAST
HE'S NOT ANSWERING HIS CELL.
YOU THINK HE TOLD HIS GRANDMA THE TRUTH AND SHE--?
WHAT? LOCKED HIM IN HIS ROOM?
ELI'S A SUPER-SOLDIER. EVEN IF HIS GRANDMA WANTED TO STOP HIM, THERE'S NOTHING SHE CAN DO.
SHE CAN MAKE HIM FEEL GUILTY.
EXCEPT THAT.
AND GRANDMA GUILT IS THE WORST.
I HATE TO EVEN ASK THIS, BUT...
...WHAT IF HE'S DONE SOMETHING STUPID?
LIKE GOING AFTER MGH DEALERS ON HIS OWN?
AND GETTING HIMSELF SHOT?
MAYBE I CAN CAST A LOCATING SPELL.
MAKE IT QUICK, BECAUSE THE LONGER WE WAIT--
BILLY, YOU'RE KINDA LEVITATING.
THAT'S HOW YOU KNOW THE SPELL'S WORKING.
FOUND HIM.
IS HE...?

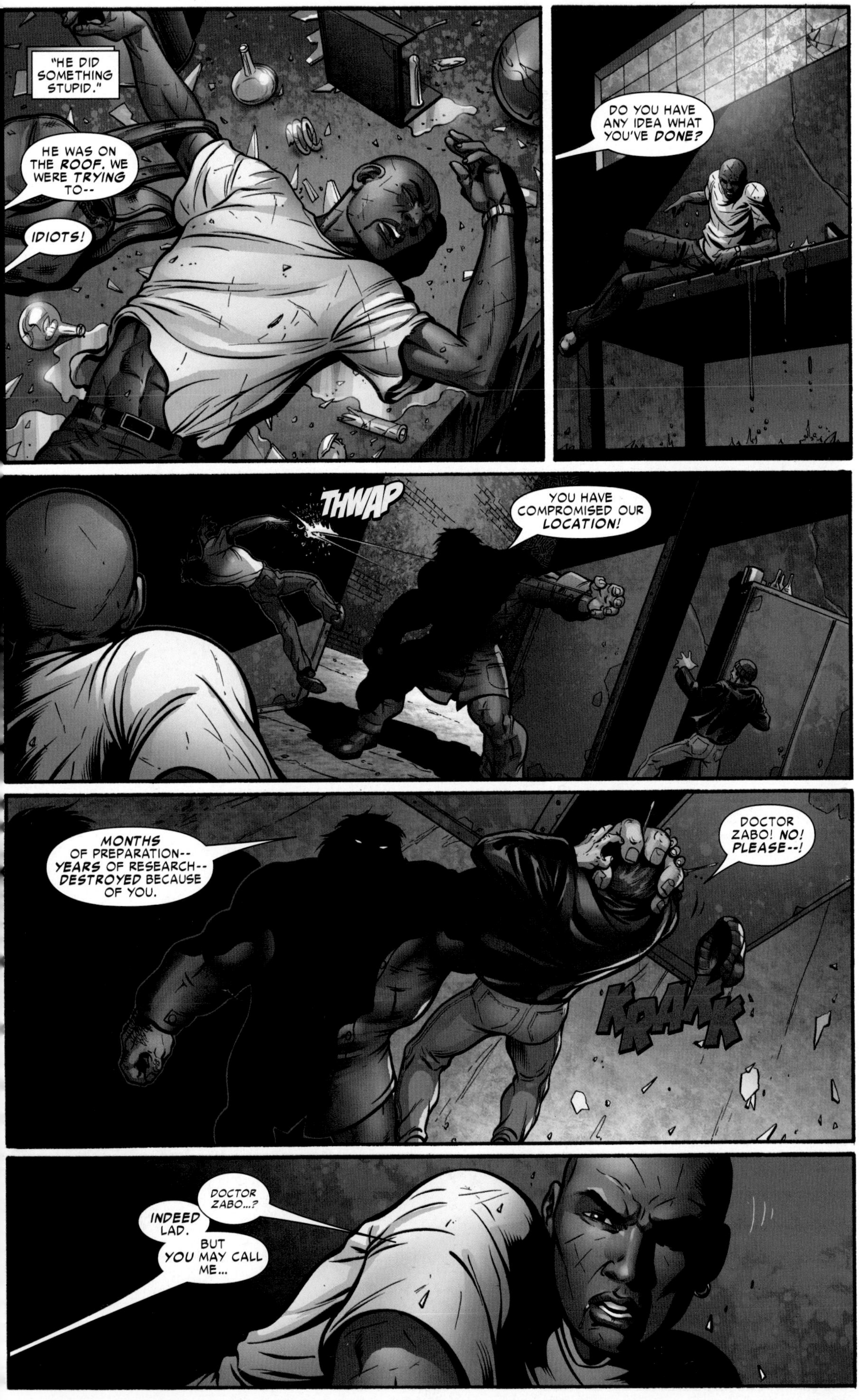
"HE DID SOMETHING STUPID."
HE WAS ON THE ROOF. WE WERE TRYING TO--
IDIOTS!
DO YOU HAVE ANY IDEA WHAT YOU'VE DONE?
THWAP
YOU HAVE COMPROMISED OUR LOCATION!
MONTHS OF PREPARATION-- YEARS OF RESEARCH-- DESTROYED BECAUSE OF YOU.
DOCTOR ZABO! NO! PLEASE--!
KRAAKK
DOCTOR ZABO...?
INDEED LAD.
BUT YOU MAY CALL ME...

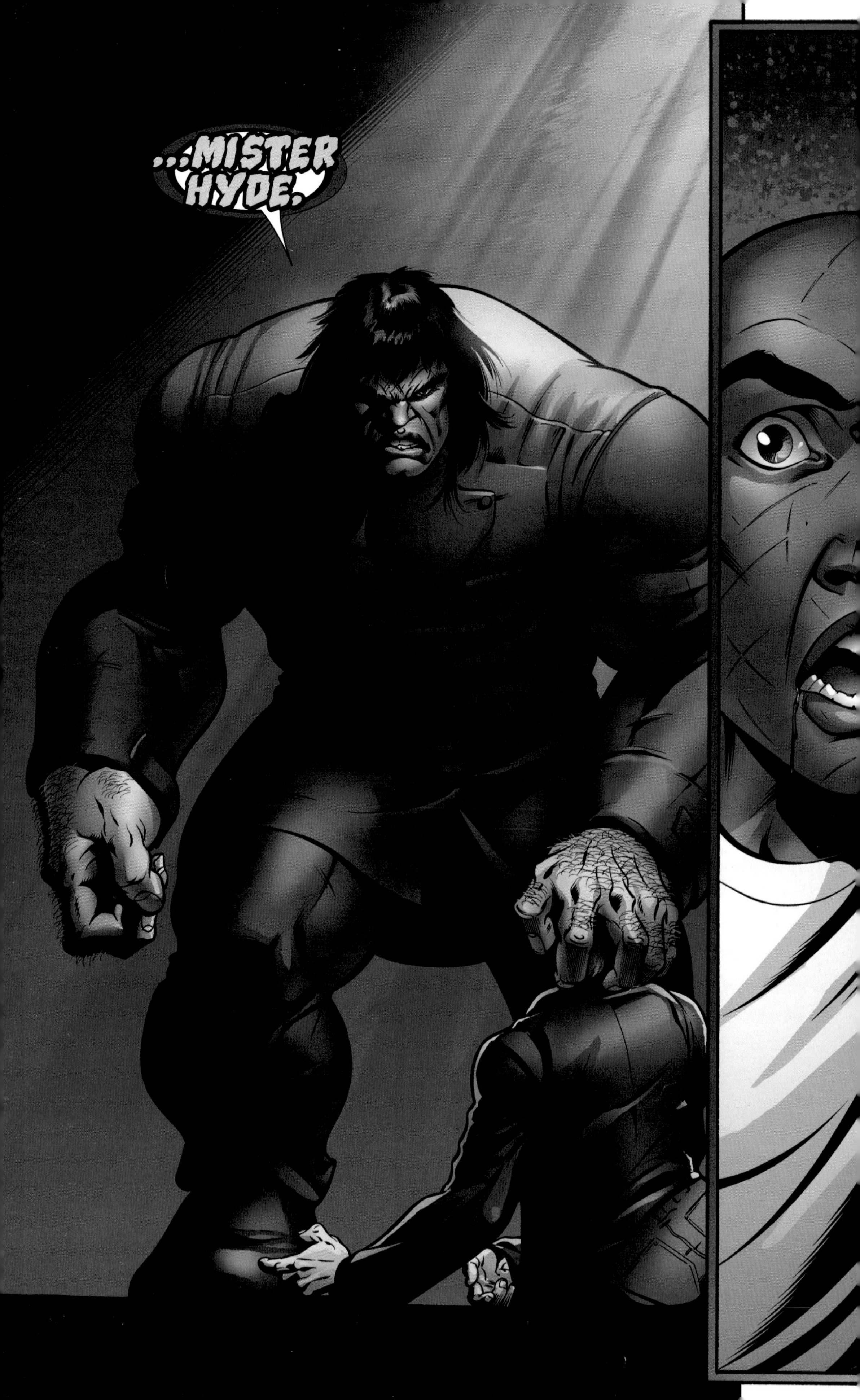
...MISTER HYDE.

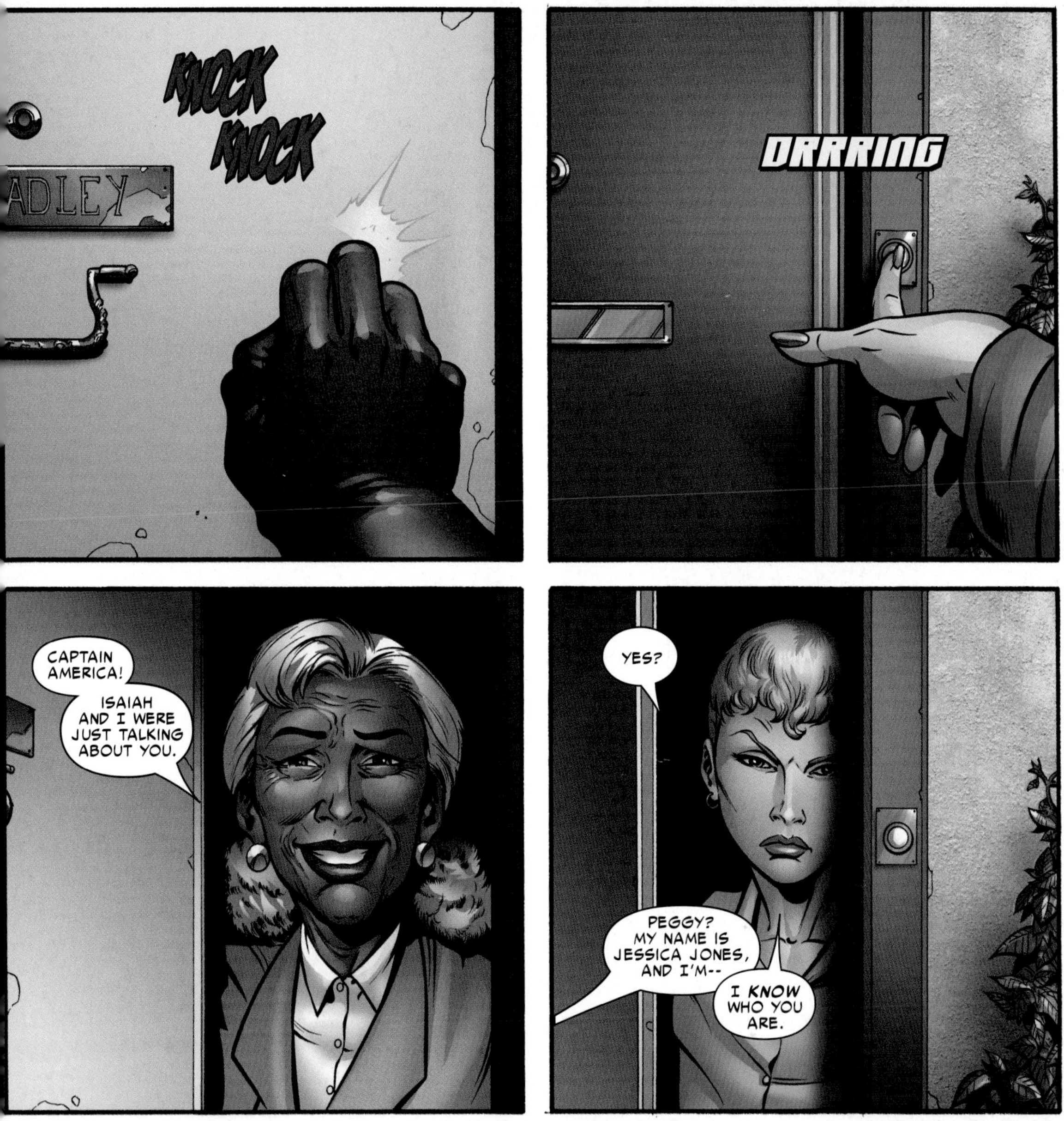
KNOCK KNOCK
ADLEY
DRRRING
CAPTAIN AMERICA!
ISAIAH AND I WERE JUST TALKING ABOUT YOU.
YES?
PEGGY? MY NAME IS JESSICA JONES, AND I'M--
I KNOW WHO YOU ARE.
SORRY TO SHOW UP UNANNOUNCED, BUT--
NONSENSE. ISAIAH WILL BE SO EXCITED TO SEE YOU.
ACTUALLY, I--
COME IN.
BIG JOHN
CAFE
IT WAS CASSIE, WASN'T IT? IN SCOTT'S COSTUME?
MRS. BURDICK, I--
COME IN.

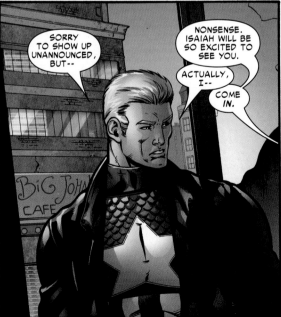

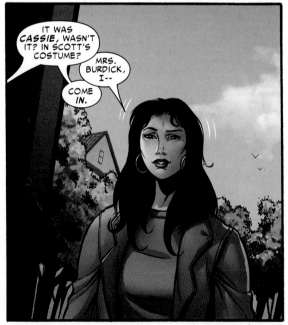

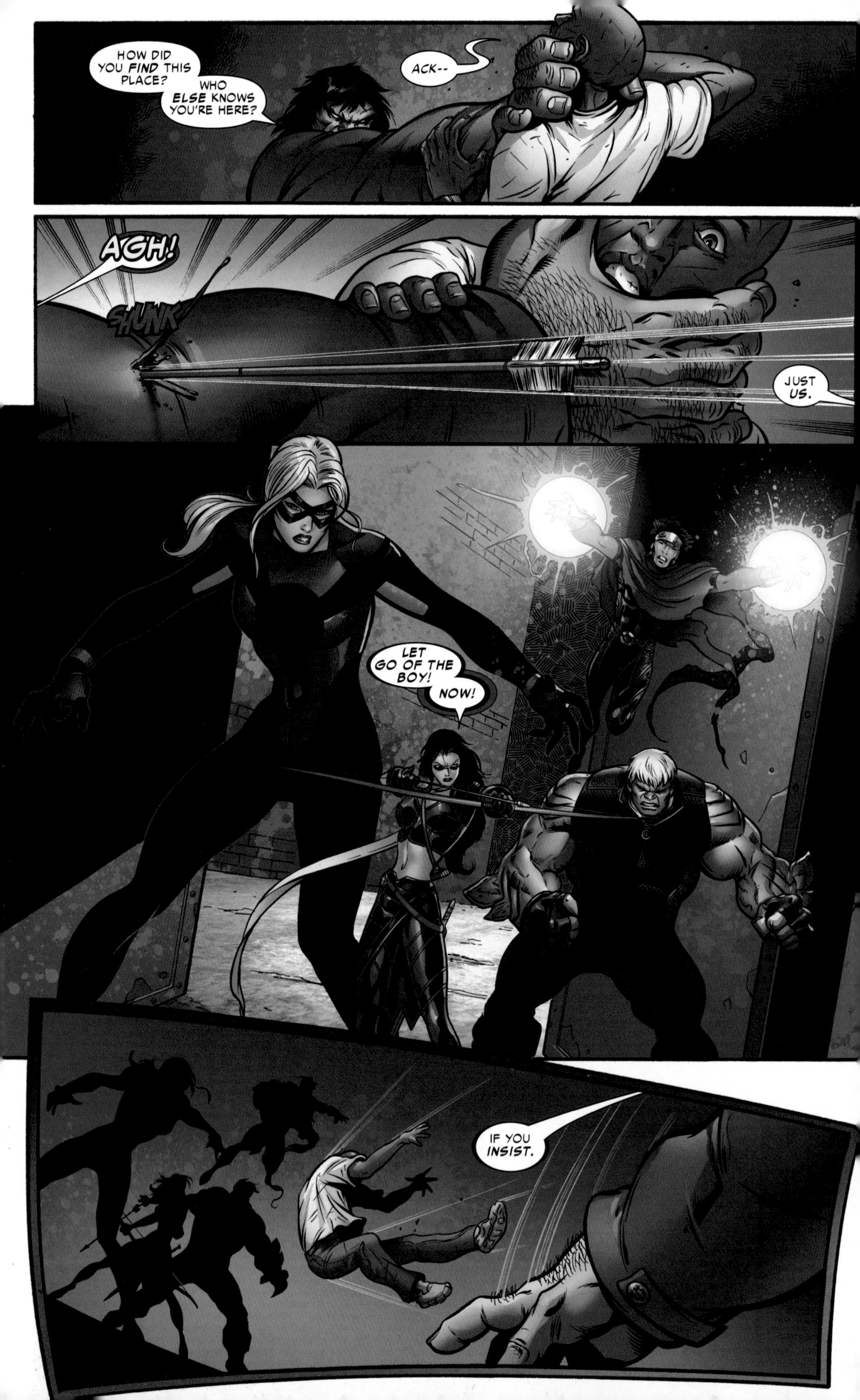
HOW DID YOU FIND THIS PLACE?
WHO ELSE KNOWS YOU'RE HERE?
ACK--
AGH!
SHUNK
JUST US.
LET GO OF THE BOY!
NOW!
IF YOU INSIST.

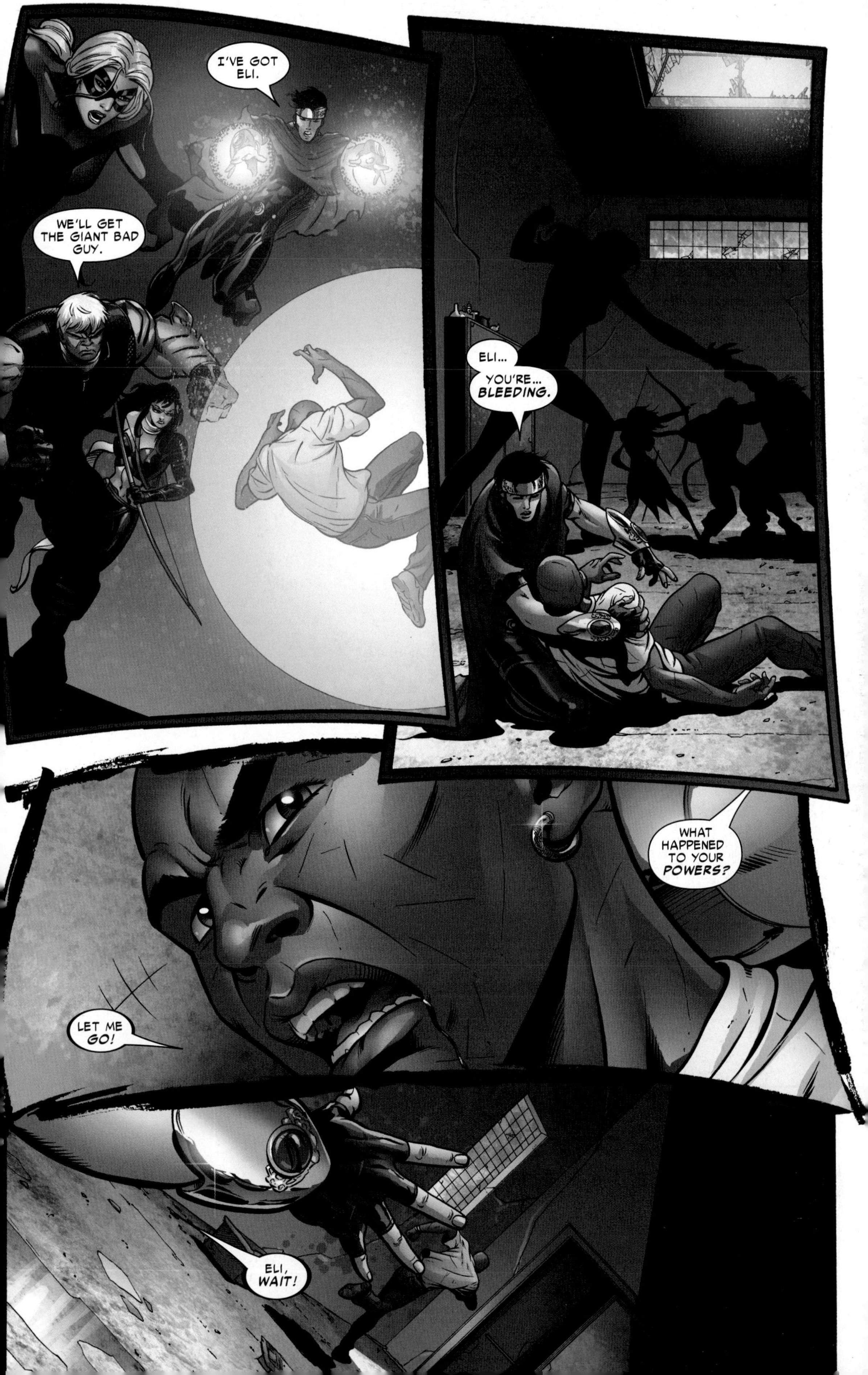
I'VE GOT ELI.
WE'LL GET THE GIANT BAD GUY.
ELI... YOU'RE... *BLEEDING.*
WHAT HAPPENED TO YOUR *POWERS?*
LET ME *GO!*
ELI, *WAIT!*

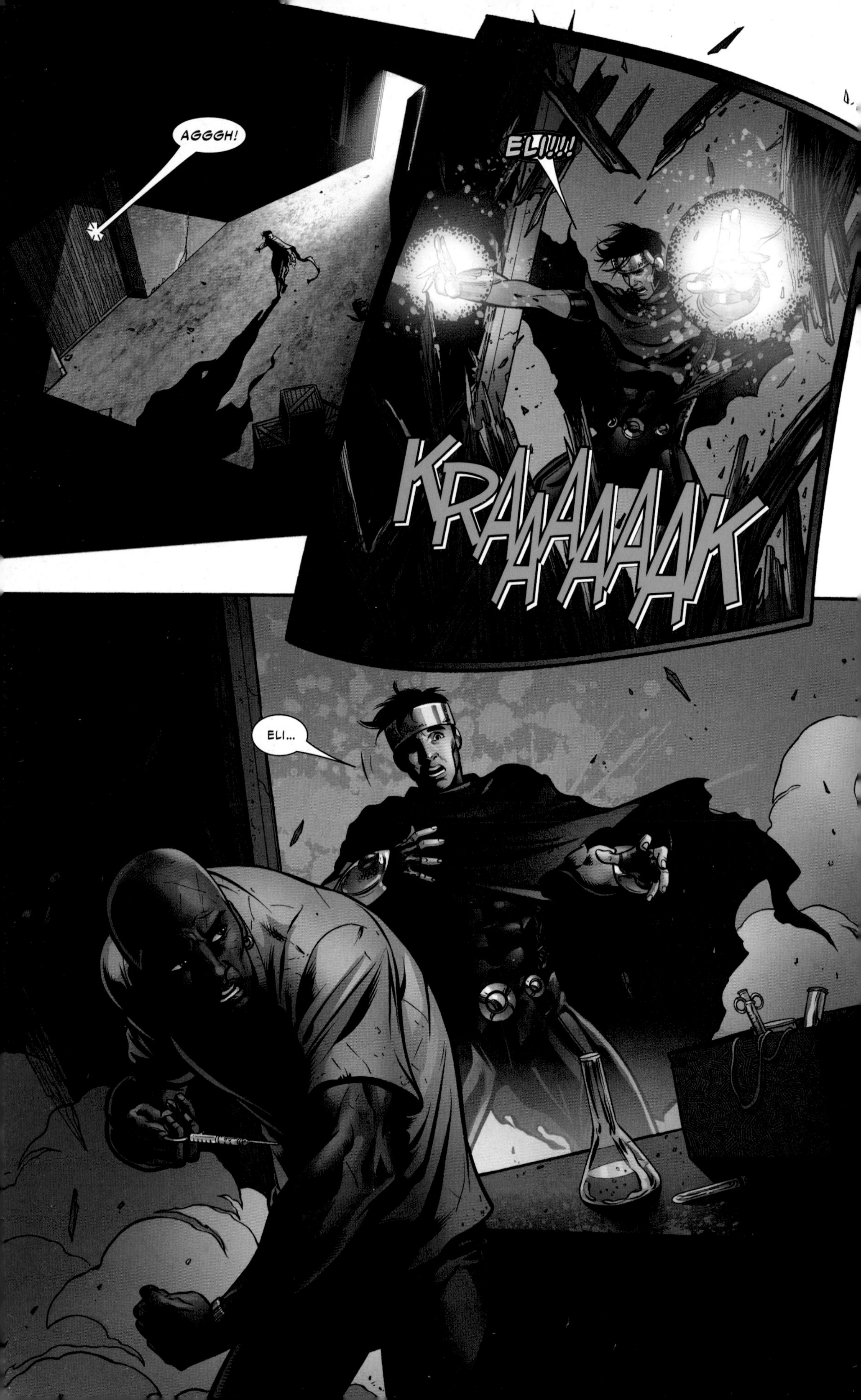
AGGGH!
ELI!!!!
KRAAAAAAAAK
ELI...

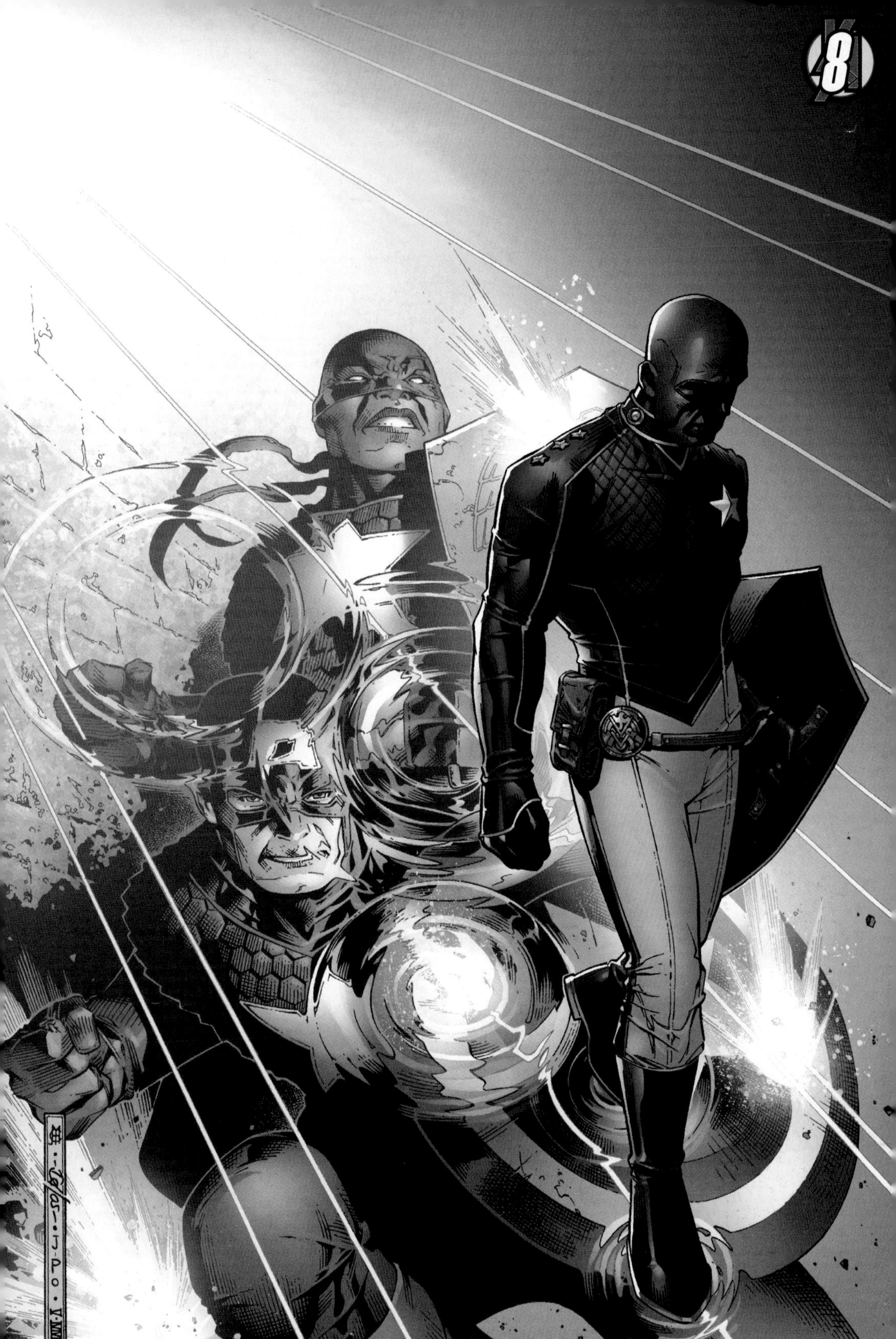

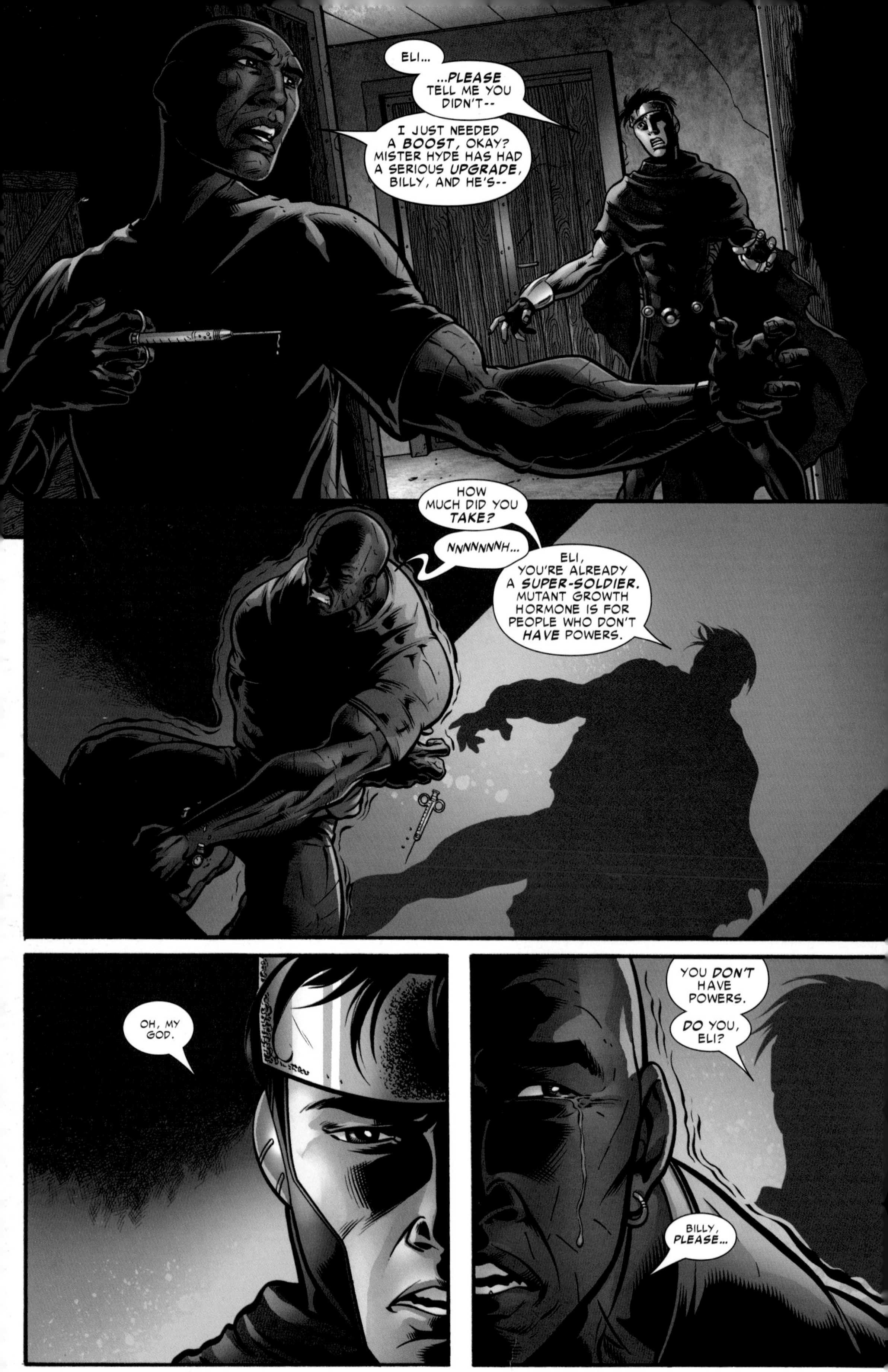
ELI...
...PLEASE TELL ME YOU DIDN'T--
I JUST NEEDED A BOOST, OKAY? MISTER HYDE HAS HAD A SERIOUS UPGRADE, BILLY, AND HE'S--
HOW MUCH DID YOU TAKE?
NNNNNNNH...
ELI, YOU'RE ALREADY A SUPER-SOLDIER. MUTANT GROWTH HORMONE IS FOR PEOPLE WHO DON'T HAVE POWERS.
OH, MY GOD.
YOU DON'T HAVE POWERS.
DO YOU, ELI?
BILLY, PLEASE...

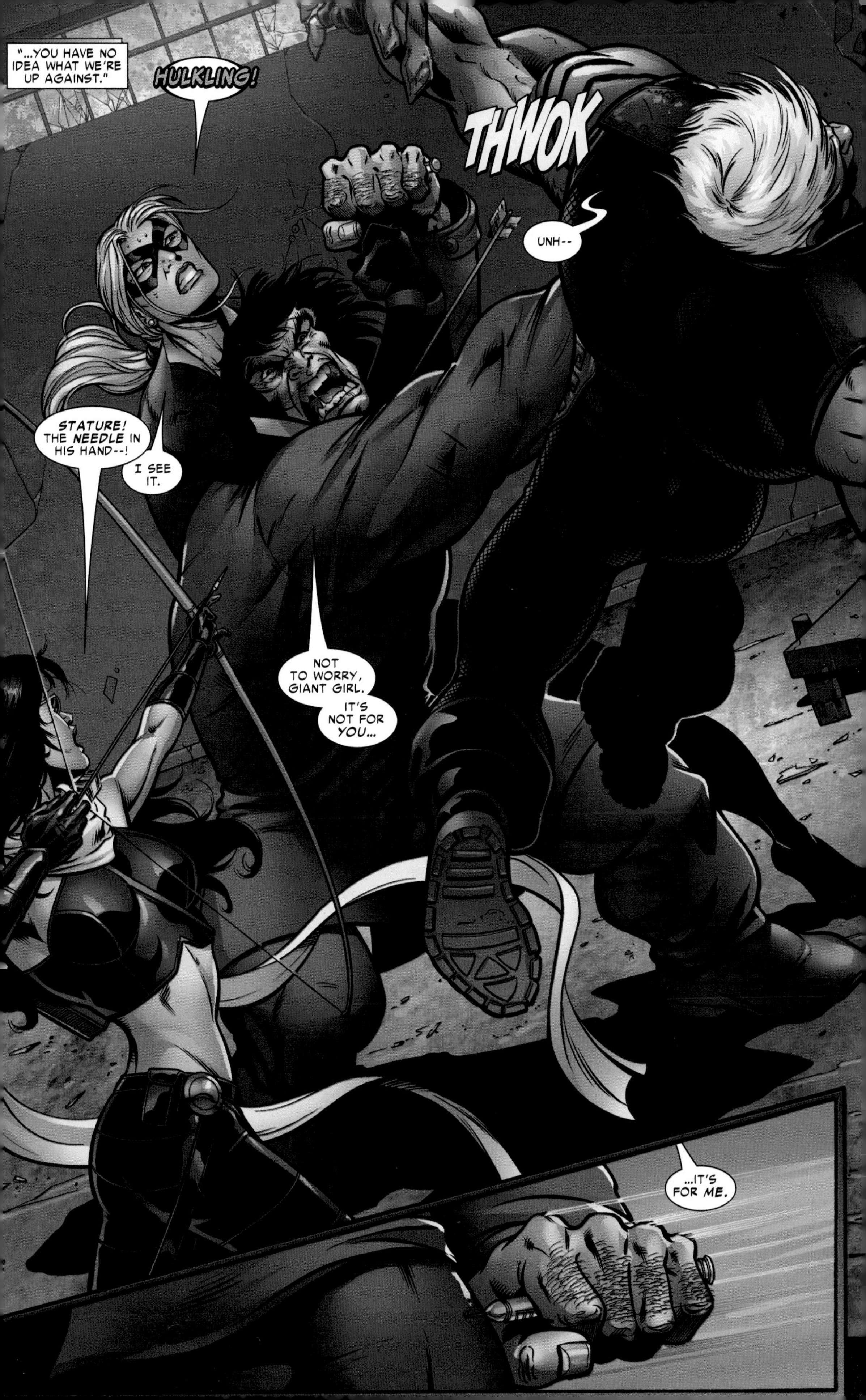
"...YOU HAVE NO IDEA WHAT WE'RE UP AGAINST."
HULKLING!
THWOK
UNH--
STATURE! THE NEEDLE IN HIS HAND--!
I SEE IT.
NOT TO WORRY, GIANT GIRL.
IT'S NOT FOR YOU...
...IT'S FOR ME.

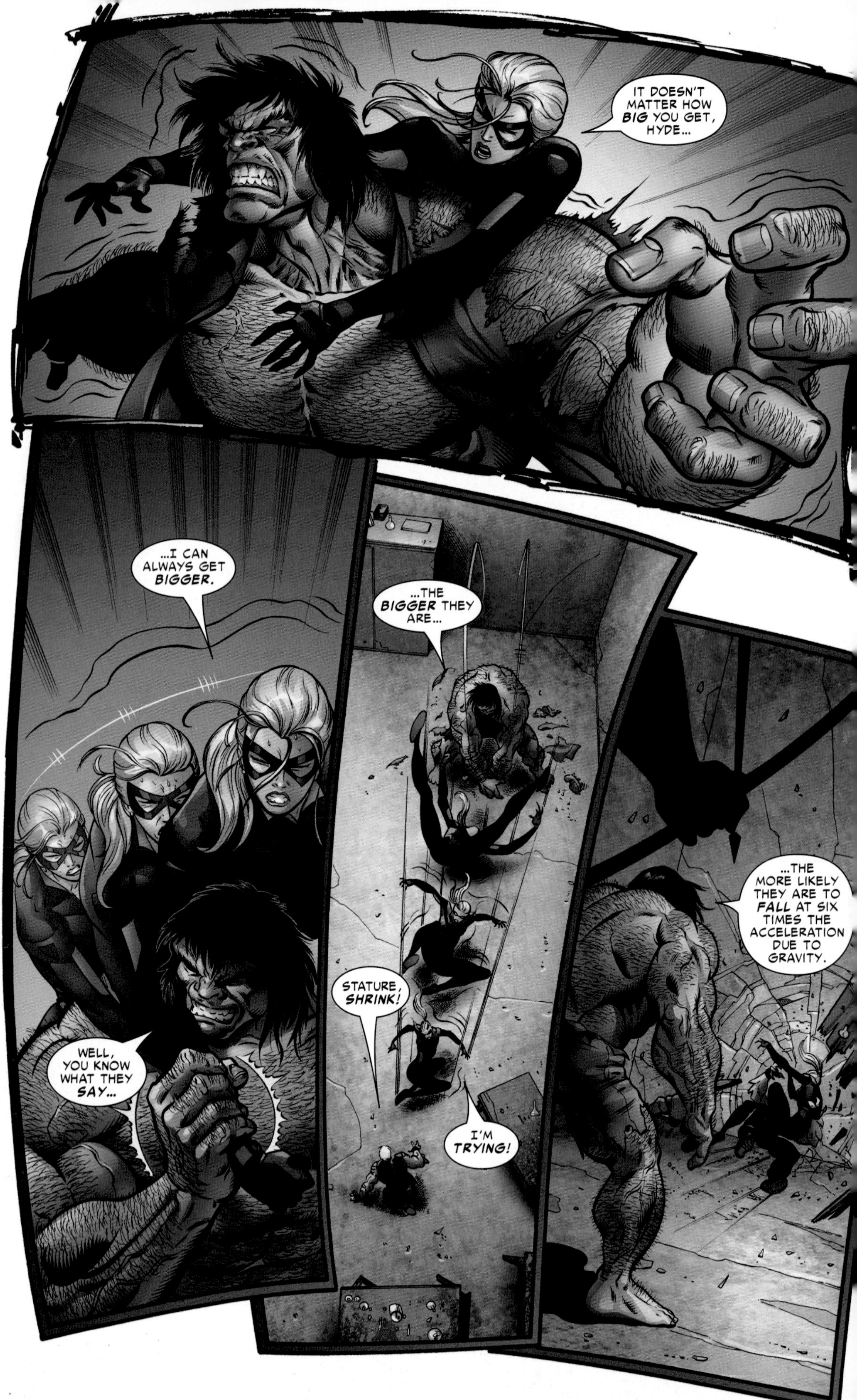
IT DOESN'T MATTER HOW BIG YOU GET, HYDE...
...I CAN ALWAYS GET BIGGER.
WELL, YOU KNOW WHAT THEY SAY...
...THE BIGGER THEY ARE...
STATURE, SHRINK!
I'M TRYING!
...THE MORE LIKELY THEY ARE TO FALL AT SIX TIMES THE ACCELERATION DUE TO GRAVITY.

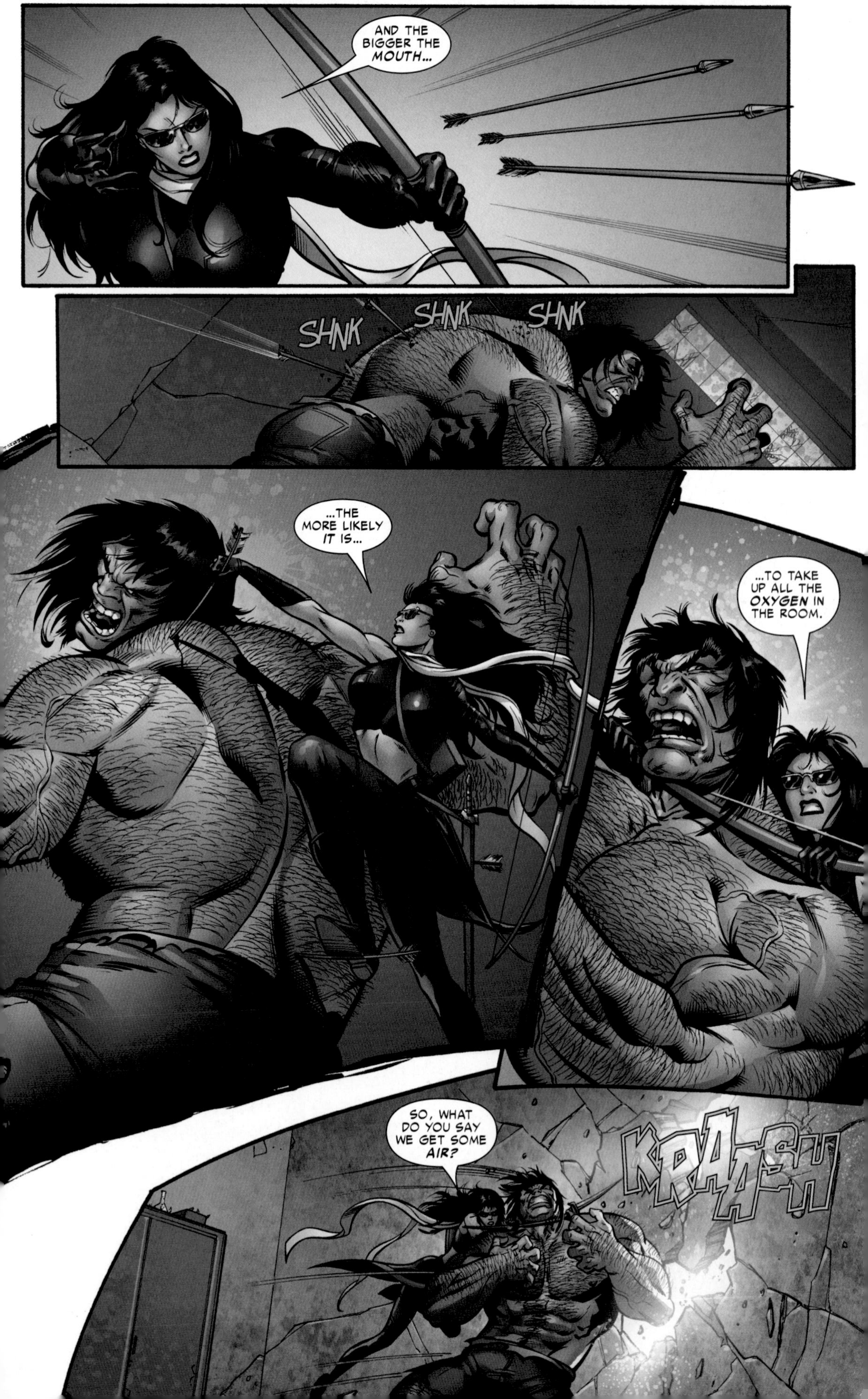

AND THE BIGGER THE MOUTH...
SHNK
SHNK
SHNK
...THE MORE LIKELY IT IS...
...TO TAKE UP ALL THE OXYGEN IN THE ROOM.
SO, WHAT DO YOU SAY WE GET SOME AIR?
KRAASH

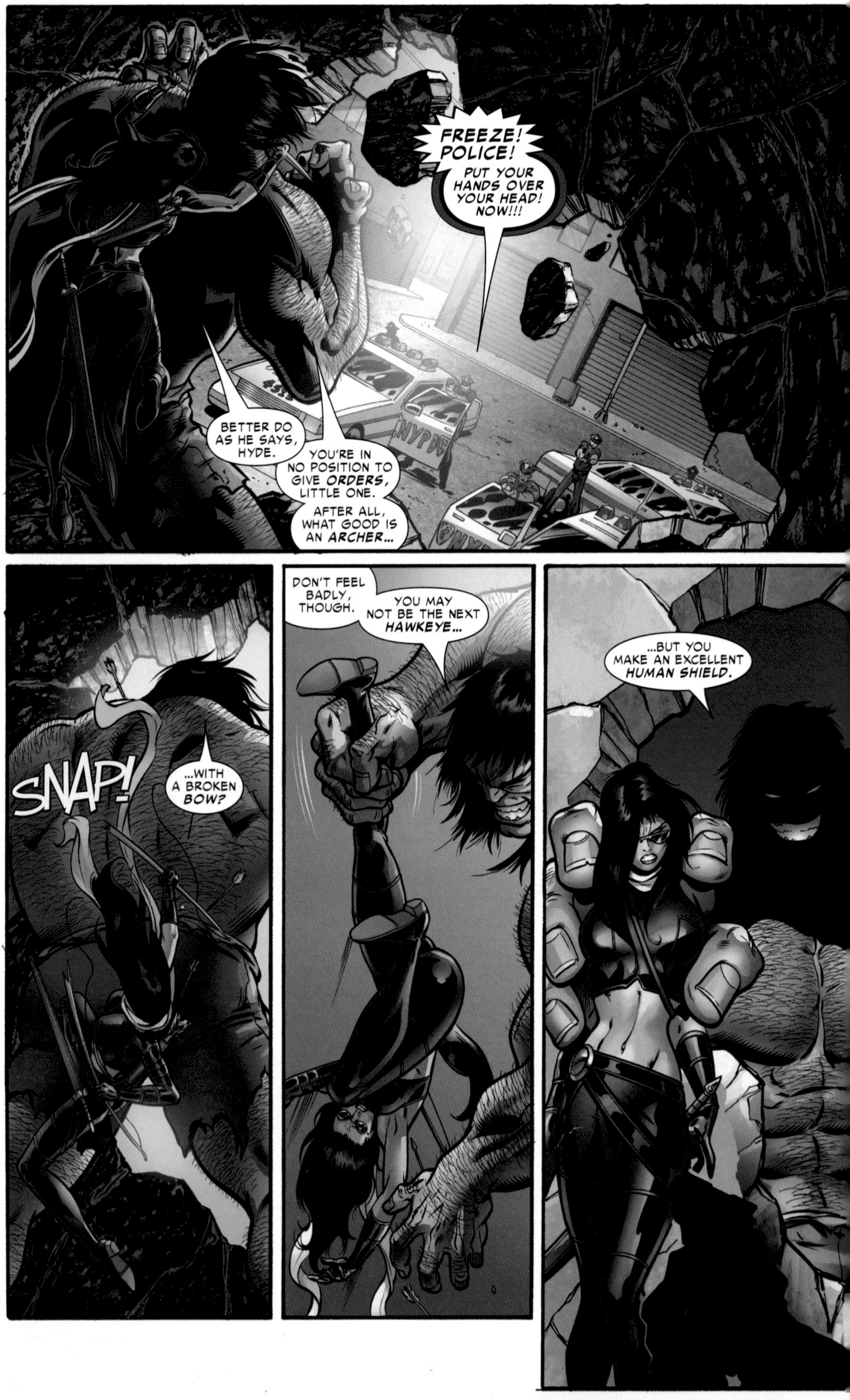

FREEZE! POLICE!
PUT YOUR HANDS OVER YOUR HEAD! NOW!!!
BETTER DO AS HE SAYS, HYDE.
YOU'RE IN NO POSITION TO GIVE ORDERS, LITTLE ONE.
AFTER ALL, WHAT GOOD IS AN ARCHER...
SNAP!
...WITH A BROKEN BOW?
DON'T FEEL BADLY, THOUGH.
YOU MAY NOT BE THE NEXT HAWKEYE...
...BUT YOU MAKE AN EXCELLENT HUMAN SHIELD.

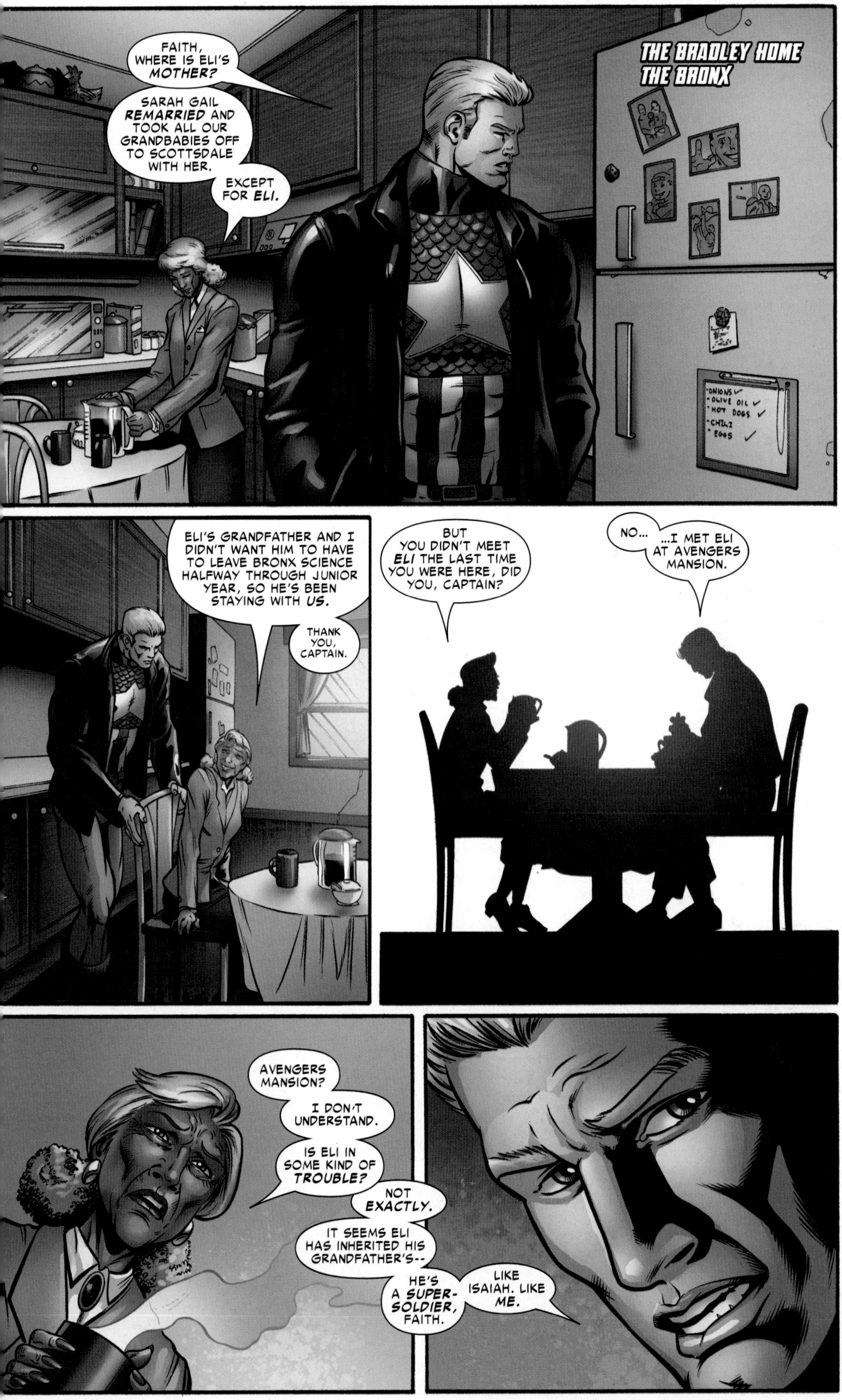
THE BRADLEY HOME THE BRONX
FAITH, WHERE IS ELI'S MOTHER?
SARAH GAIL REMARRIED AND TOOK ALL OUR GRANDBABIES OFF TO SCOTTSDALE WITH HER.
EXCEPT FOR ELI.
•ONIONS •OLIVE OIL •HOT DOGS •CHILI •EGGS
ELI'S GRANDFATHER AND I DIDN'T WANT HIM TO HAVE TO LEAVE BRONX SCIENCE HALFWAY THROUGH JUNIOR YEAR, SO HE'S BEEN STAYING WITH US.
THANK YOU, CAPTAIN.
BUT YOU DIDN'T MEET ELI THE LAST TIME YOU WERE HERE, DID YOU, CAPTAIN?
NO...
...I MET ELI AT AVENGERS MANSION.
AVENGERS MANSION?
I DON'T UNDERSTAND.
IS ELI IN SOME KIND OF TROUBLE?
NOT EXACTLY.
IT SEEMS ELI HAS INHERITED HIS GRANDFATHER'S--
HE'S A SUPER-SOLDIER, FAITH.
LIKE ISAIAH. LIKE ME.

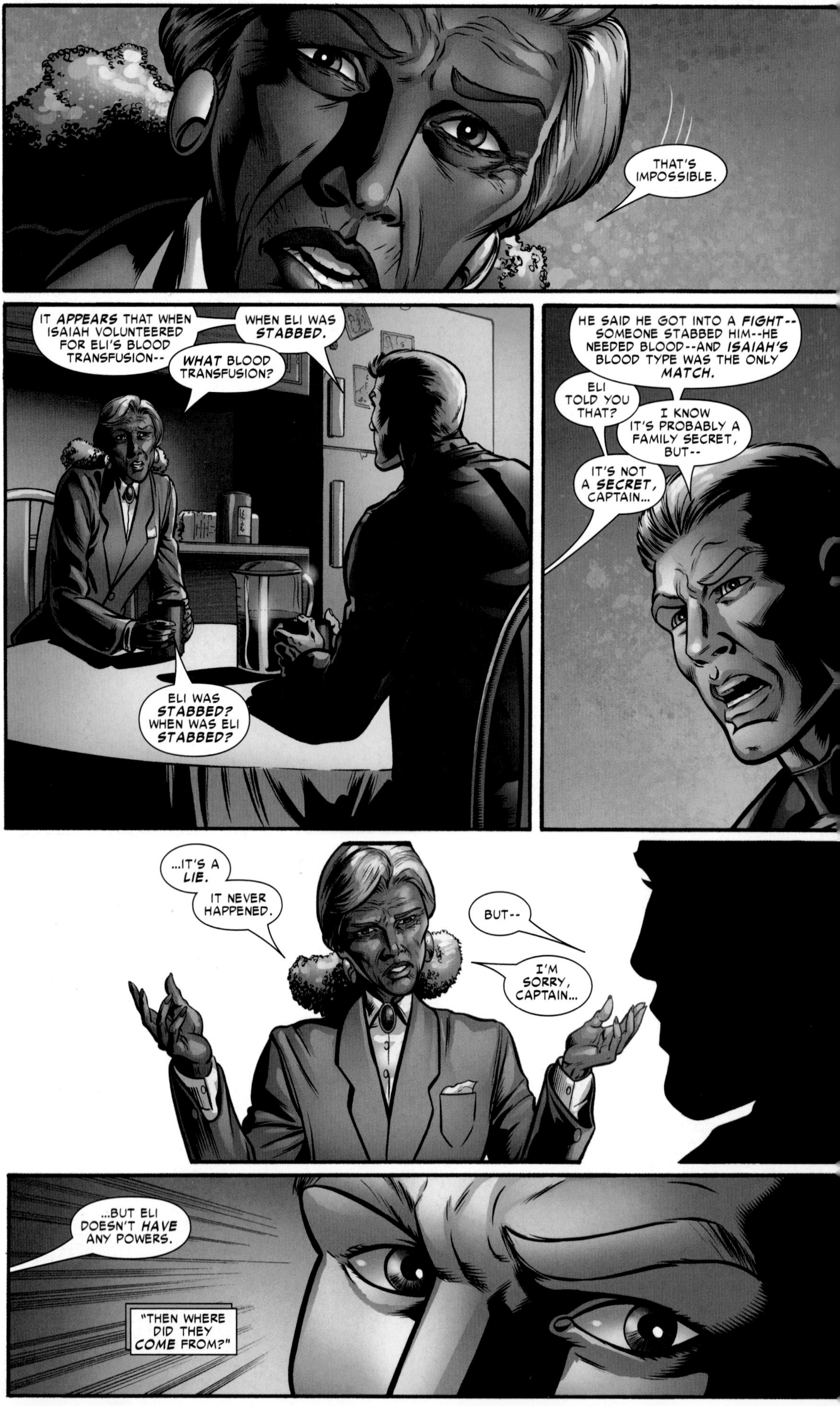
THAT'S IMPOSSIBLE.
IT APPEARS THAT WHEN ISAIAH VOLUNTEERED FOR ELI'S BLOOD TRANSFUSION--
WHEN ELI WAS STABBED.
WHAT BLOOD TRANSFUSION?
ELI WAS STABBED? WHEN WAS ELI STABBED?
HE SAID HE GOT INTO A FIGHT--SOMEONE STABBED HIM--HE NEEDED BLOOD--AND ISAIAH'S BLOOD TYPE WAS THE ONLY MATCH.
ELI TOLD YOU THAT?
I KNOW IT'S PROBABLY A FAMILY SECRET, BUT--
IT'S NOT A SECRET, CAPTAIN...
...IT'S A LIE.
IT NEVER HAPPENED.
BUT--
I'M SORRY, CAPTAIN...
...BUT ELI DOESN'T HAVE ANY POWERS.
"THEN WHERE DID THEY COME FROM?"

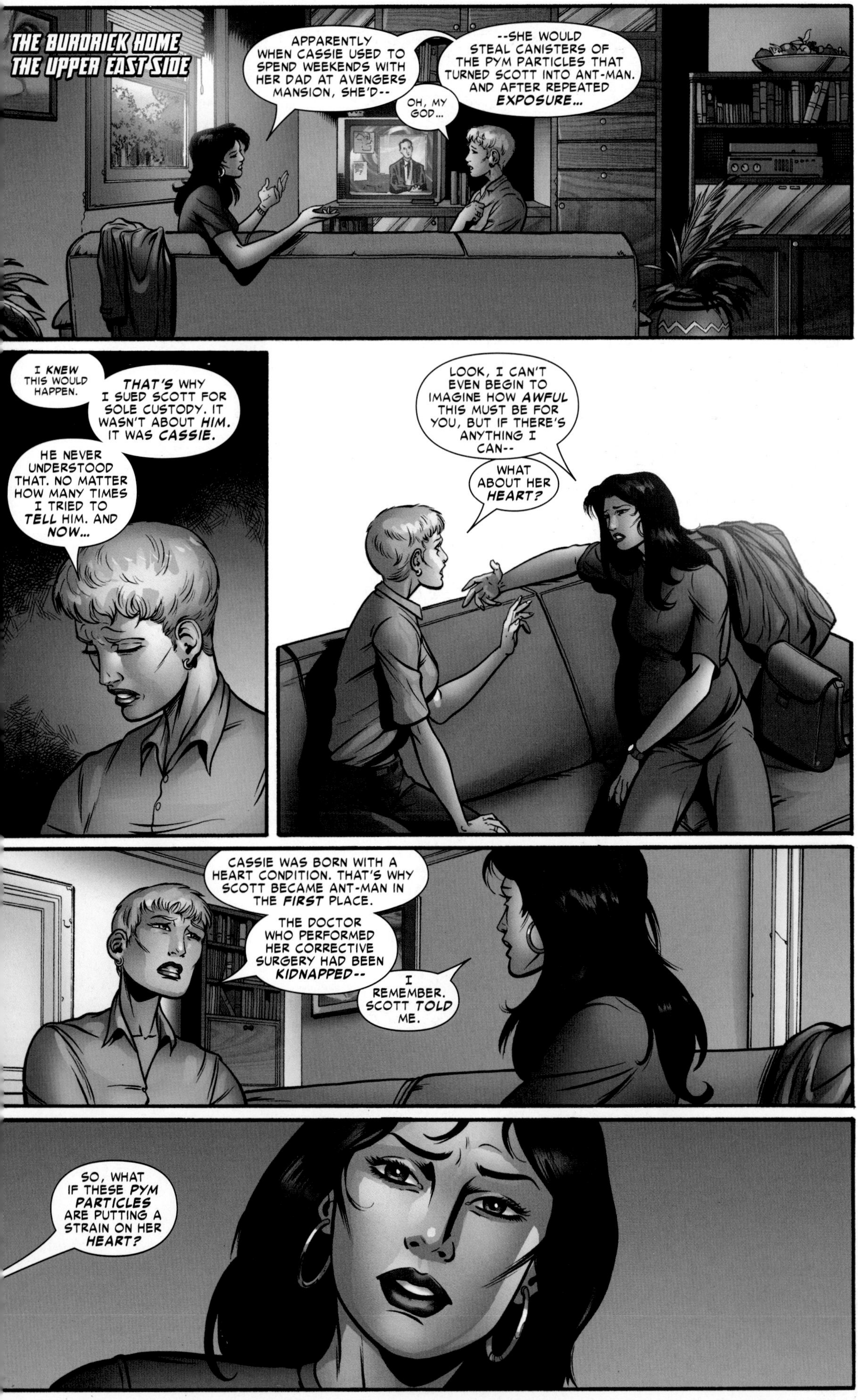
THE BURDRICK HOME
THE UPPER EAST SIDE
APPARENTLY WHEN CASSIE USED TO SPEND WEEKENDS WITH HER DAD AT AVENGERS MANSION, SHE'D--
OH, MY GOD...
--SHE WOULD STEAL CANISTERS OF THE PYM PARTICLES THAT TURNED SCOTT INTO ANT-MAN. AND AFTER REPEATED EXPOSURE...
I KNEW THIS WOULD HAPPEN.
THAT'S WHY I SUED SCOTT FOR SOLE CUSTODY. IT WASN'T ABOUT HIM. IT WAS CASSIE.
HE NEVER UNDERSTOOD THAT. NO MATTER HOW MANY TIMES I TRIED TO TELL HIM. AND NOW...
LOOK, I CAN'T EVEN BEGIN TO IMAGINE HOW AWFUL THIS MUST BE FOR YOU, BUT IF THERE'S ANYTHING I CAN--
WHAT ABOUT HER HEART?
CASSIE WAS BORN WITH A HEART CONDITION. THAT'S WHY SCOTT BECAME ANT-MAN IN THE FIRST PLACE.
THE DOCTOR WHO PERFORMED HER CORRECTIVE SURGERY HAD BEEN KIDNAPPED--
I REMEMBER. SCOTT TOLD ME.
SO, WHAT IF THESE PYM PARTICLES ARE PUTTING A STRAIN ON HER HEART?

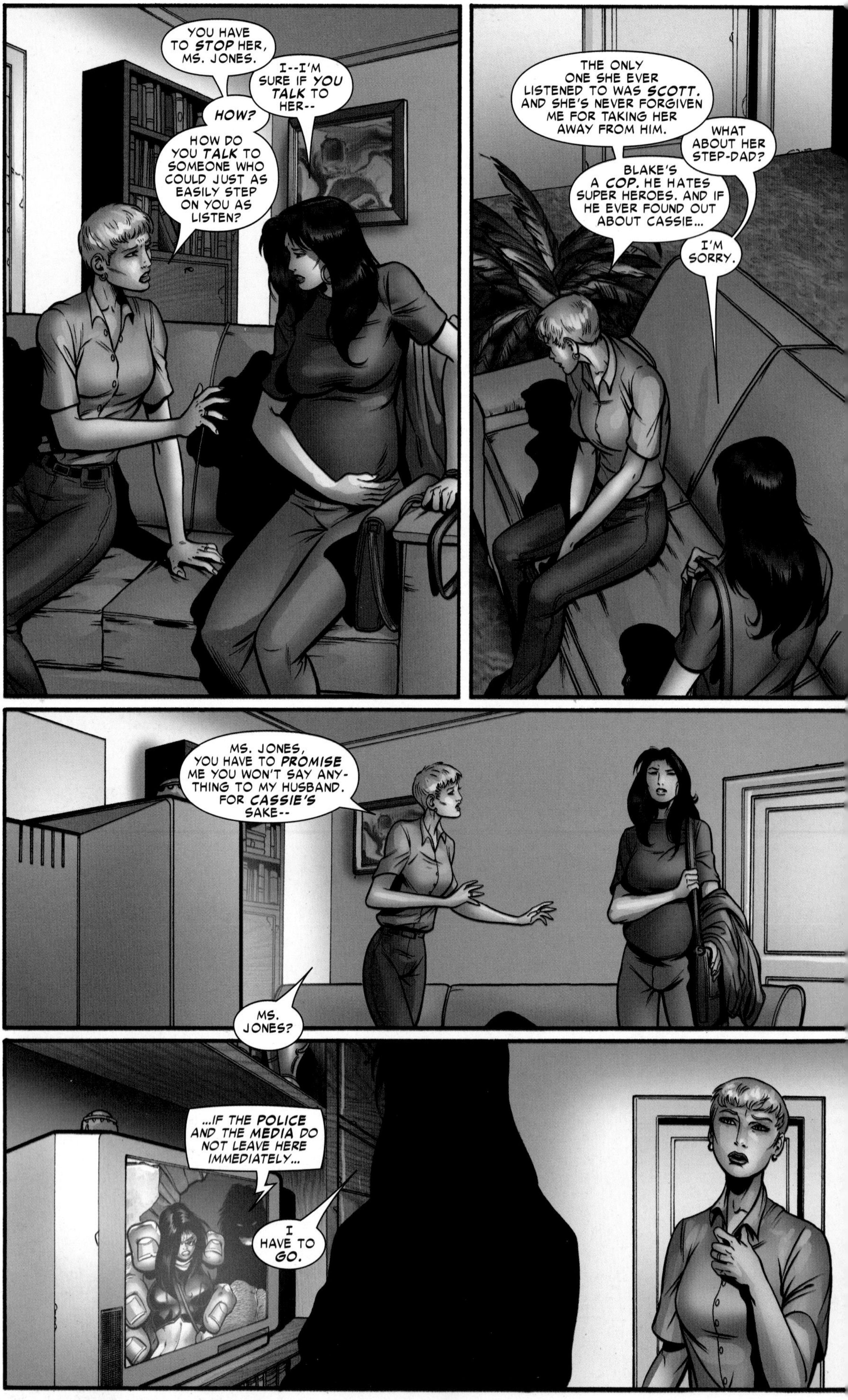
YOU HAVE TO STOP HER, MS. JONES.
I--I'M SURE IF YOU TALK TO HER--
HOW?
HOW DO YOU TALK TO SOMEONE WHO COULD JUST AS EASILY STEP ON YOU AS LISTEN?
THE ONLY ONE SHE EVER LISTENED TO WAS SCOTT. AND SHE'S NEVER FORGIVEN ME FOR TAKING HER AWAY FROM HIM.
WHAT ABOUT HER STEP-DAD?
BLAKE'S A COP. HE HATES SUPER HEROES. AND IF HE EVER FOUND OUT ABOUT CASSIE...
I'M SORRY.
MS. JONES, YOU HAVE TO PROMISE ME YOU WON'T SAY ANYTHING TO MY HUSBAND. FOR CASSIE'S SAKE--
MS. JONES?
...IF THE POLICE AND THE MEDIA DO NOT LEAVE HERE IMMEDIATELY...
I HAVE TO GO.

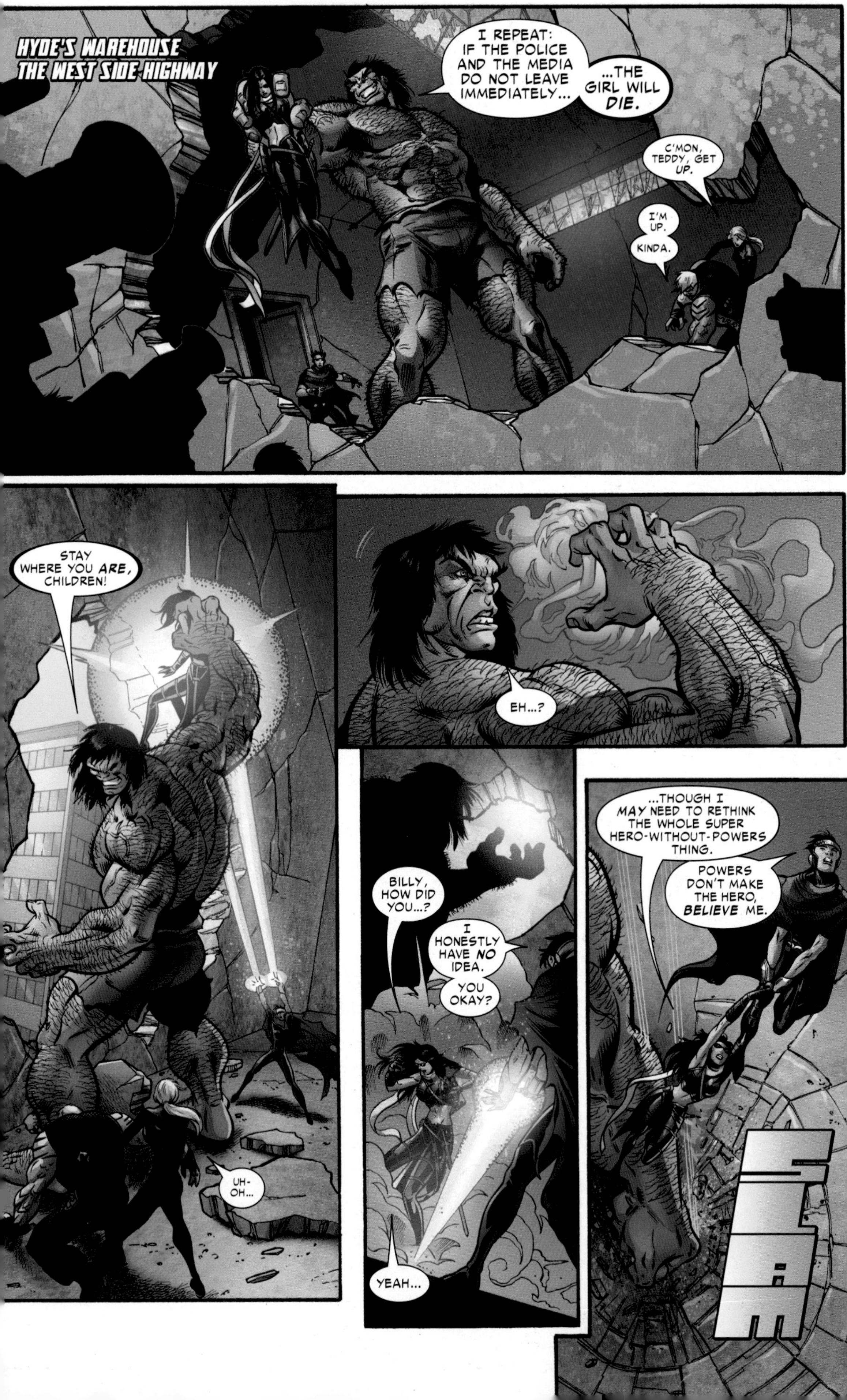
HYDE'S WAREHOUSE
THE WEST SIDE HIGHWAY
I REPEAT: IF THE POLICE AND THE MEDIA DO NOT LEAVE IMMEDIATELY...
...THE GIRL WILL DIE.
C'MON, TEDDY, GET UP.
I'M UP.
KINDA.
STAY WHERE YOU ARE, CHILDREN!
UH-OH...
EH...?
BILLY, HOW DID YOU...?
I HONESTLY HAVE NO IDEA.
YOU OKAY?
YEAH...
...THOUGH I MAY NEED TO RETHINK THE WHOLE SUPER HERO-WITHOUT-POWERS THING.
POWERS DON'T MAKE THE HERO, BELIEVE ME.

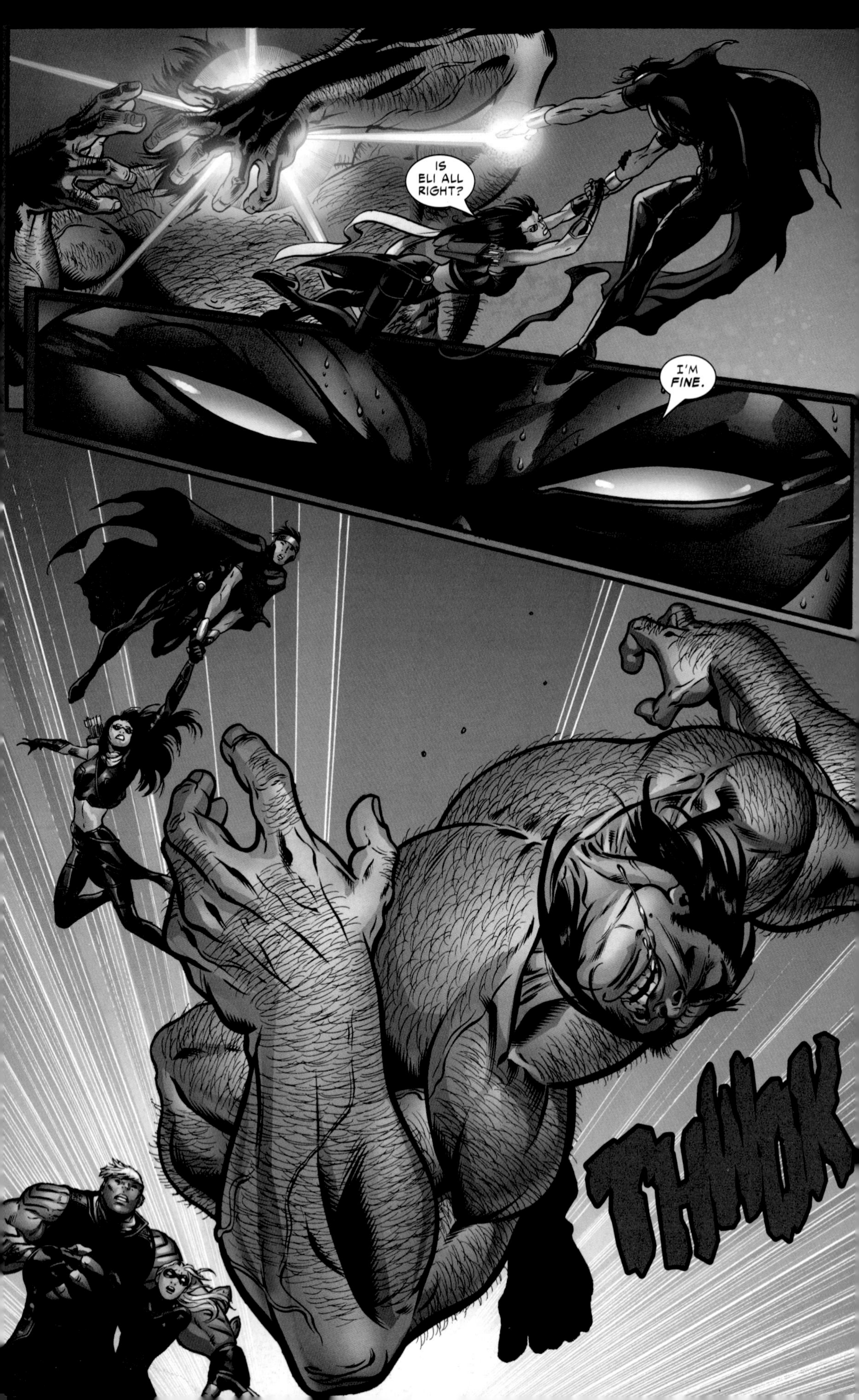
IS ELI ALL RIGHT?
I'M FINE.
THWOK

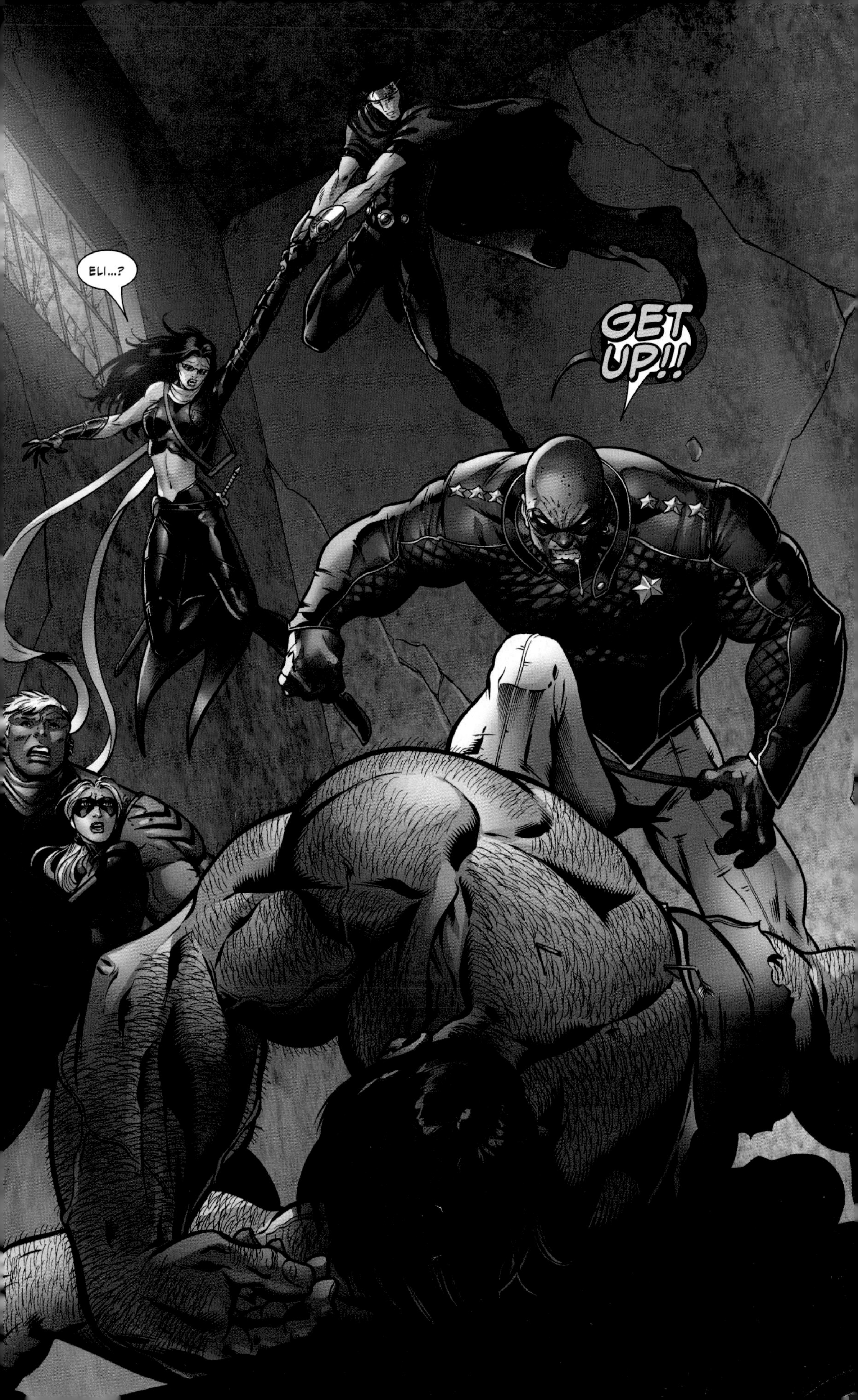
ELI...?
GET UP!!

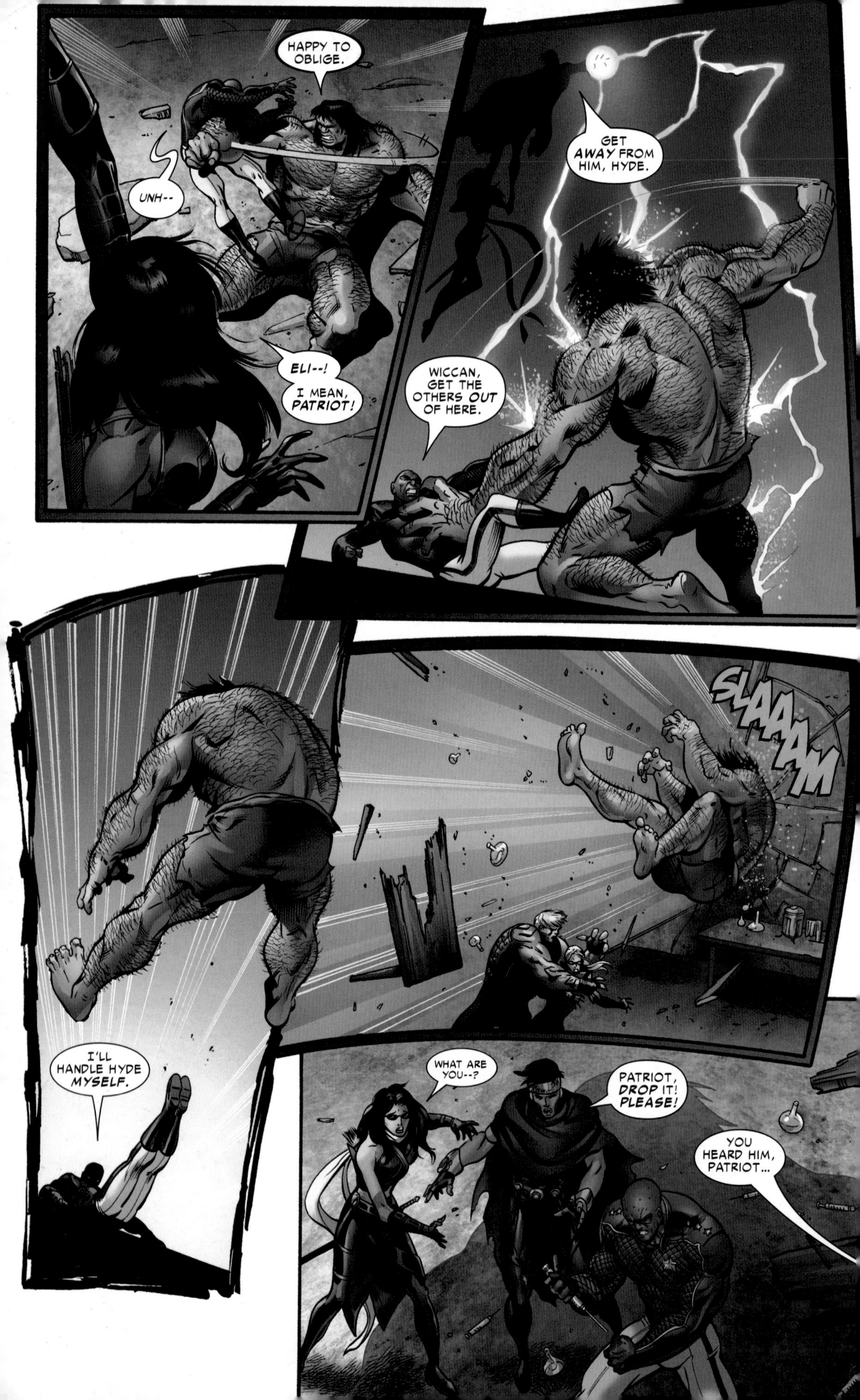
HAPPY TO OBLIGE.
UNH--
ELI--! I MEAN, PATRIOT!
GET AWAY FROM HIM, HYDE.
WICCAN, GET THE OTHERS OUT OF HERE.
SLAAAAM
I'LL HANDLE HYDE MYSELF.
WHAT ARE YOU--?
PATRIOT, DROP IT! PLEASE!
YOU HEARD HIM, PATRIOT...

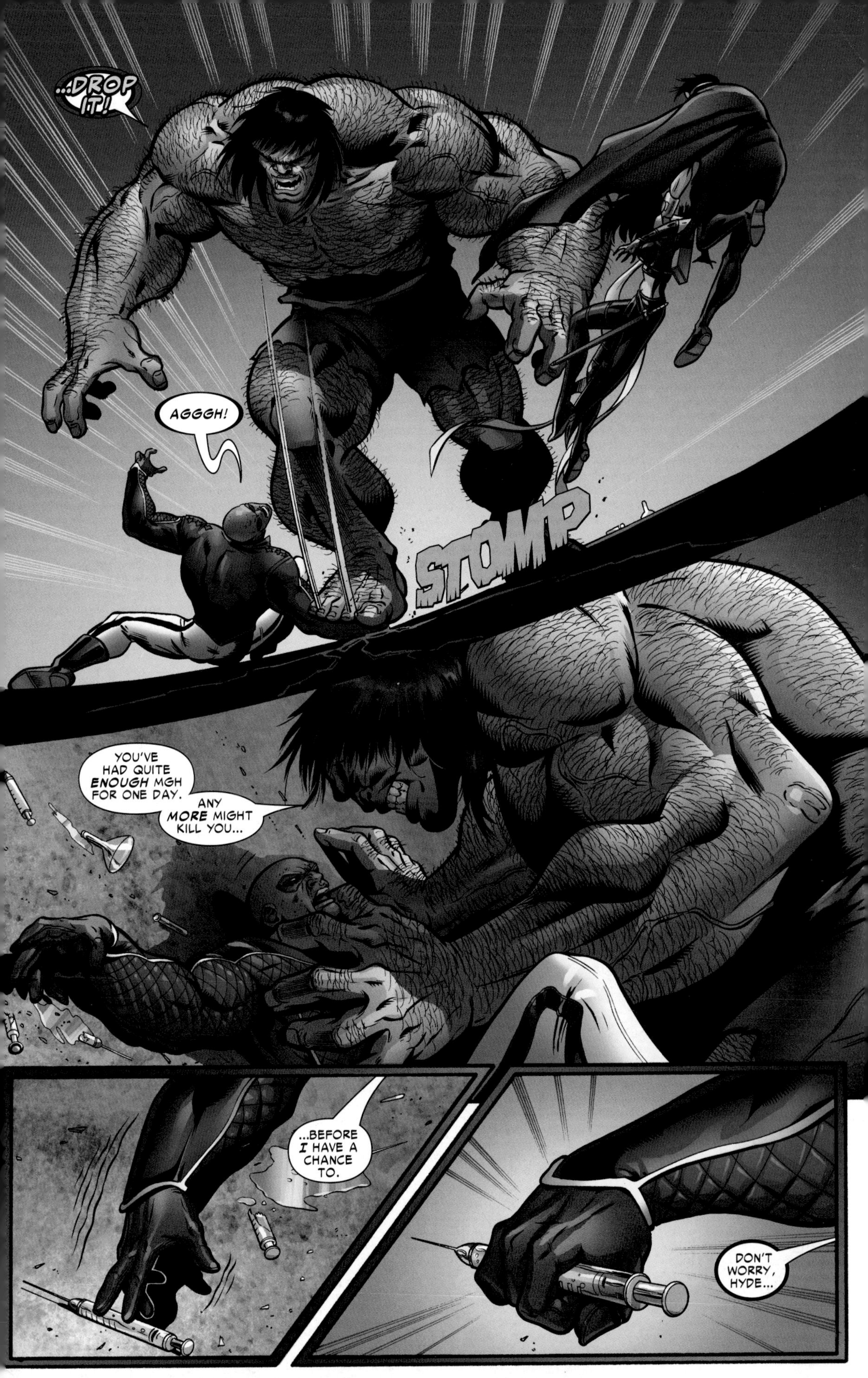
...DROP IT!
AGGGH!
STOMP
YOU'VE HAD QUITE ENOUGH MGH FOR ONE DAY.
ANY MORE MIGHT KILL YOU...
...BEFORE I HAVE A CHANCE TO.
DON'T WORRY, HYDE...

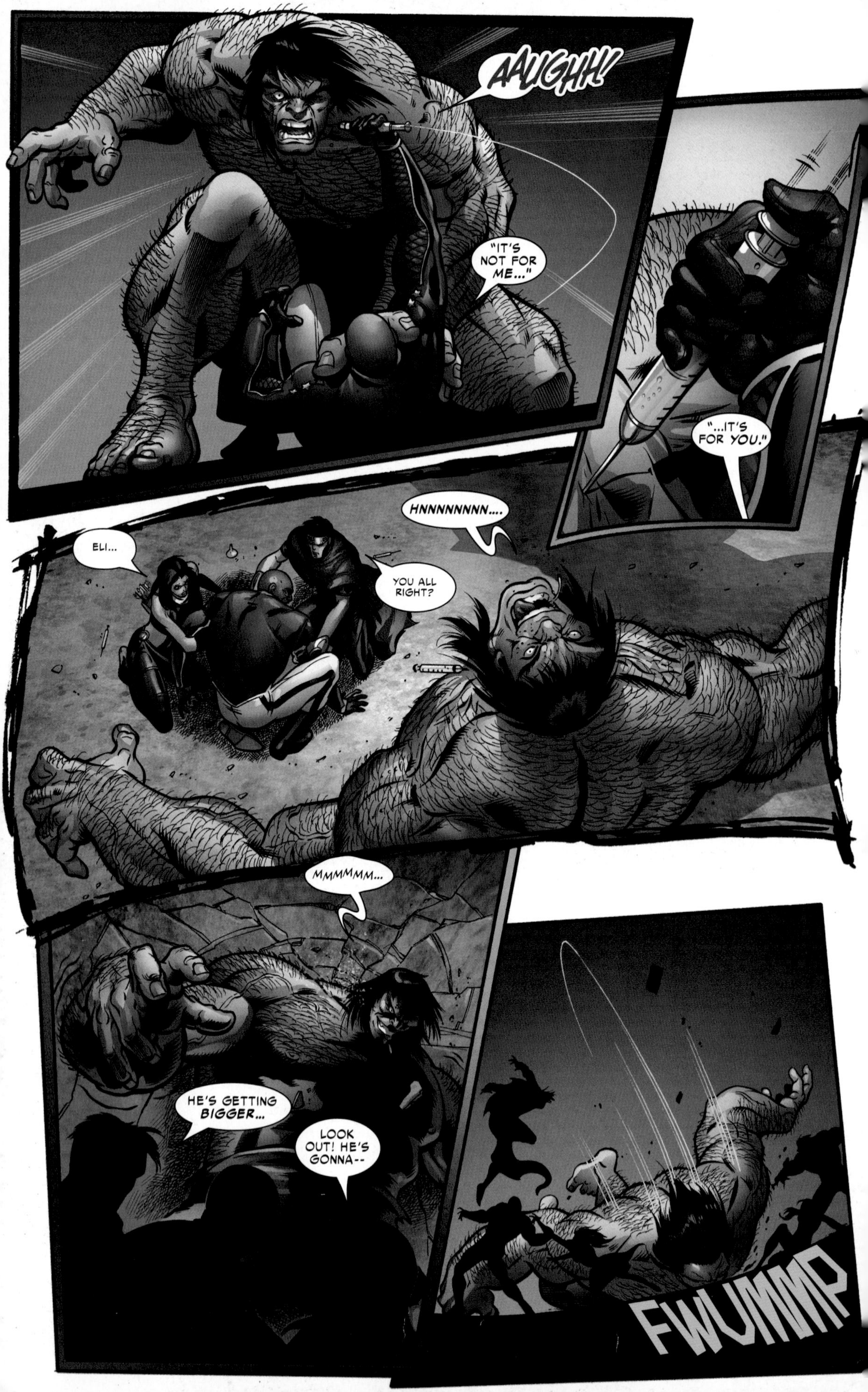
AAUGHH!
"IT'S NOT FOR ME..."
"...IT'S FOR YOU."
HNNNNNNNN....
ELI...
YOU ALL RIGHT?
MMMMMM...
HE'S GETTING BIGGER...
LOOK OUT! HE'S GONNA--
FWUMMP

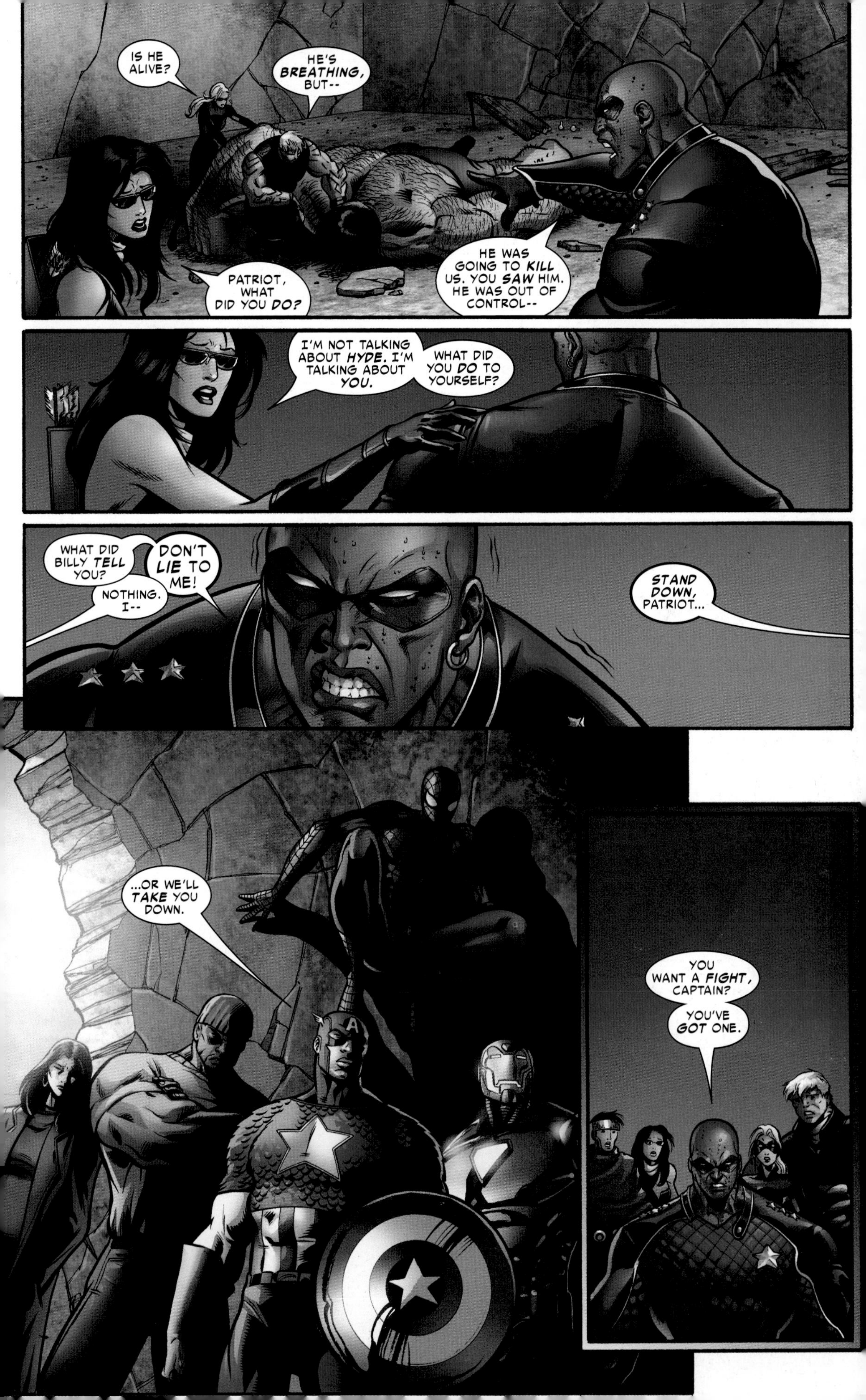
IS HE ALIVE?
HE'S BREATHING, BUT--
PATRIOT, WHAT DID YOU DO?
HE WAS GOING TO KILL US. YOU SAW HIM. HE WAS OUT OF CONTROL--
I'M NOT TALKING ABOUT HYDE. I'M TALKING ABOUT YOU.
WHAT DID YOU DO TO YOURSELF?
WHAT DID BILLY TELL YOU?
NOTHING. I--
DON'T LIE TO ME!
STAND DOWN, PATRIOT...
...OR WE'LL TAKE YOU DOWN.
YOU WANT A FIGHT, CAPTAIN?
YOU'VE GOT ONE.

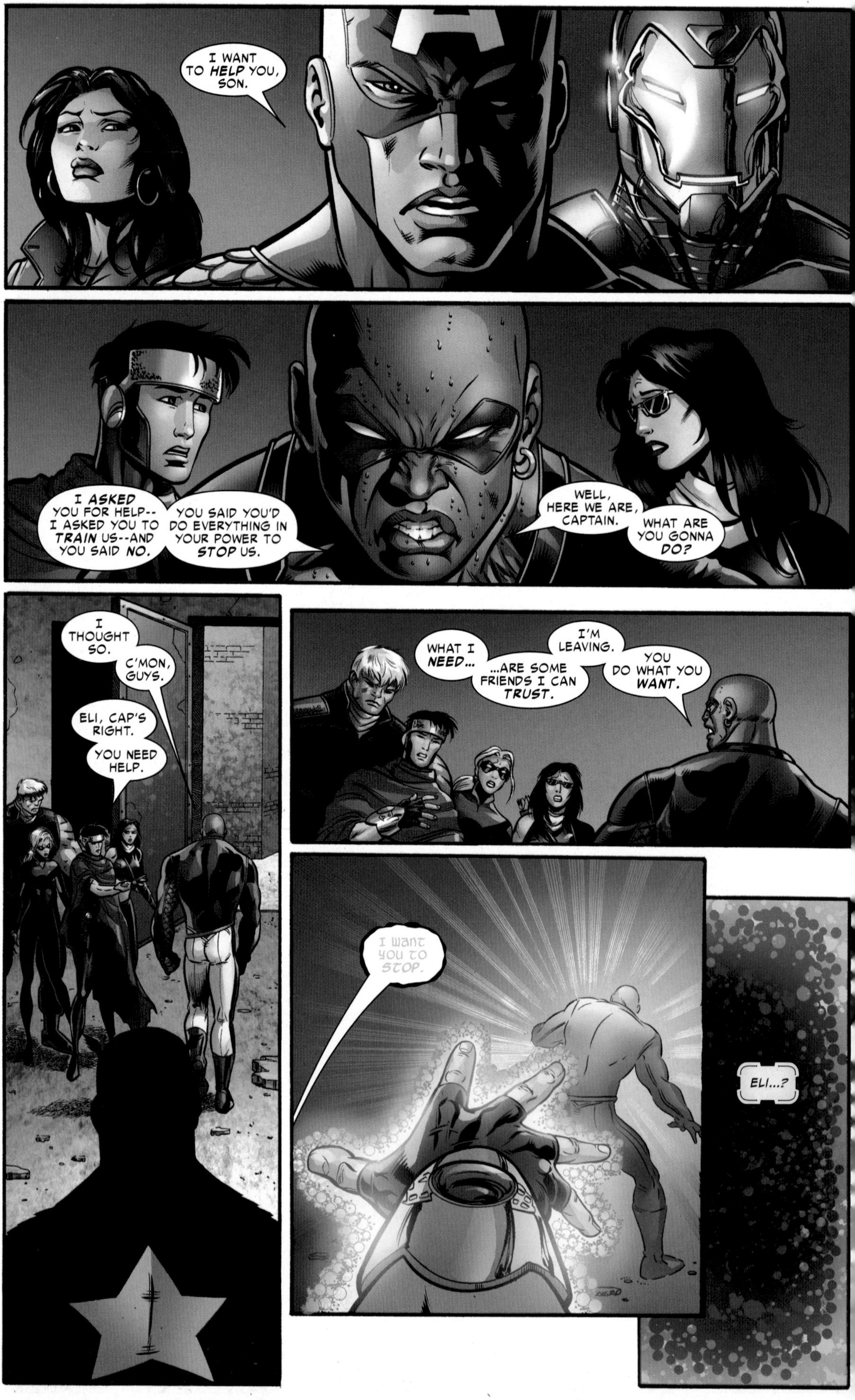

I WANT TO HELP YOU, SON.
I ASKED YOU FOR HELP-- I ASKED YOU TO TRAIN US--AND YOU SAID NO.
YOU SAID YOU'D DO EVERYTHING IN YOUR POWER TO STOP US.
WELL, HERE WE ARE, CAPTAIN.
WHAT ARE YOU GONNA DO?
I THOUGHT SO.
C'MON, GUYS.
ELI, CAP'S RIGHT.
YOU NEED HELP.
WHAT I NEED...
...ARE SOME FRIENDS I CAN TRUST.
I'M LEAVING.
YOU DO WHAT YOU WANT.
I WANT YOU TO STOP.
ELI...?

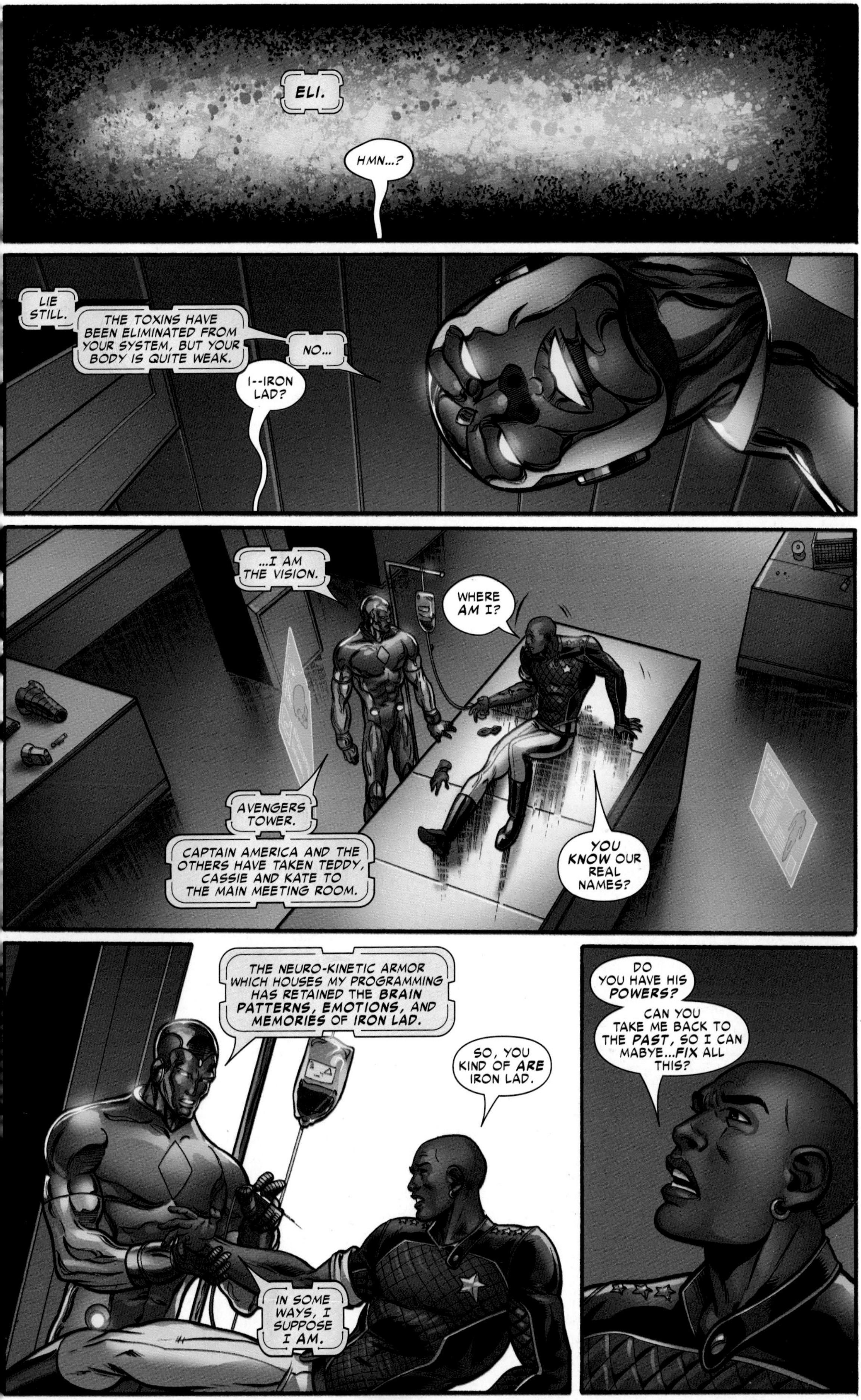
ELI.
HMN...?
LIE STILL.
THE TOXINS HAVE BEEN ELIMINATED FROM YOUR SYSTEM, BUT YOUR BODY IS QUITE WEAK.
NO...
I--IRON LAD?
...I AM THE VISION.
WHERE AM I?
AVENGERS TOWER.
CAPTAIN AMERICA AND THE OTHERS HAVE TAKEN TEDDY, CASSIE AND KATE TO THE MAIN MEETING ROOM.
YOU KNOW OUR REAL NAMES?
THE NEURO-KINETIC ARMOR WHICH HOUSES MY PROGRAMMING HAS RETAINED THE BRAIN PATTERNS, EMOTIONS, AND MEMORIES OF IRON LAD.
SO, YOU KIND OF ARE IRON LAD.
IN SOME WAYS, I SUPPOSE I AM.
DO YOU HAVE HIS POWERS?
CAN YOU TAKE ME BACK TO THE PAST, SO I CAN MABYE...FIX ALL THIS?

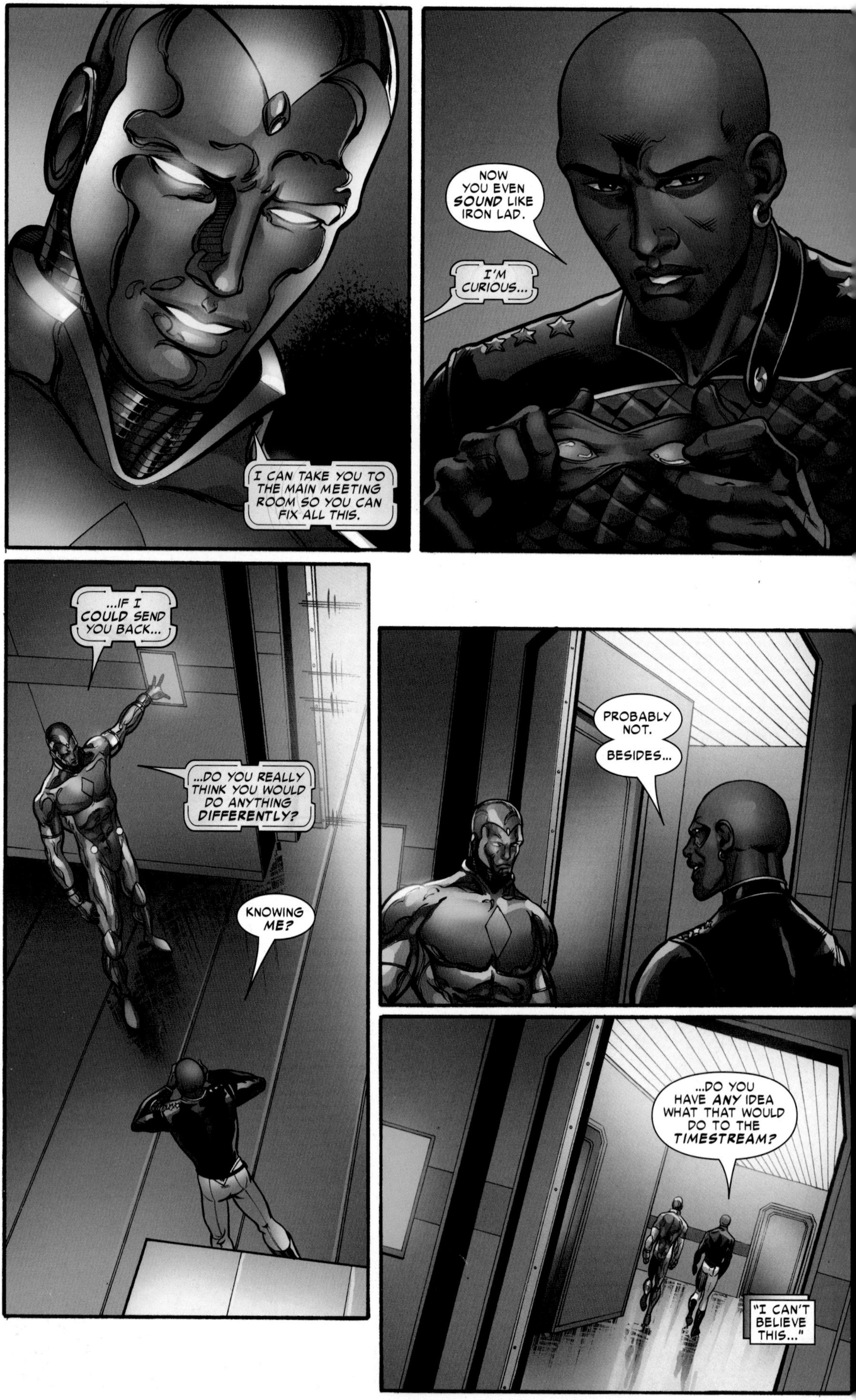

I CAN TAKE YOU TO THE MAIN MEETING ROOM SO YOU CAN FIX ALL THIS.
NOW YOU EVEN SOUND LIKE IRON LAD.
I'M CURIOUS...
...IF I COULD SEND YOU BACK...
...DO YOU REALLY THINK YOU WOULD DO ANYTHING DIFFERENTLY?
KNOWING ME?
PROBABLY NOT.
BESIDES...
...DO YOU HAVE ANY IDEA WHAT THAT WOULD DO TO THE TIMESTREAM?
"I CAN'T BELIEVE THIS..."

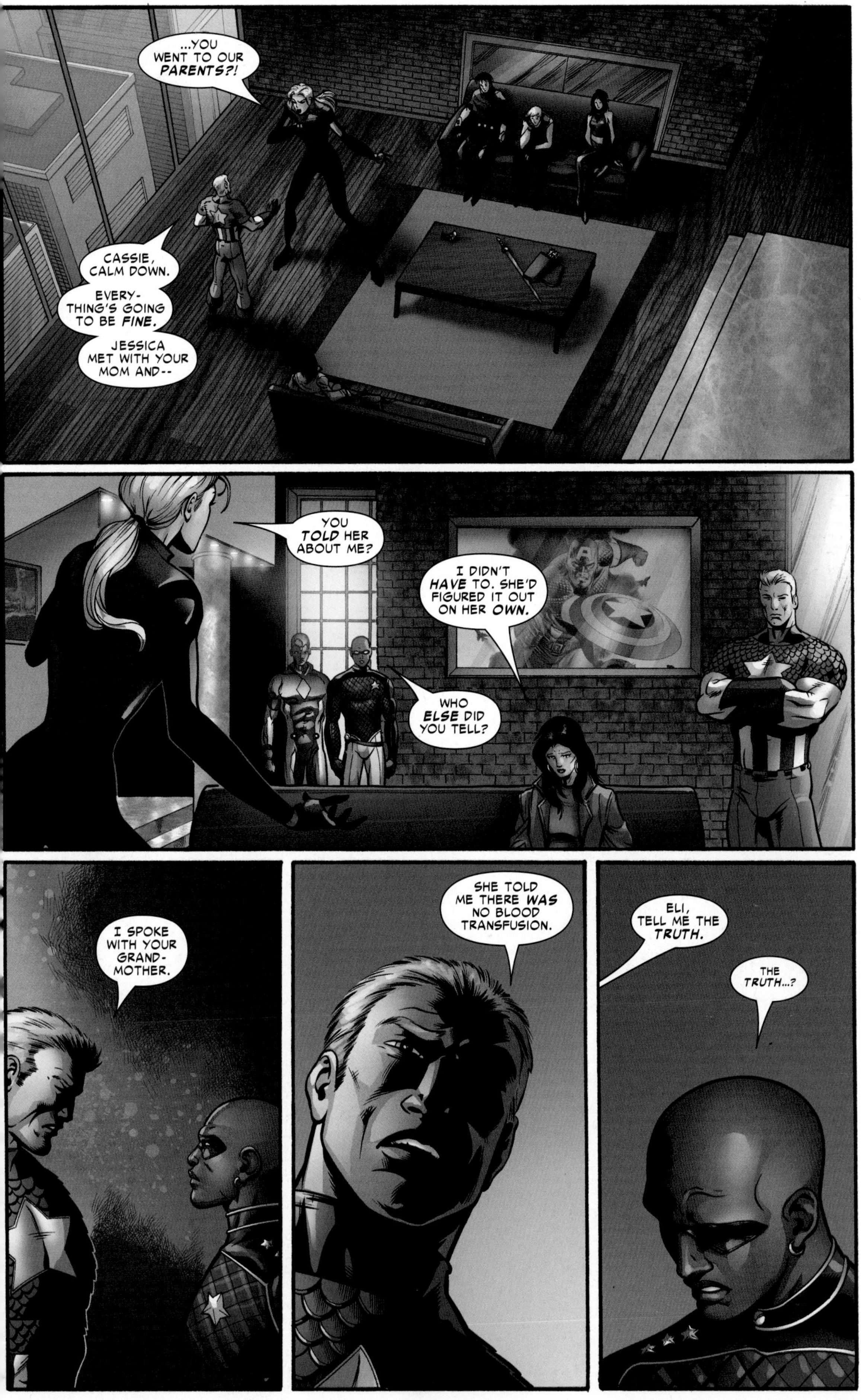
...YOU WENT TO OUR PARENTS?!
CASSIE, CALM DOWN.
EVERY-THING'S GOING TO BE FINE.
JESSICA MET WITH YOUR MOM AND--
YOU TOLD HER ABOUT ME?
I DIDN'T HAVE TO. SHE'D FIGURED IT OUT ON HER OWN.
WHO ELSE DID YOU TELL?
I SPOKE WITH YOUR GRAND-MOTHER.
SHE TOLD ME THERE WAS NO BLOOD TRANSFUSION.
ELI, TELL ME THE TRUTH.
THE TRUTH...?

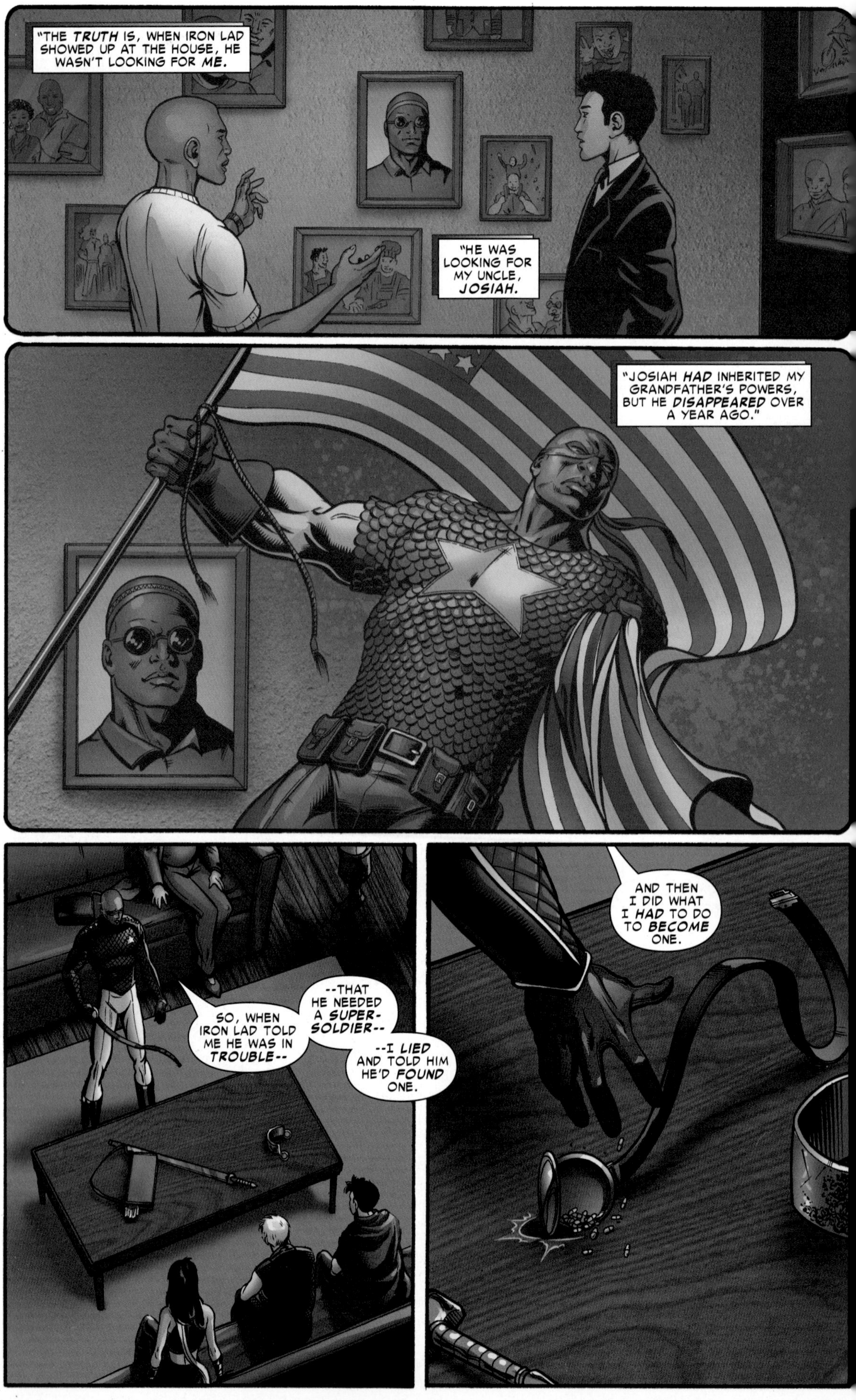
"THE TRUTH IS, WHEN IRON LAD SHOWED UP AT THE HOUSE, HE WASN'T LOOKING FOR ME.
"HE WAS LOOKING FOR MY UNCLE, JOSIAH.
"JOSIAH HAD INHERITED MY GRANDFATHER'S POWERS, BUT HE DISAPPEARED OVER A YEAR AGO."
SO, WHEN IRON LAD TOLD ME HE WAS IN TROUBLE--
--THAT HE NEEDED A SUPER-SOLDIER--
--I LIED AND TOLD HIM HE'D FOUND ONE.
AND THEN I DID WHAT I HAD TO DO TO BECOME ONE.

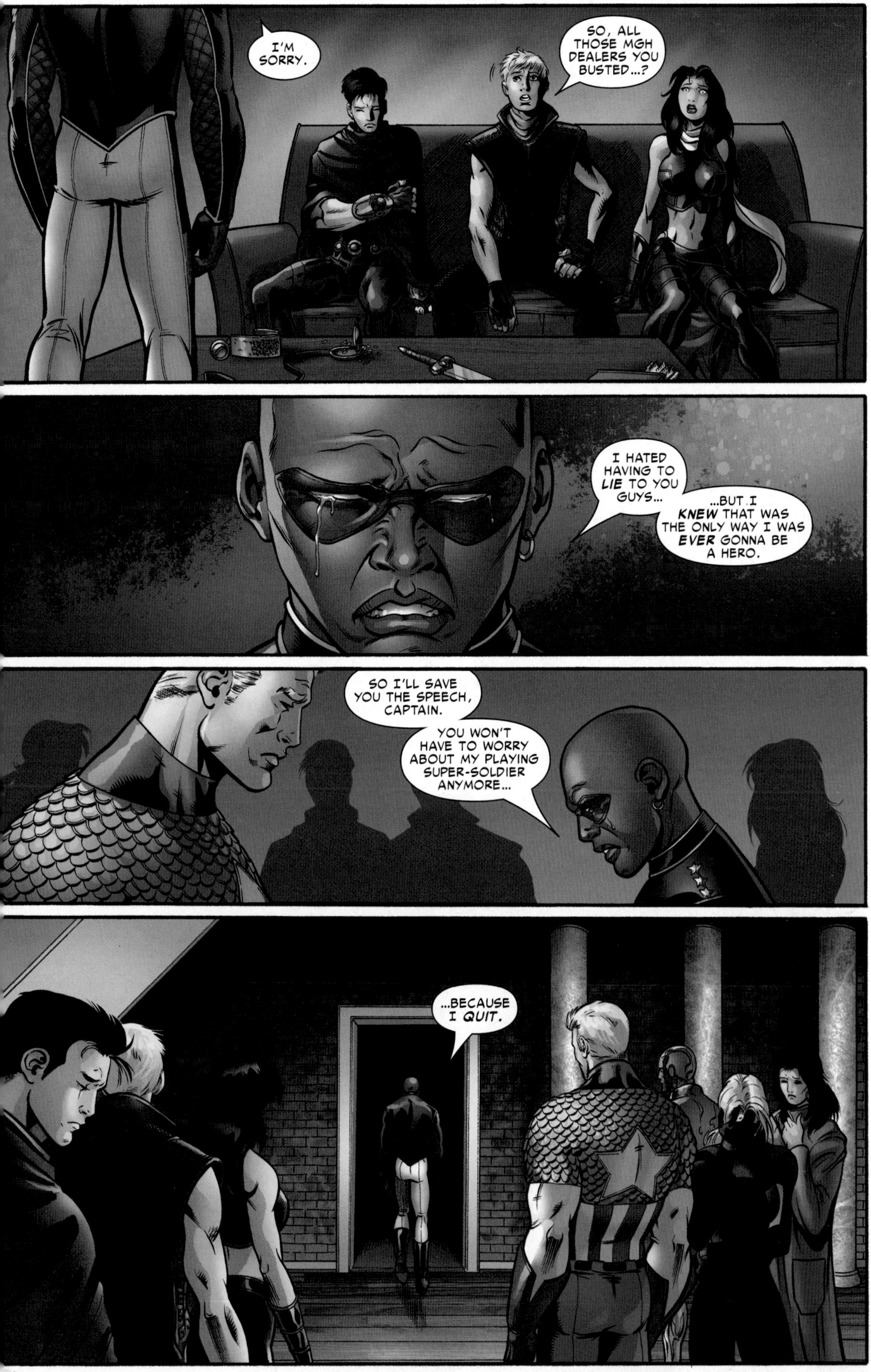
I'M SORRY.
SO, ALL THOSE MGH DEALERS YOU BUSTED...?
I HATED HAVING TO LIE TO YOU GUYS...
...BUT I KNEW THAT WAS THE ONLY WAY I WAS EVER GONNA BE A HERO.
SO I'LL SAVE YOU THE SPEECH, CAPTAIN.
YOU WON'T HAVE TO WORRY ABOUT MY PLAYING SUPER-SOLDIER ANYMORE...
...BECAUSE I QUIT.

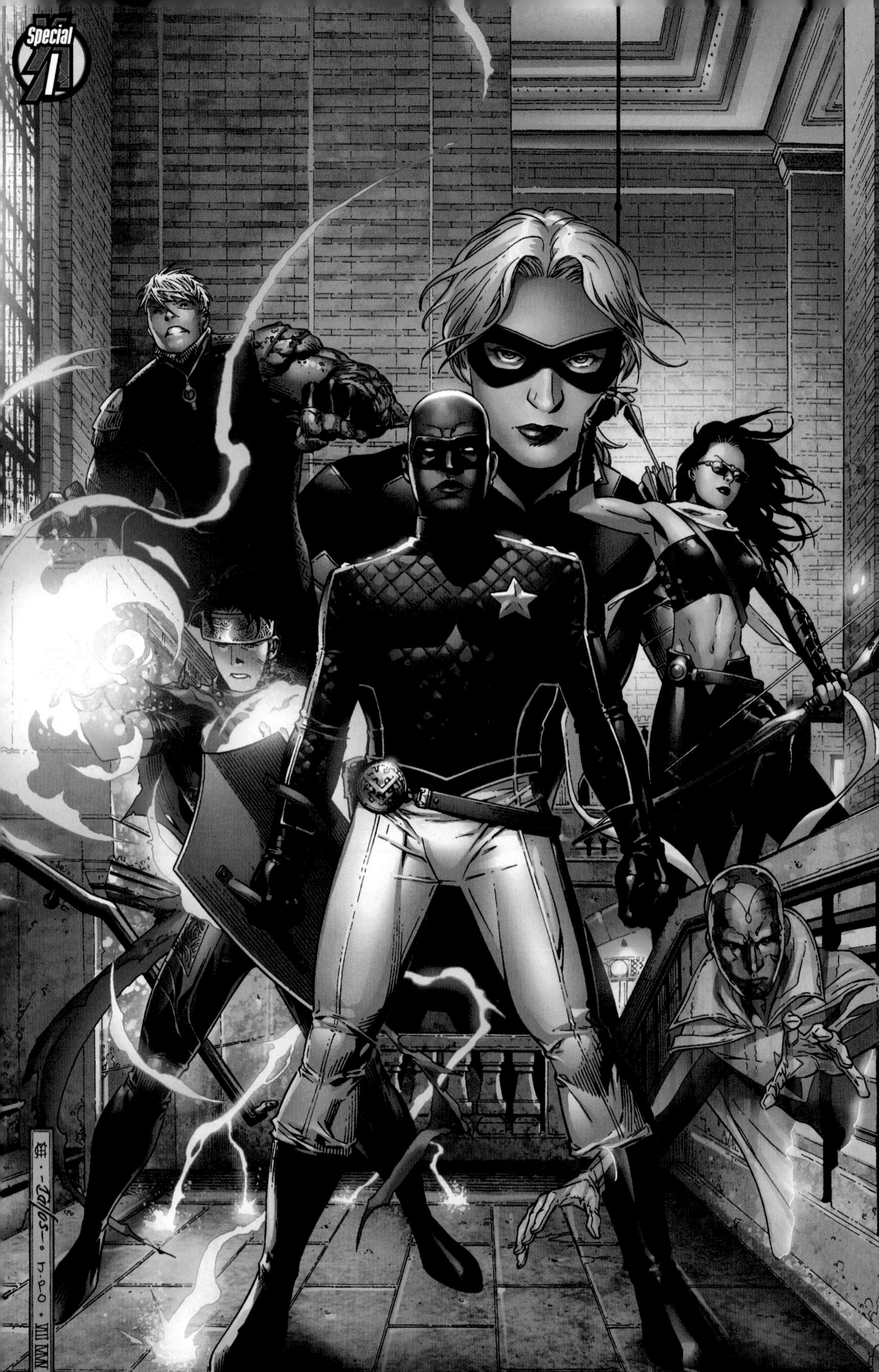
Special

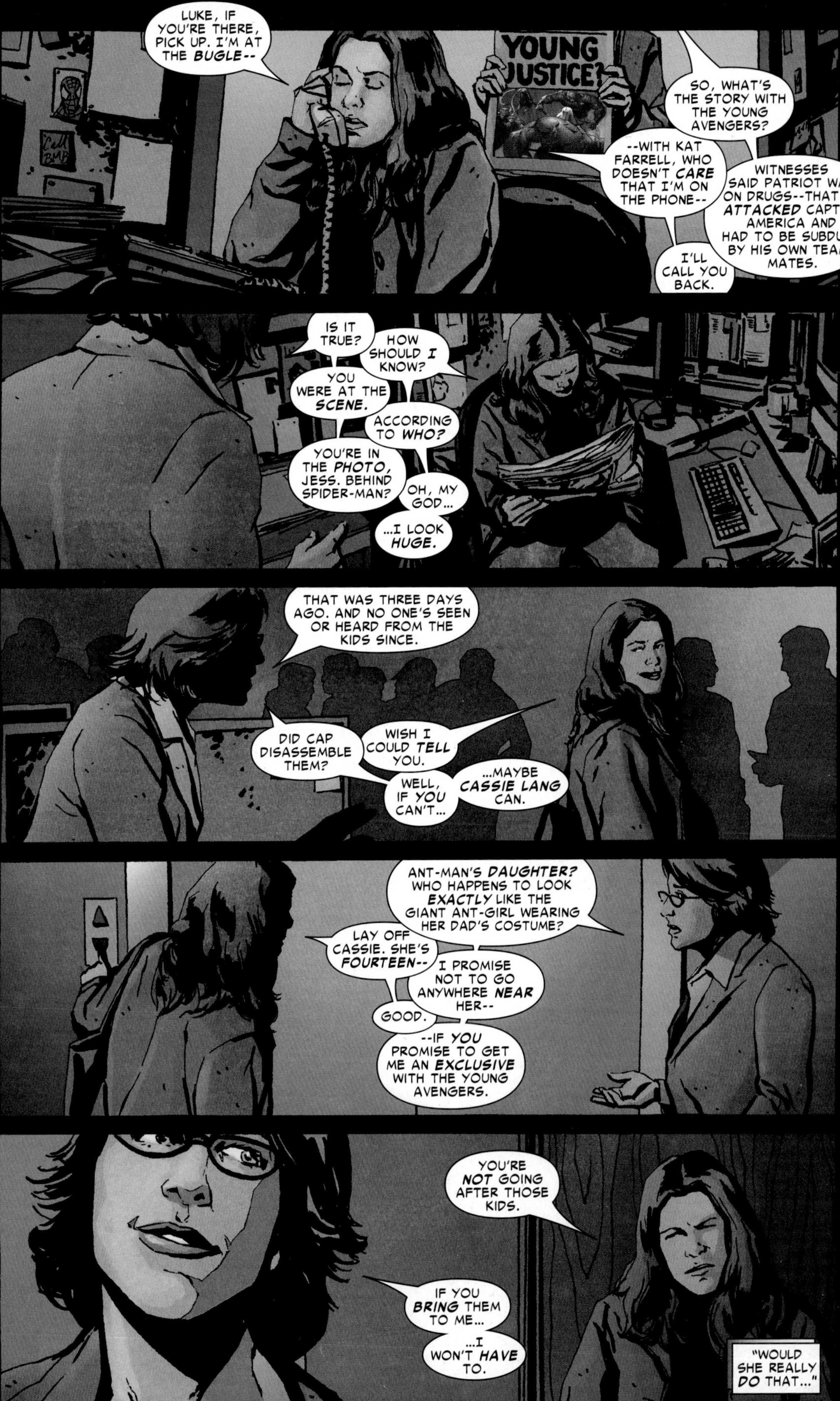
LUKE, IF YOU'RE THERE, PICK UP. I'M AT THE BUGLE--
YOUNG JUSTICE?
SO, WHAT'S THE STORY WITH THE YOUNG AVENGERS?
--WITH KAT FARRELL, WHO DOESN'T CARE THAT I'M ON THE PHONE--
WITNESSES SAID PATRIOT WAS ON DRUGS--THAT HE ATTACKED CAPTAIN AMERICA AND HAD TO BE SUBDUED BY HIS OWN TEAM-MATES.
I'LL CALL YOU BACK.
IS IT TRUE?
HOW SHOULD I KNOW?
YOU WERE AT THE SCENE.
ACCORDING TO WHO?
YOU'RE IN THE PHOTO, JESS. BEHIND SPIDER-MAN?
OH, MY GOD...
...I LOOK HUGE.
THAT WAS THREE DAYS AGO. AND NO ONE'S SEEN OR HEARD FROM THE KIDS SINCE.
DID CAP DISASSEMBLE THEM?
WISH I COULD TELL YOU.
WELL, IF YOU CAN'T...
...MAYBE CASSIE LANG CAN.
ANT-MAN'S DAUGHTER? WHO HAPPENS TO LOOK EXACTLY LIKE THE GIANT ANT-GIRL WEARING HER DAD'S COSTUME?
LAY OFF CASSIE. SHE'S FOURTEEN--
I PROMISE NOT TO GO ANYWHERE NEAR HER--
GOOD.
--IF YOU PROMISE TO GET ME AN EXCLUSIVE WITH THE YOUNG AVENGERS.
YOU'RE NOT GOING AFTER THOSE KIDS.
IF YOU BRING THEM TO ME...
...I WON'T HAVE TO.
"WOULD SHE REALLY DO THAT..."

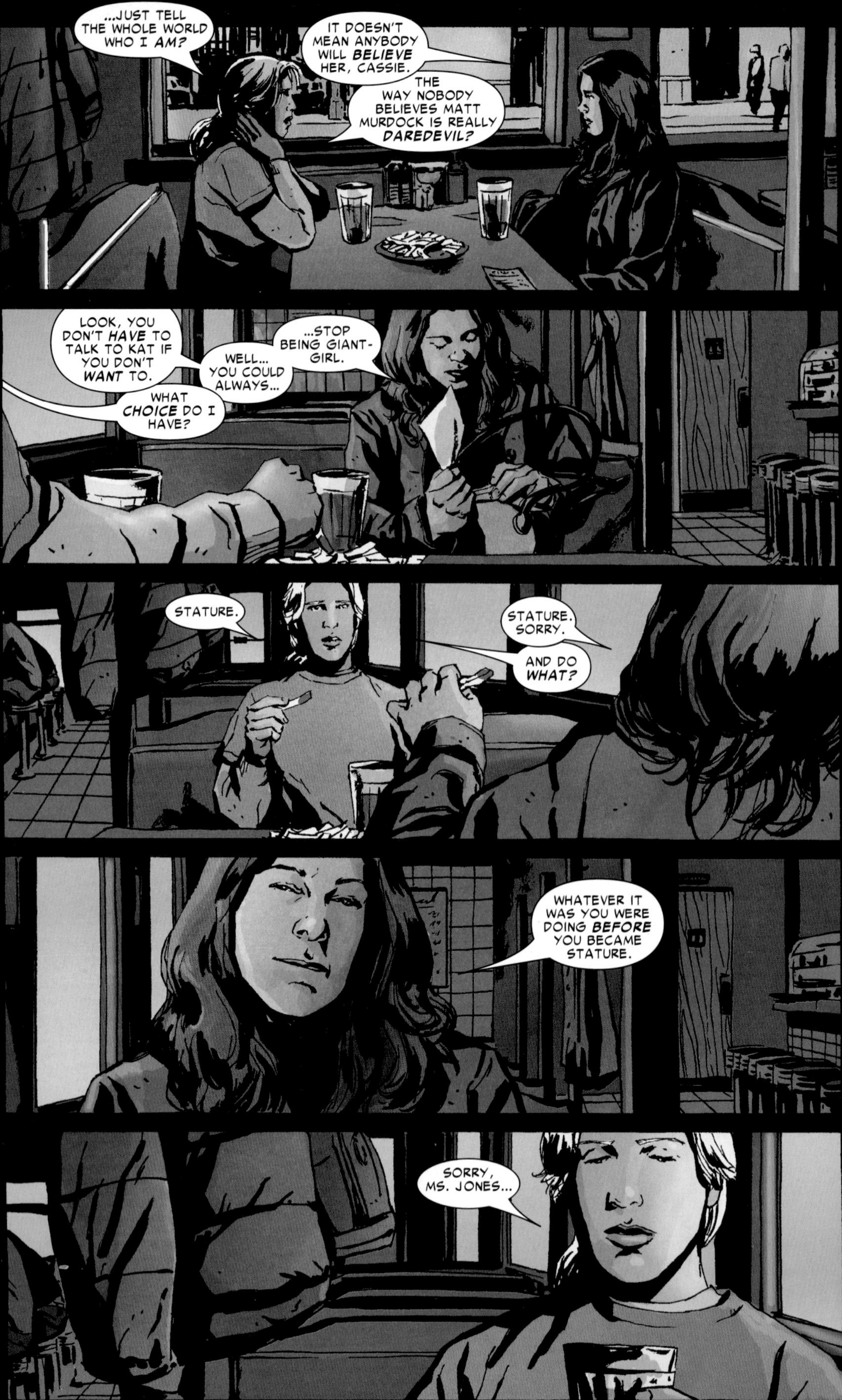

...JUST TELL THE WHOLE WORLD WHO I AM?
IT DOESN'T MEAN ANYBODY WILL BELIEVE HER, CASSIE.
THE WAY NOBODY BELIEVES MATT MURDOCK IS REALLY DAREDEVIL?
LOOK, YOU DON'T HAVE TO TALK TO KAT IF YOU DON'T WANT TO.
WHAT CHOICE DO I HAVE?
WELL... YOU COULD ALWAYS...
...STOP BEING GIANT-GIRL.
STATURE.
STATURE. SORRY.
AND DO WHAT?
WHATEVER IT WAS YOU WERE DOING BEFORE YOU BECAME STATURE.
SORRY, MS. JONES...

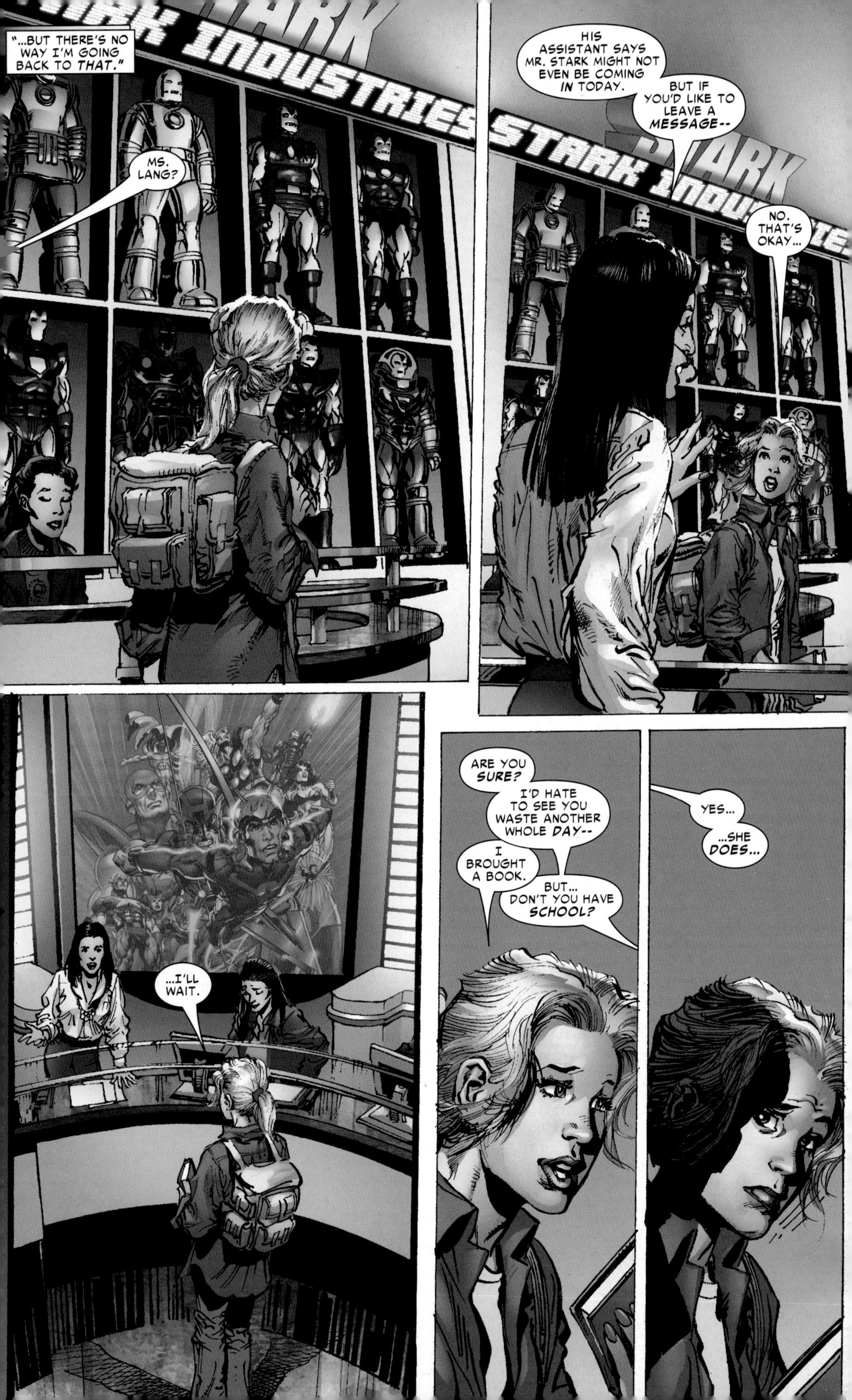
"...BUT THERE'S NO WAY I'M GOING BACK TO THAT."
STARK INDUSTRIES
MS. LANG?
HIS ASSISTANT SAYS MR. STARK MIGHT NOT EVEN BE COMING IN TODAY.
BUT IF YOU'D LIKE TO LEAVE A MESSAGE--
NO. THAT'S OKAY...
...I'LL WAIT.
ARE YOU SURE?
I'D HATE TO SEE YOU WASTE ANOTHER WHOLE DAY--
I BROUGHT A BOOK.
BUT... DON'T YOU HAVE SCHOOL?
YES...
...SHE DOES...

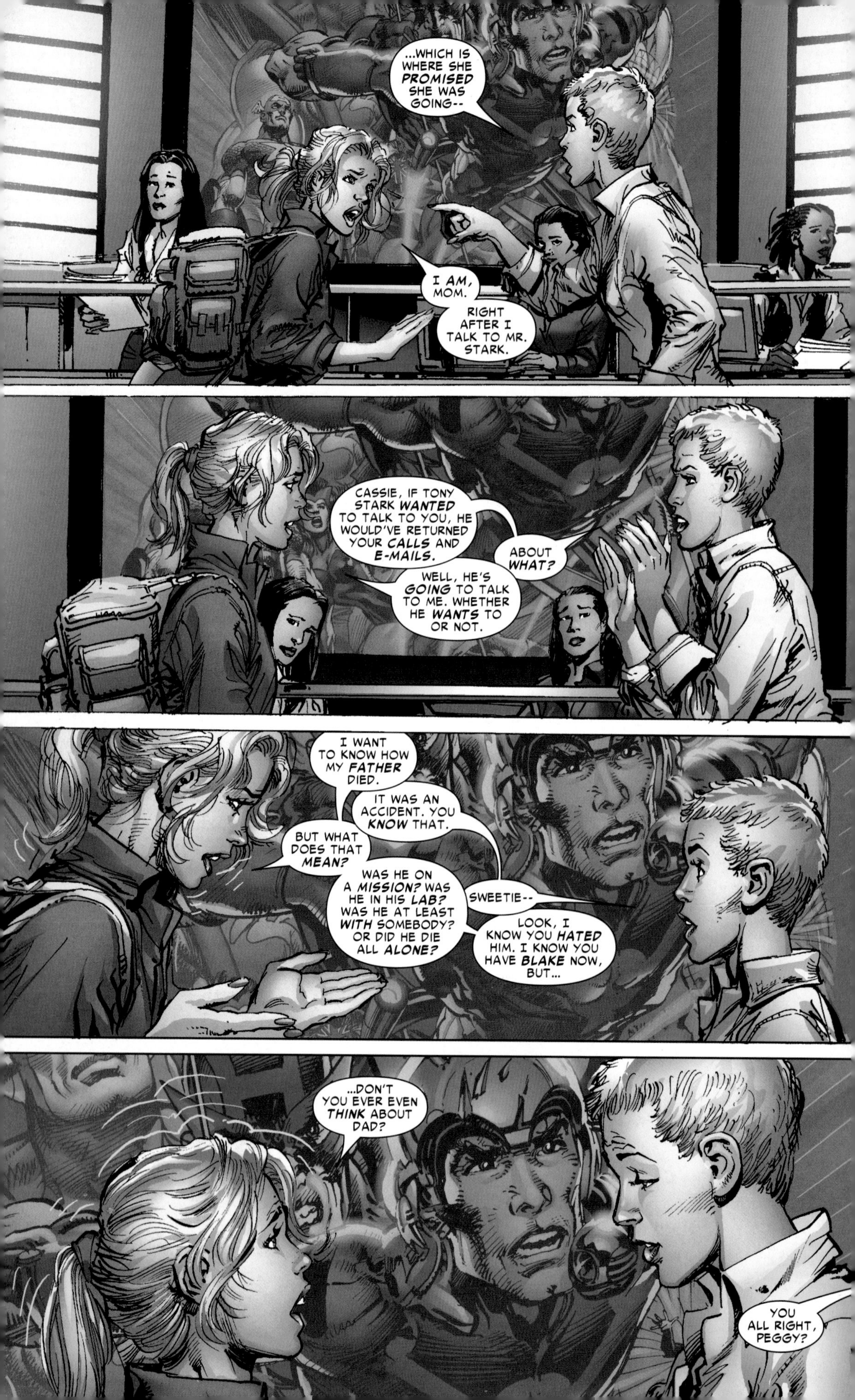
...WHICH IS WHERE SHE *PROMISED* SHE WAS GOING--
I *AM*, MOM.
RIGHT AFTER I TALK TO MR. STARK.
CASSIE, IF TONY STARK *WANTED* TO TALK TO YOU, HE WOULD'VE RETURNED YOUR *CALLS* AND *E-MAILS*.
WELL, HE'S *GOING* TO TALK TO ME. WHETHER HE *WANTS* TO OR NOT.
ABOUT *WHAT?*
I WANT TO KNOW HOW MY *FATHER* DIED.
IT WAS AN ACCIDENT. YOU *KNOW* THAT.
BUT WHAT DOES THAT *MEAN?*
WAS HE ON A *MISSION?* WAS HE IN HIS *LAB?* WAS HE AT LEAST *WITH* SOMEBODY? OR DID HE DIE ALL *ALONE?*
SWEETIE--
LOOK, I KNOW YOU *HATED* HIM. I KNOW YOU HAVE *BLAKE* NOW, BUT...
...DON'T YOU EVER EVEN *THINK* ABOUT DAD?
YOU ALL RIGHT, PEGGY?

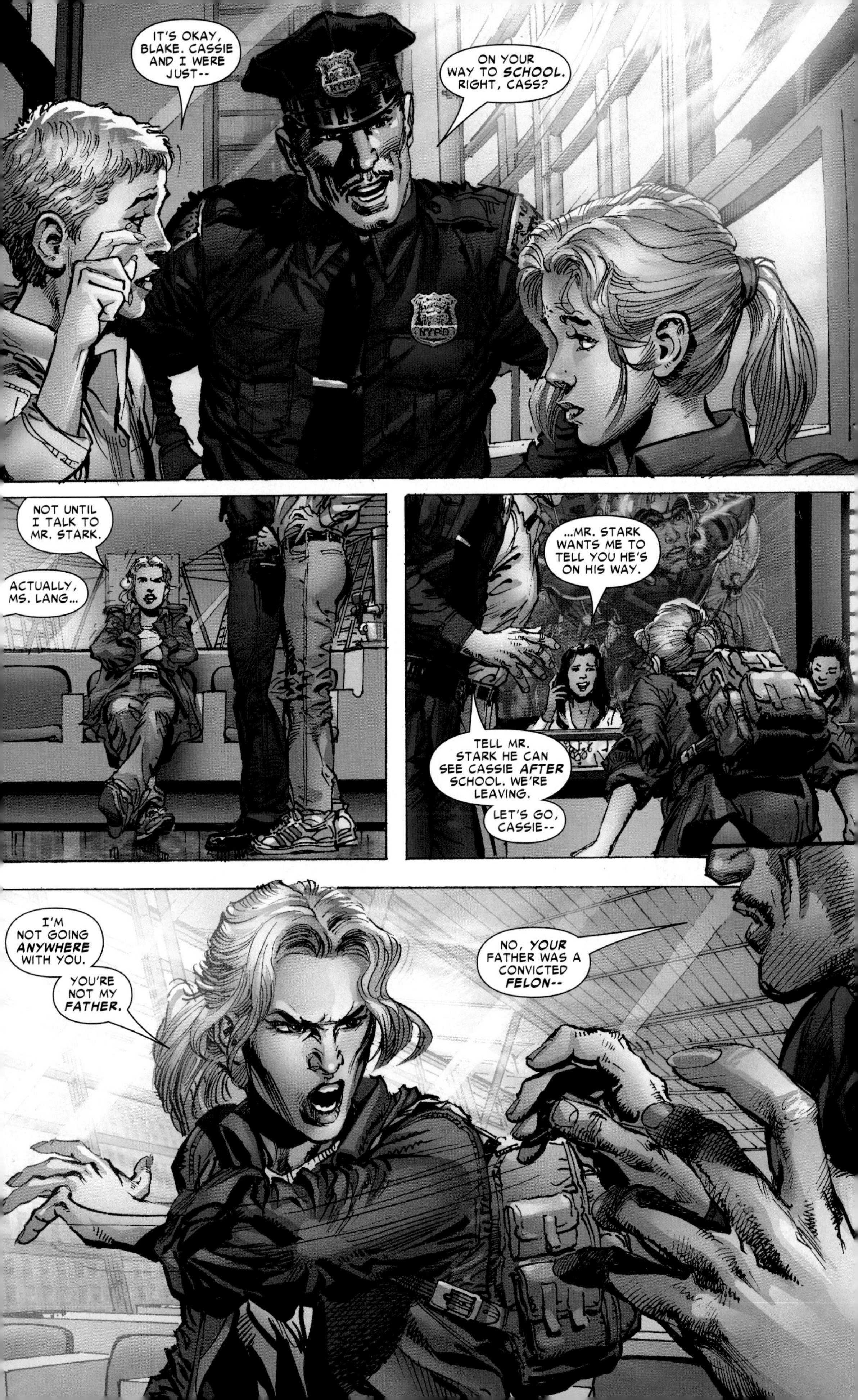

IT'S OKAY, BLAKE. CASSIE AND I WERE JUST--
ON YOUR WAY TO SCHOOL. RIGHT, CASS?
NOT UNTIL I TALK TO MR. STARK.
ACTUALLY, MS. LANG...
...MR. STARK WANTS ME TO TELL YOU HE'S ON HIS WAY.
TELL MR. STARK HE CAN SEE CASSIE AFTER SCHOOL. WE'RE LEAVING.
LET'S GO, CASSIE--
I'M NOT GOING ANYWHERE WITH YOU.
YOU'RE NOT MY FATHER.
NO, YOUR FATHER WAS A CONVICTED FELON--

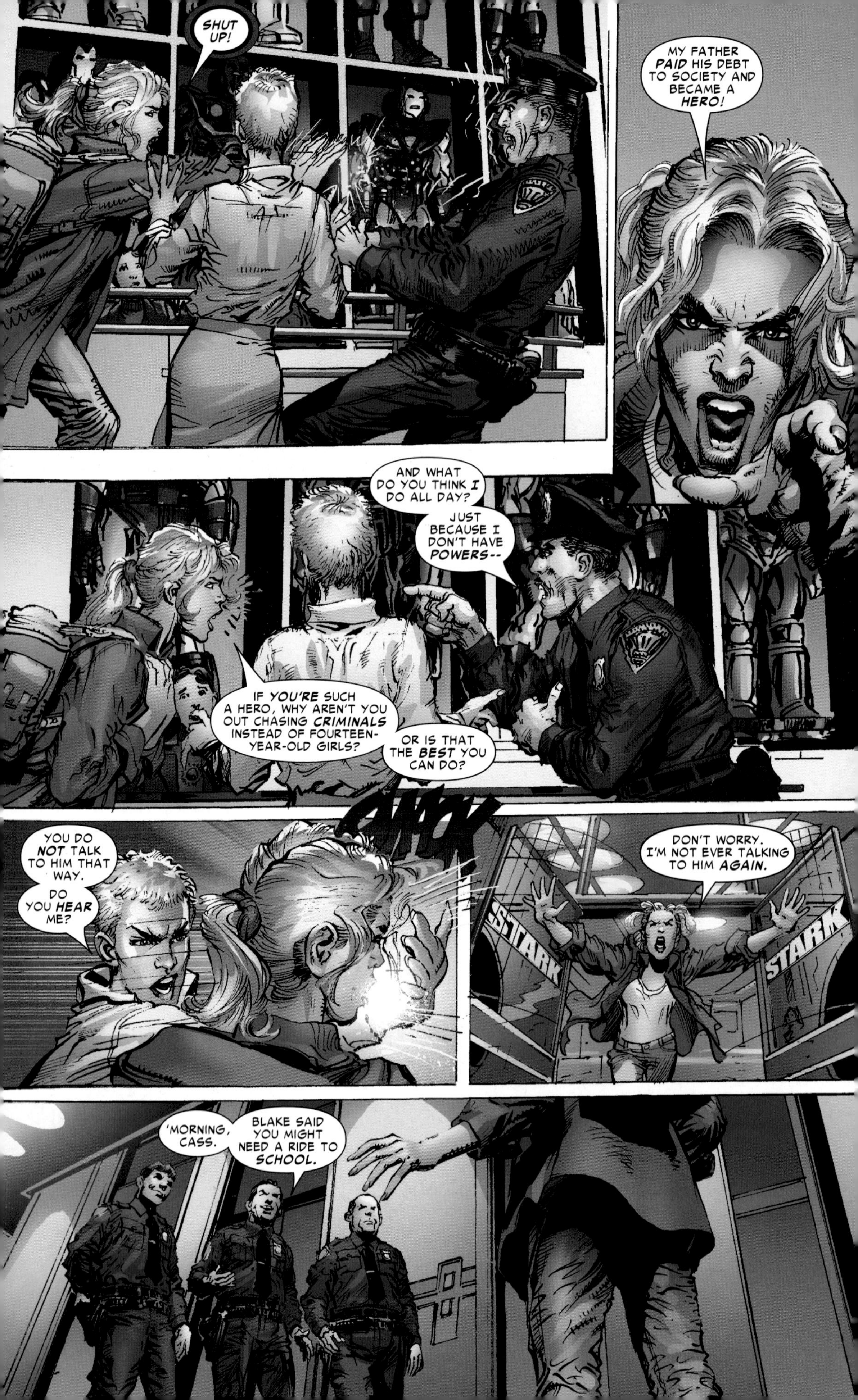

SHUT UP!
MY FATHER PAID HIS DEBT TO SOCIETY AND BECAME A HERO!
AND WHAT DO YOU THINK I DO ALL DAY?
JUST BECAUSE I DON'T HAVE POWERS--
IF YOU'RE SUCH A HERO, WHY AREN'T YOU OUT CHASING CRIMINALS INSTEAD OF FOURTEEN-YEAR-OLD GIRLS?
OR IS THAT THE BEST YOU CAN DO?
YOU DO NOT TALK TO HIM THAT WAY.
DO YOU HEAR ME?
DON'T WORRY. I'M NOT EVER TALKING TO HIM AGAIN.
STARK
STARK
'MORNING, CASS.
BLAKE SAID YOU MIGHT NEED A RIDE TO SCHOOL.

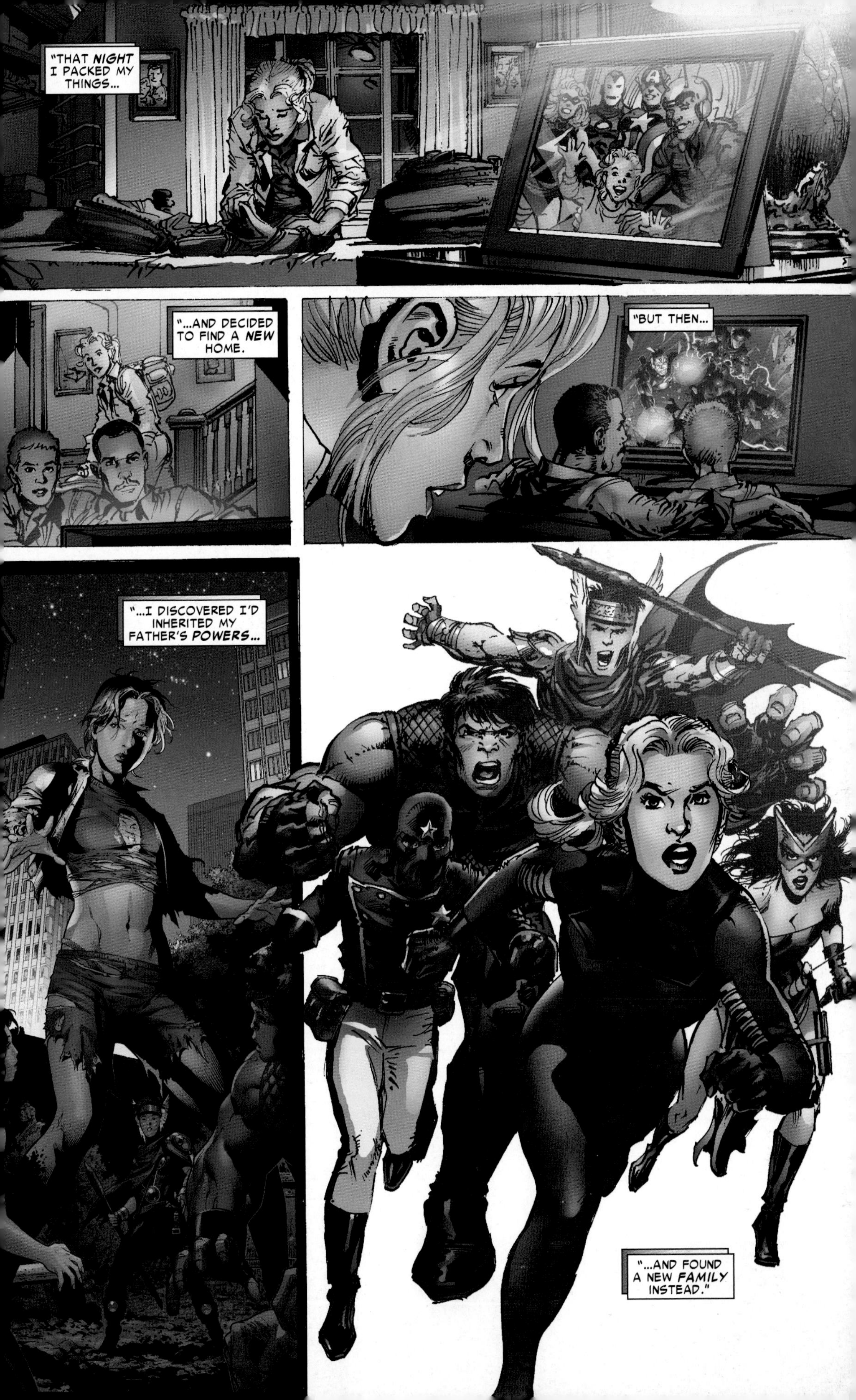
"THAT NIGHT I PACKED MY THINGS...
"...AND DECIDED TO FIND A NEW HOME.
"BUT THEN...
"...I DISCOVERED I'D INHERITED MY FATHER'S POWERS...
"...AND FOUND A NEW FAMILY INSTEAD."

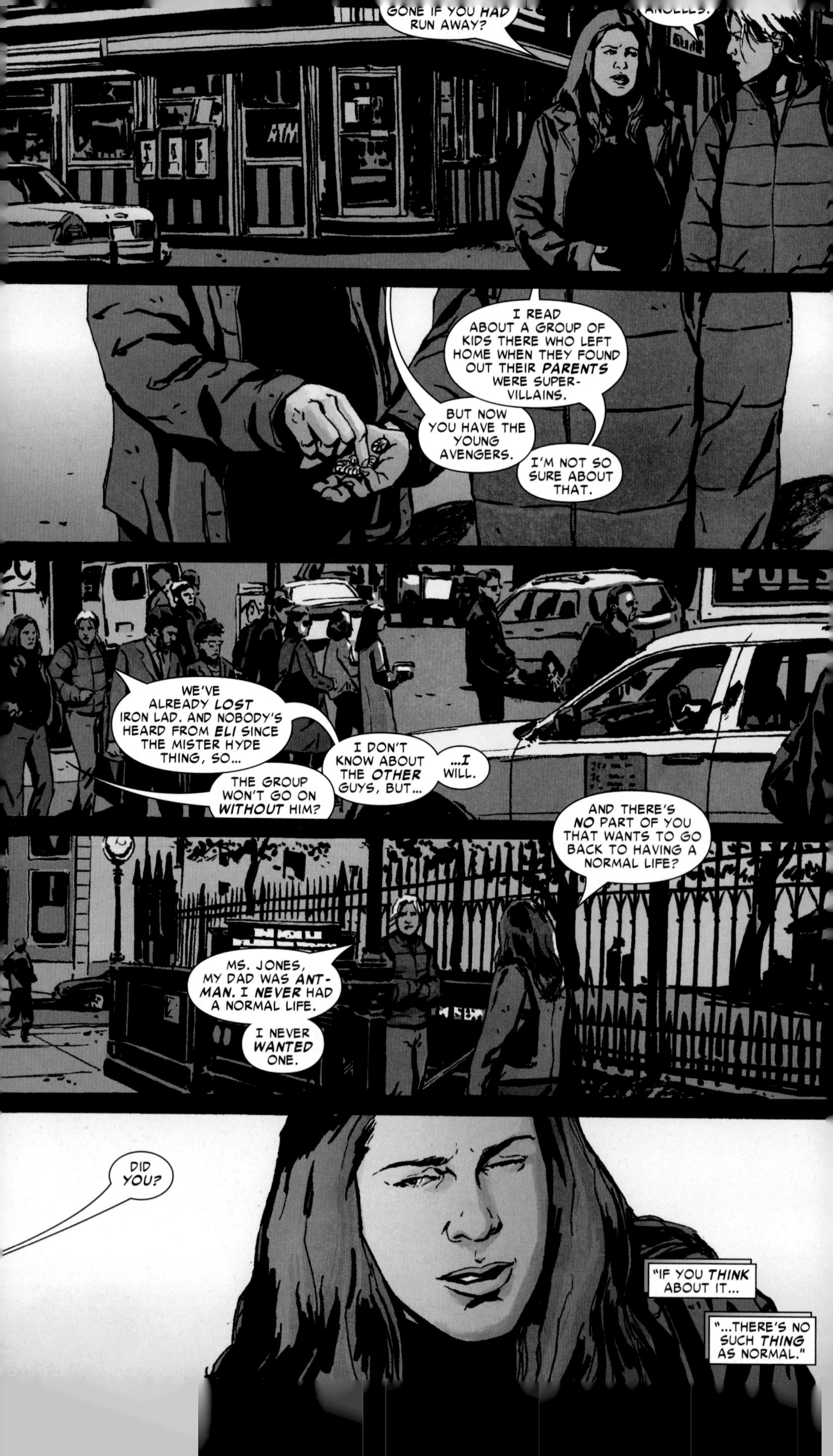
GONE IF YOU HAD RUN AWAY?
I READ ABOUT A GROUP OF KIDS THERE WHO LEFT HOME WHEN THEY FOUND OUT THEIR PARENTS WERE SUPER-VILLAINS.
BUT NOW YOU HAVE THE YOUNG AVENGERS.
I'M NOT SO SURE ABOUT THAT.
WE'VE ALREADY LOST IRON LAD. AND NOBODY'S HEARD FROM ELI SINCE THE MISTER HYDE THING, SO...
THE GROUP WON'T GO ON WITHOUT HIM?
I DON'T KNOW ABOUT THE OTHER GUYS, BUT...
...I WILL.
AND THERE'S NO PART OF YOU THAT WANTS TO GO BACK TO HAVING A NORMAL LIFE?
MS. JONES, MY DAD WAS ANT-MAN. I NEVER HAD A NORMAL LIFE.
I NEVER WANTED ONE.
DID YOU?
"IF YOU THINK ABOUT IT...
"...THERE'S NO SUCH THING AS NORMAL."

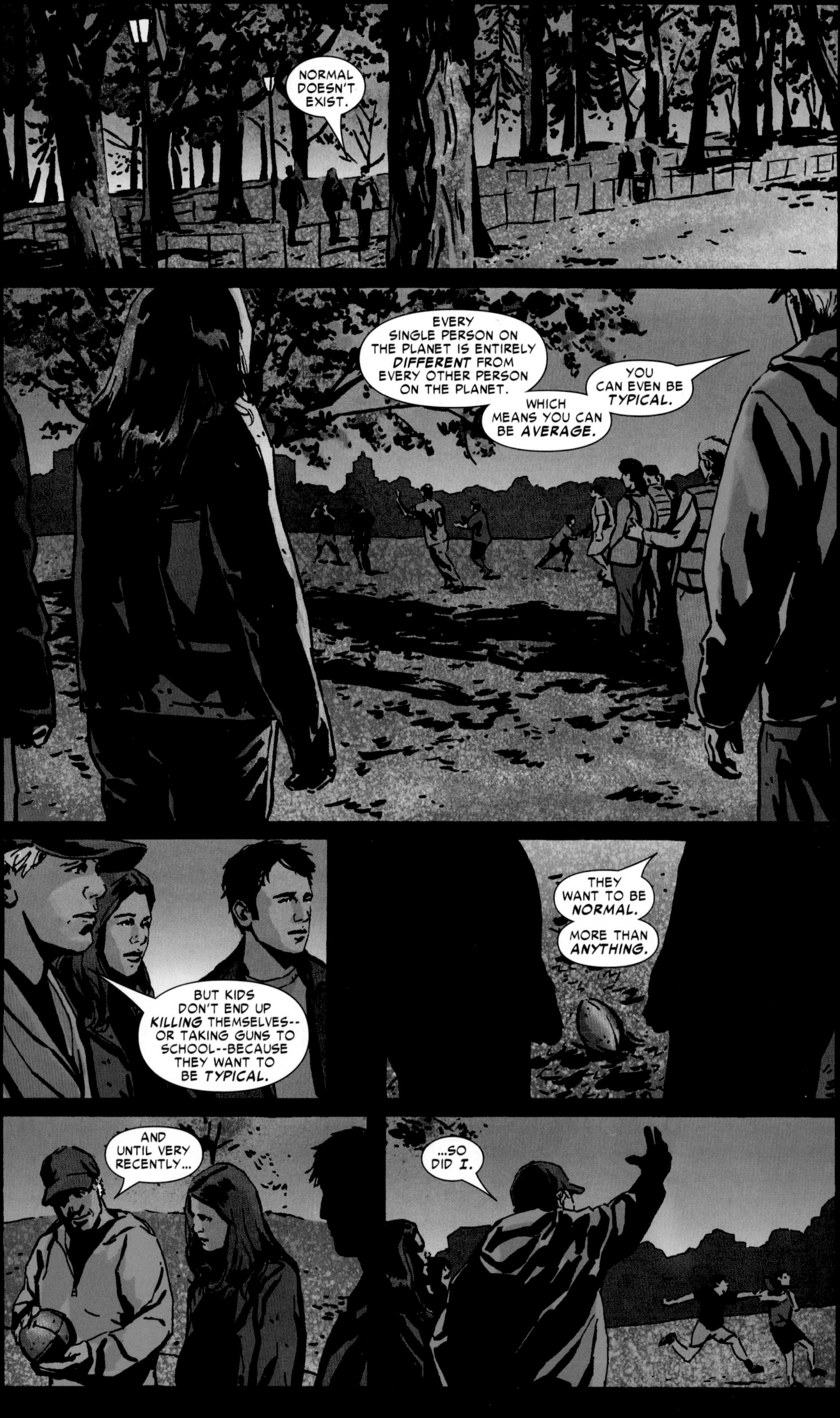
NORMAL DOESN'T EXIST.
EVERY SINGLE PERSON ON THE PLANET IS ENTIRELY DIFFERENT FROM EVERY OTHER PERSON ON THE PLANET.
WHICH MEANS YOU CAN BE AVERAGE.
YOU CAN EVEN BE TYPICAL.
BUT KIDS DON'T END UP KILLING THEMSELVES--OR TAKING GUNS TO SCHOOL--BECAUSE THEY WANT TO BE TYPICAL.
THEY WANT TO BE NORMAL.
MORE THAN ANYTHING.
AND UNTIL VERY RECENTLY...
...SO DID I.

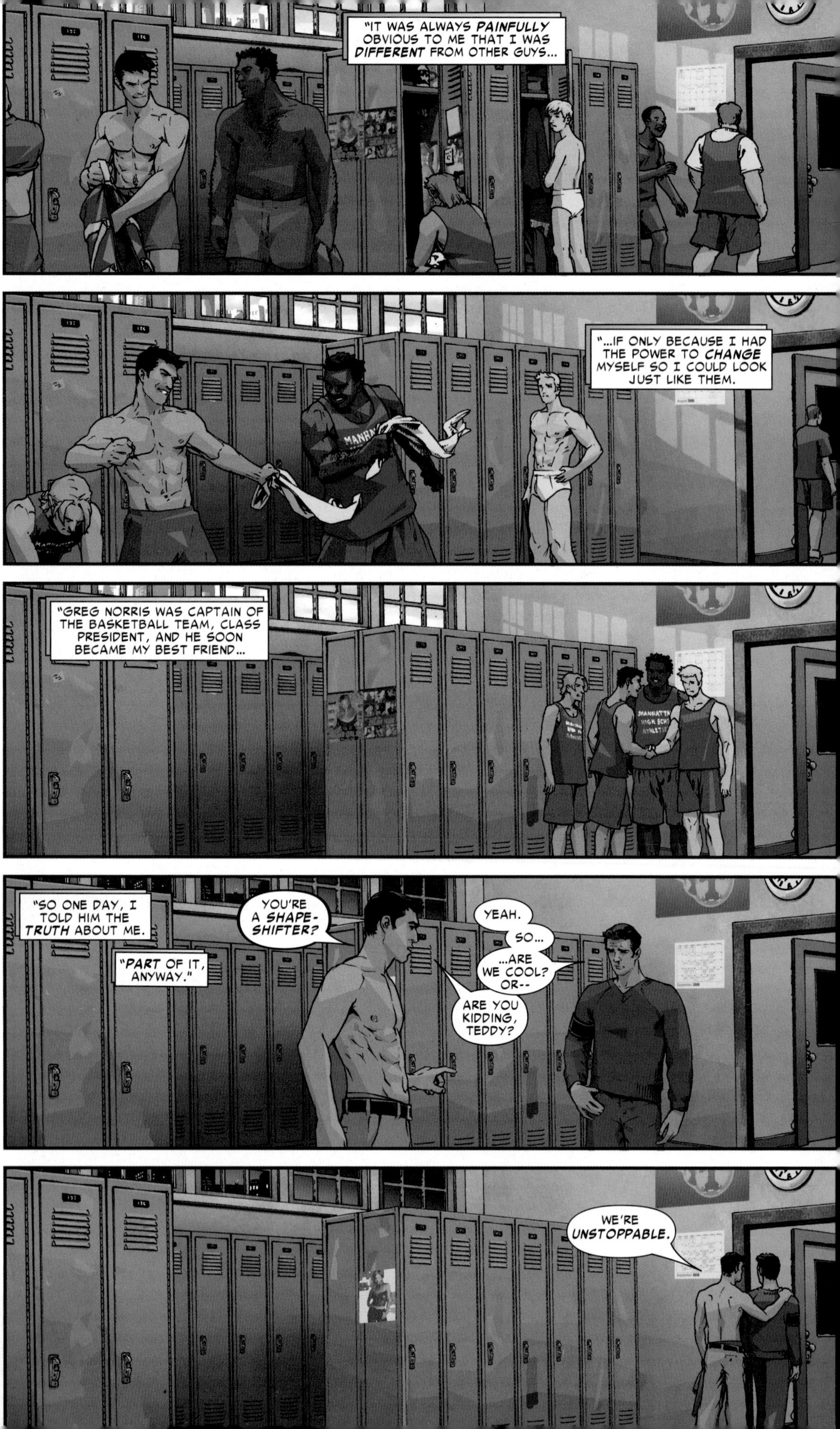
"IT WAS ALWAYS PAINFULLY OBVIOUS TO ME THAT I WAS DIFFERENT FROM OTHER GUYS...
"...IF ONLY BECAUSE I HAD THE POWER TO CHANGE MYSELF SO I COULD LOOK JUST LIKE THEM.
"GREG NORRIS WAS CAPTAIN OF THE BASKETBALL TEAM, CLASS PRESIDENT, AND HE SOON BECAME MY BEST FRIEND...
"SO ONE DAY, I TOLD HIM THE TRUTH ABOUT ME.
"PART OF IT, ANYWAY."
YOU'RE A SHAPE-SHIFTER?
YEAH.
SO...
...ARE WE COOL? OR--
ARE YOU KIDDING, TEDDY?
WE'RE UNSTOPPABLE.

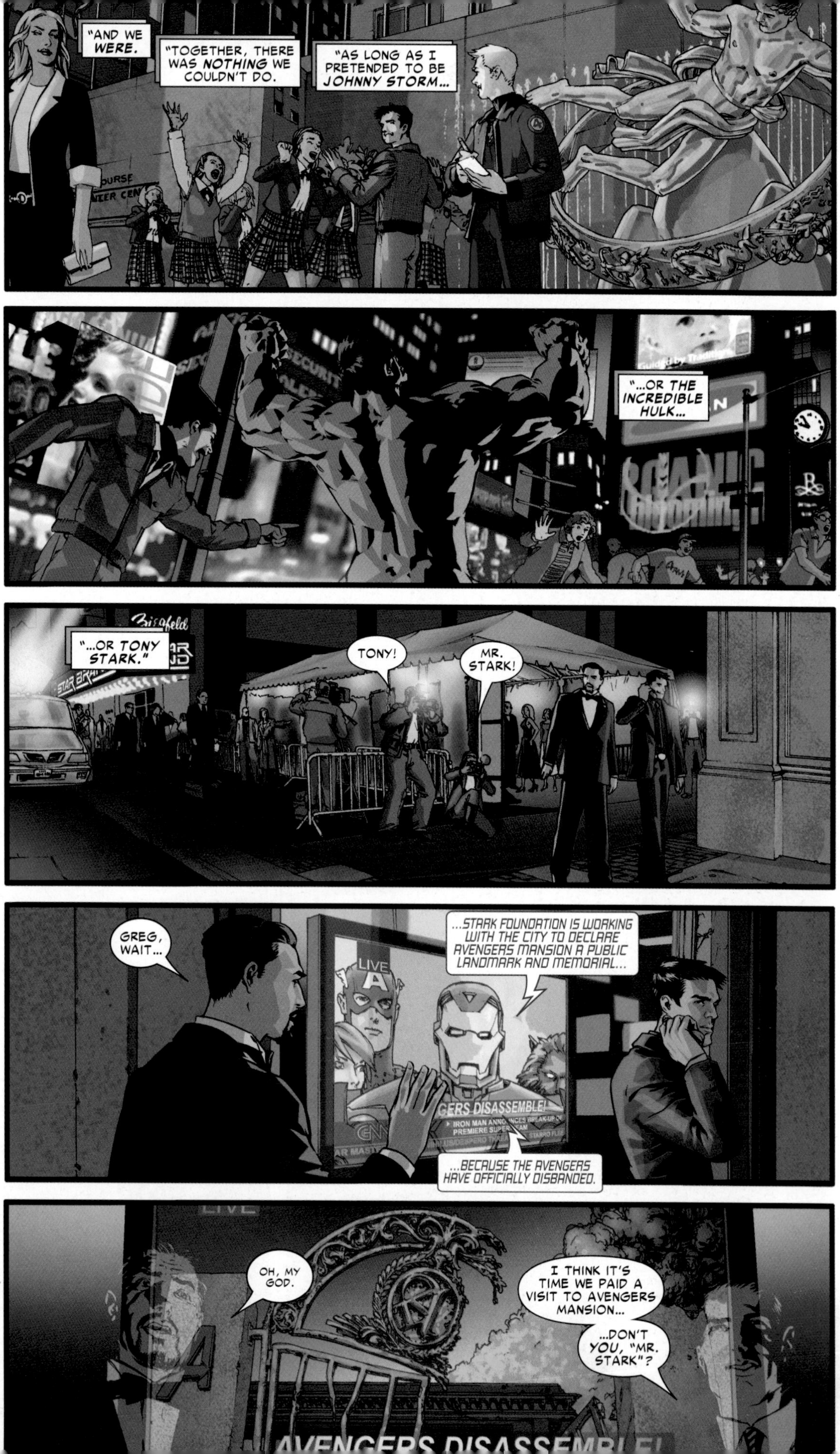
"AND WE WERE.
"TOGETHER, THERE WAS NOTHING WE COULDN'T DO.
"AS LONG AS I PRETENDED TO BE JOHNNY STORM...
"...OR THE INCREDIBLE HULK...
"...OR TONY STARK."
TONY!
MR. STARK!
GREG, WAIT...
...STARK FOUNDATION IS WORKING WITH THE CITY TO DECLARE AVENGERS MANSION A PUBLIC LANDMARK AND MEMORIAL...
LIVE
...BECAUSE THE AVENGERS HAVE OFFICIALLY DISBANDED.
OH, MY GOD.
I THINK IT'S TIME WE PAID A VISIT TO AVENGERS MANSION...
...DON'T YOU, "MR. STARK"?

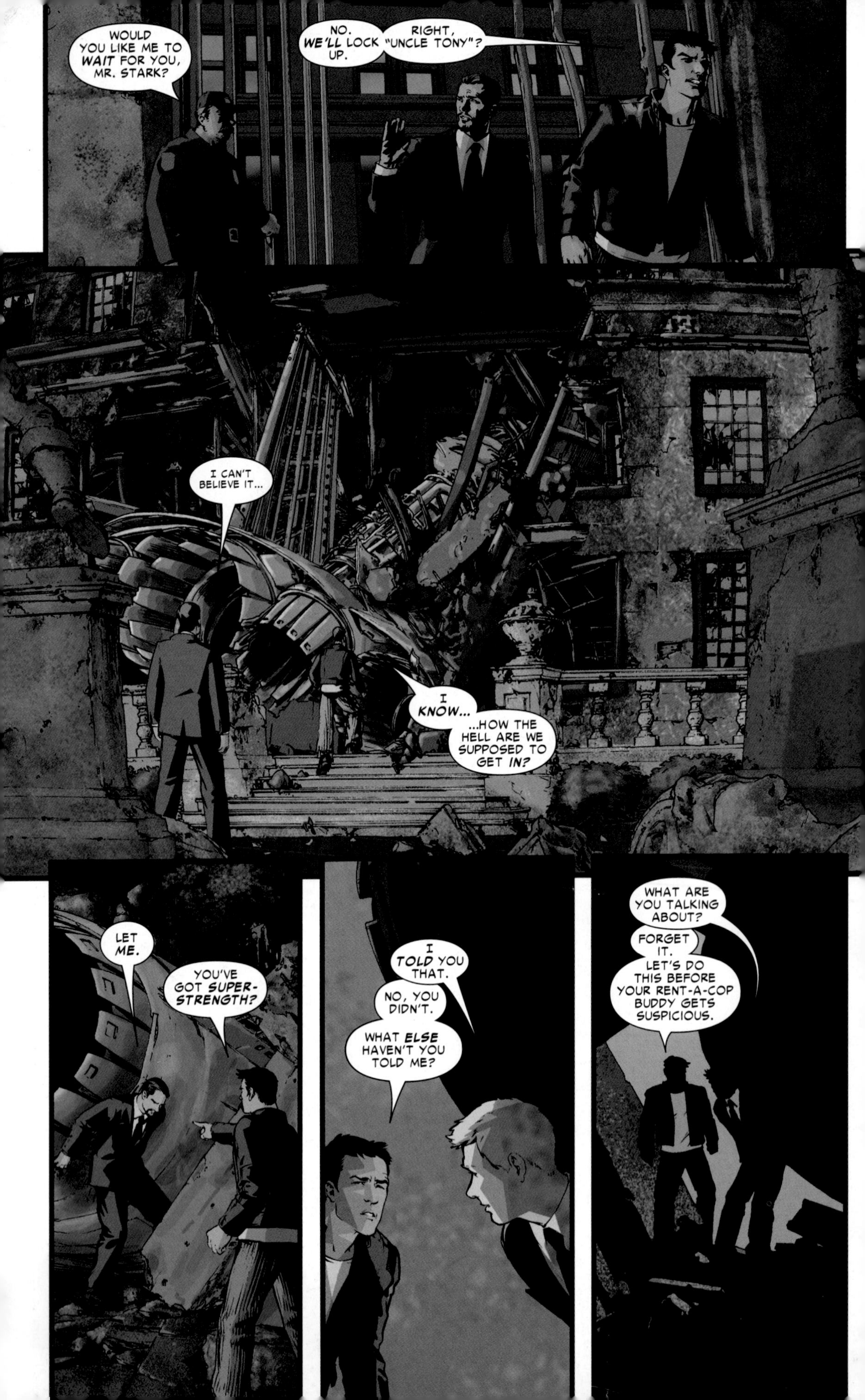

WOULD YOU LIKE ME TO WAIT FOR YOU, MR. STARK?
NO. WE'LL LOCK UP.
RIGHT, "UNCLE TONY"?
I CAN'T BELIEVE IT...
I KNOW...
...HOW THE HELL ARE WE SUPPOSED TO GET IN?
LET ME.
YOU'VE GOT SUPER-STRENGTH?
I TOLD YOU THAT.
NO, YOU DIDN'T.
WHAT ELSE HAVEN'T YOU TOLD ME?
WHAT ARE YOU TALKING ABOUT?
FORGET IT.
LET'S DO THIS BEFORE YOUR RENT-A-COP BUDDY GETS SUSPICIOUS.

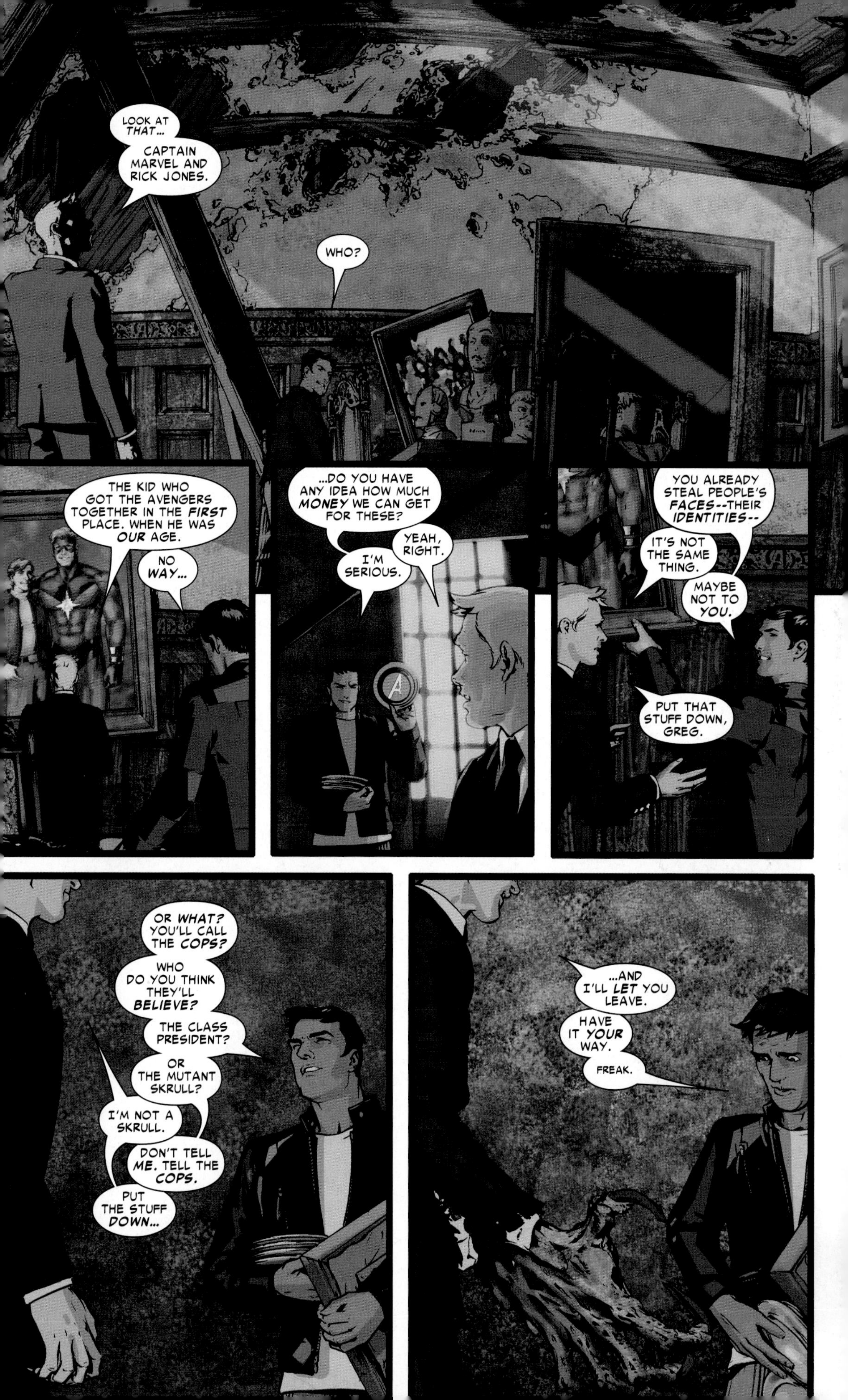
LOOK AT *THAT*...
CAPTAIN MARVEL AND RICK JONES.
WHO?
THE KID WHO GOT THE AVENGERS TOGETHER IN THE *FIRST* PLACE. WHEN HE WAS *OUR* AGE.
NO *WAY*...
...DO YOU HAVE ANY IDEA HOW MUCH *MONEY* WE CAN GET FOR THESE?
YEAH, RIGHT.
I'M SERIOUS.
YOU ALREADY STEAL PEOPLE'S *FACES*--THEIR *IDENTITIES*--
IT'S NOT THE SAME THING.
MAYBE NOT TO *YOU*.
PUT THAT STUFF DOWN, GREG.
OR *WHAT*? YOU'LL CALL THE *COPS*?
WHO DO YOU THINK THEY'LL *BELIEVE*?
THE CLASS PRESIDENT?
OR THE MUTANT SKRULL?
I'M NOT A SKRULL.
DON'T TELL *ME*. TELL THE *COPS*.
PUT THE STUFF *DOWN*...
...AND I'LL *LET* YOU LEAVE.
HAVE IT *YOUR* WAY.
FREAK.

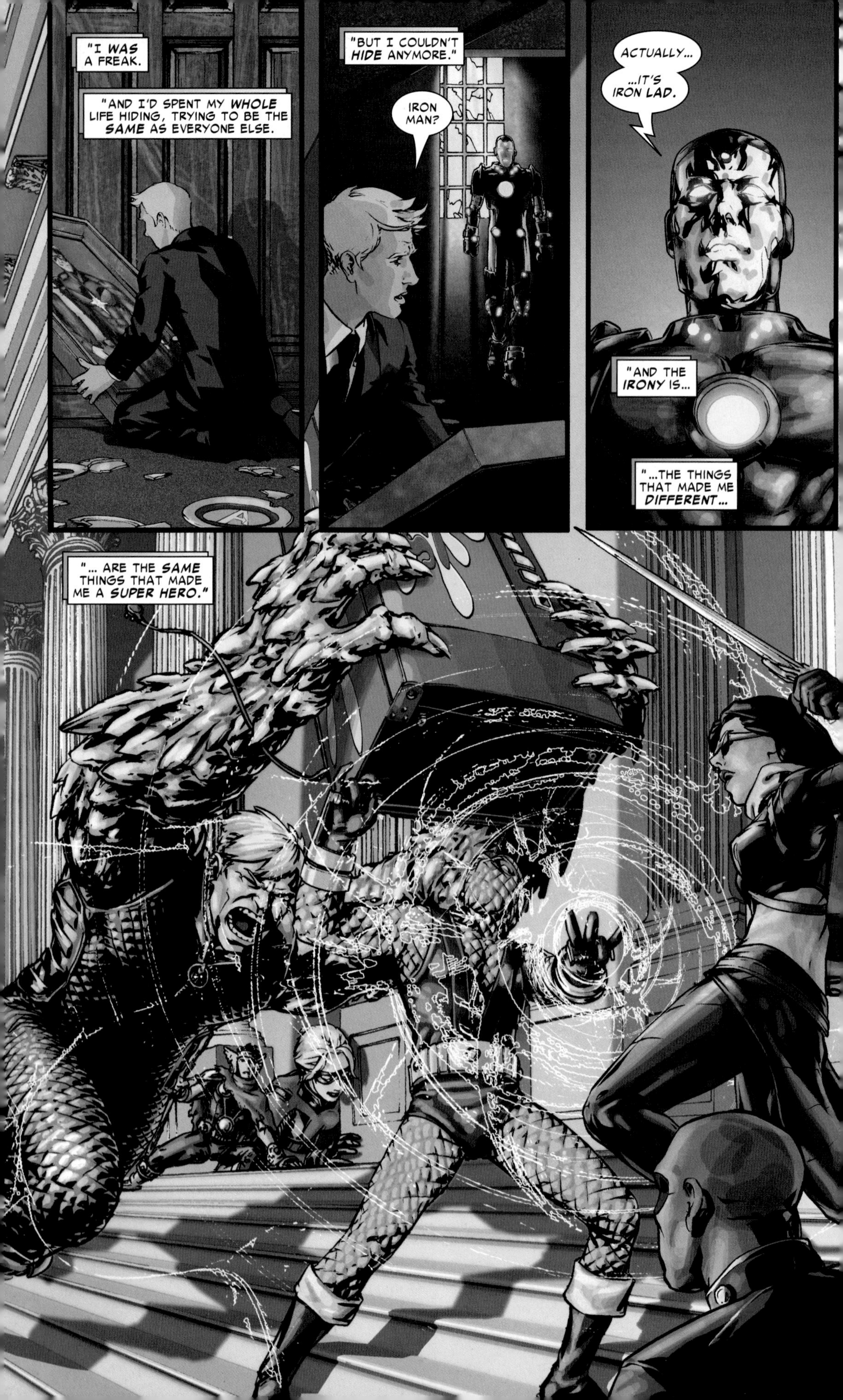
"I WAS A FREAK.
"AND I'D SPENT MY WHOLE LIFE HIDING, TRYING TO BE THE SAME AS EVERYONE ELSE.
"BUT I COULDN'T HIDE ANYMORE."
IRON MAN?
ACTUALLY...
...IT'S IRON LAD.
"AND THE IRONY IS...
"...THE THINGS THAT MADE ME DIFFERENT...
"... ARE THE SAME THINGS THAT MADE ME A SUPER HERO."

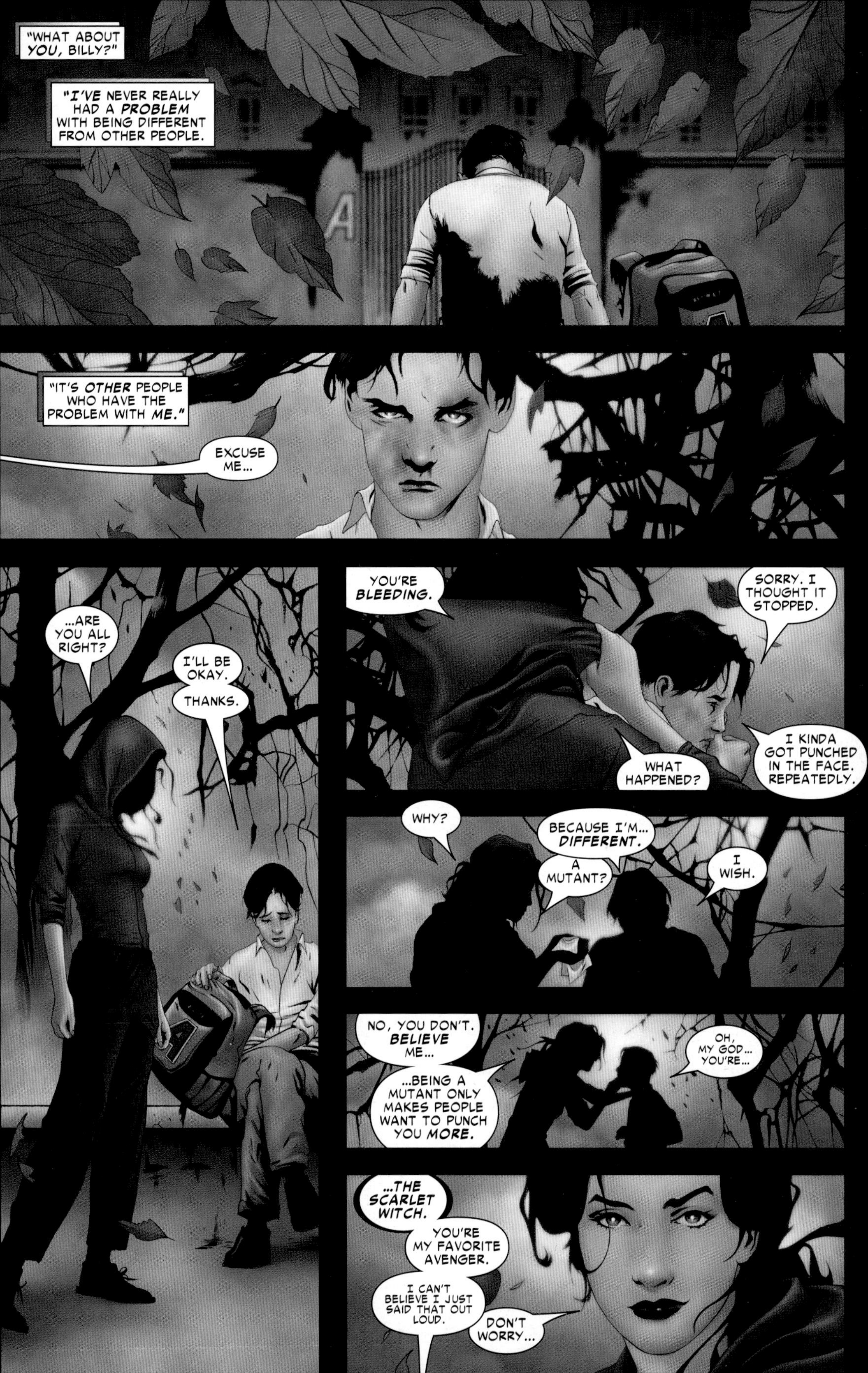
"WHAT ABOUT YOU, BILLY?"
"I'VE NEVER REALLY HAD A PROBLEM WITH BEING DIFFERENT FROM OTHER PEOPLE.
"IT'S OTHER PEOPLE WHO HAVE THE PROBLEM WITH ME."
EXCUSE ME...
...ARE YOU ALL RIGHT?
I'LL BE OKAY.
THANKS.
YOU'RE BLEEDING.
SORRY. I THOUGHT IT STOPPED.
WHAT HAPPENED?
I KINDA GOT PUNCHED IN THE FACE. REPEATEDLY.
WHY?
BECAUSE I'M... DIFFERENT.
A MUTANT?
I WISH.
NO, YOU DON'T. BELIEVE ME...
...BEING A MUTANT ONLY MAKES PEOPLE WANT TO PUNCH YOU MORE.
OH, MY GOD... YOU'RE...
...THE SCARLET WITCH.
YOU'RE MY FAVORITE AVENGER.
I CAN'T BELIEVE I JUST SAID THAT OUT LOUD.
DON'T WORRY...

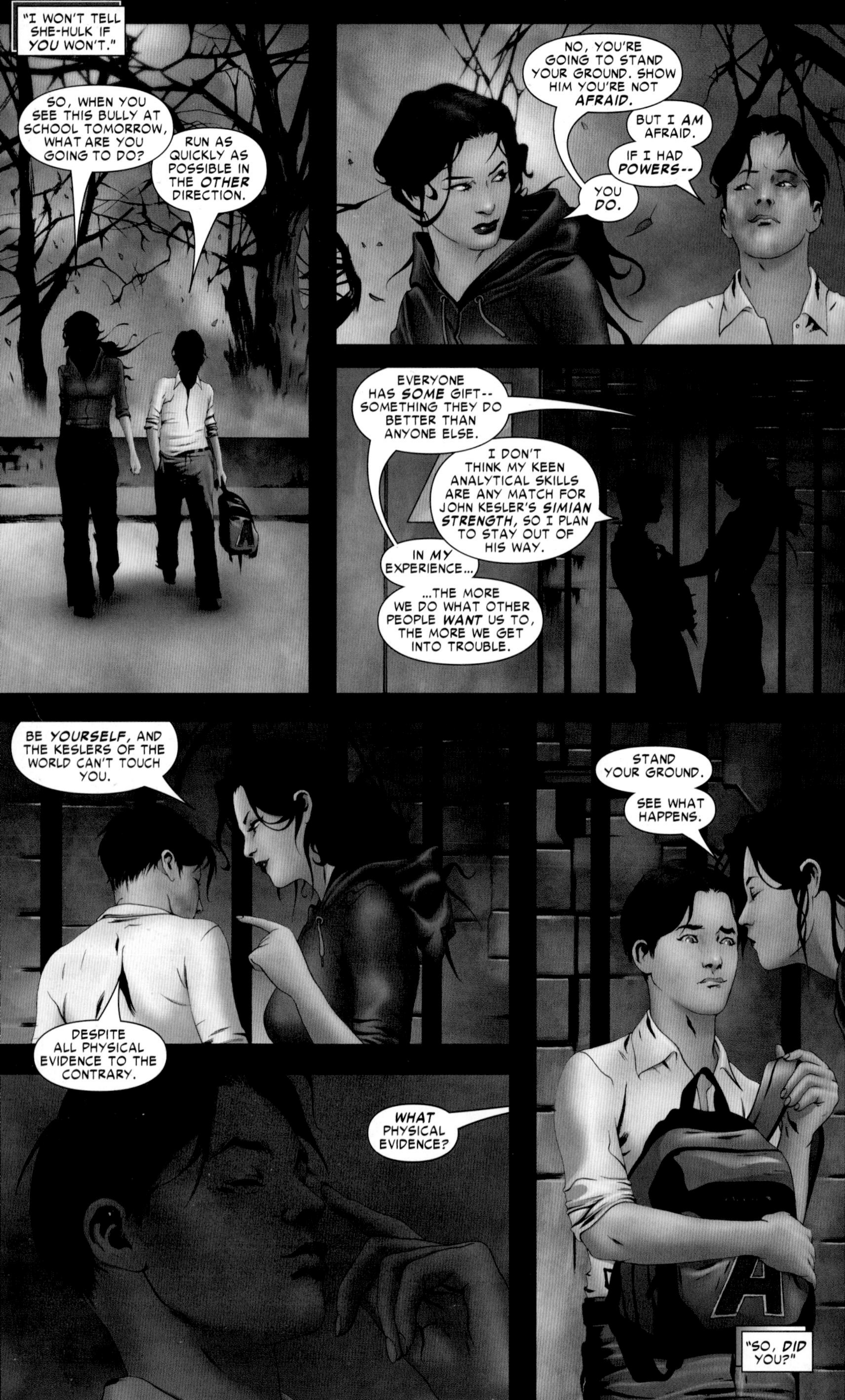
"I WON'T TELL SHE-HULK IF YOU WON'T."
SO, WHEN YOU SEE THIS BULLY AT SCHOOL TOMORROW, WHAT ARE YOU GOING TO DO?
RUN AS QUICKLY AS POSSIBLE IN THE OTHER DIRECTION.
NO, YOU'RE GOING TO STAND YOUR GROUND. SHOW HIM YOU'RE NOT AFRAID.
BUT I AM AFRAID.
IF I HAD POWERS--
YOU DO.
EVERYONE HAS SOME GIFT-- SOMETHING THEY DO BETTER THAN ANYONE ELSE.
I DON'T THINK MY KEEN ANALYTICAL SKILLS ARE ANY MATCH FOR JOHN KESLER'S SIMIAN STRENGTH, SO I PLAN TO STAY OUT OF HIS WAY.
IN MY EXPERIENCE...
...THE MORE WE DO WHAT OTHER PEOPLE WANT US TO, THE MORE WE GET INTO TROUBLE.
BE YOURSELF, AND THE KESLERS OF THE WORLD CAN'T TOUCH YOU.
DESPITE ALL PHYSICAL EVIDENCE TO THE CONTRARY.
WHAT PHYSICAL EVIDENCE?
STAND YOUR GROUND.
SEE WHAT HAPPENS.
"SO, DID YOU?"

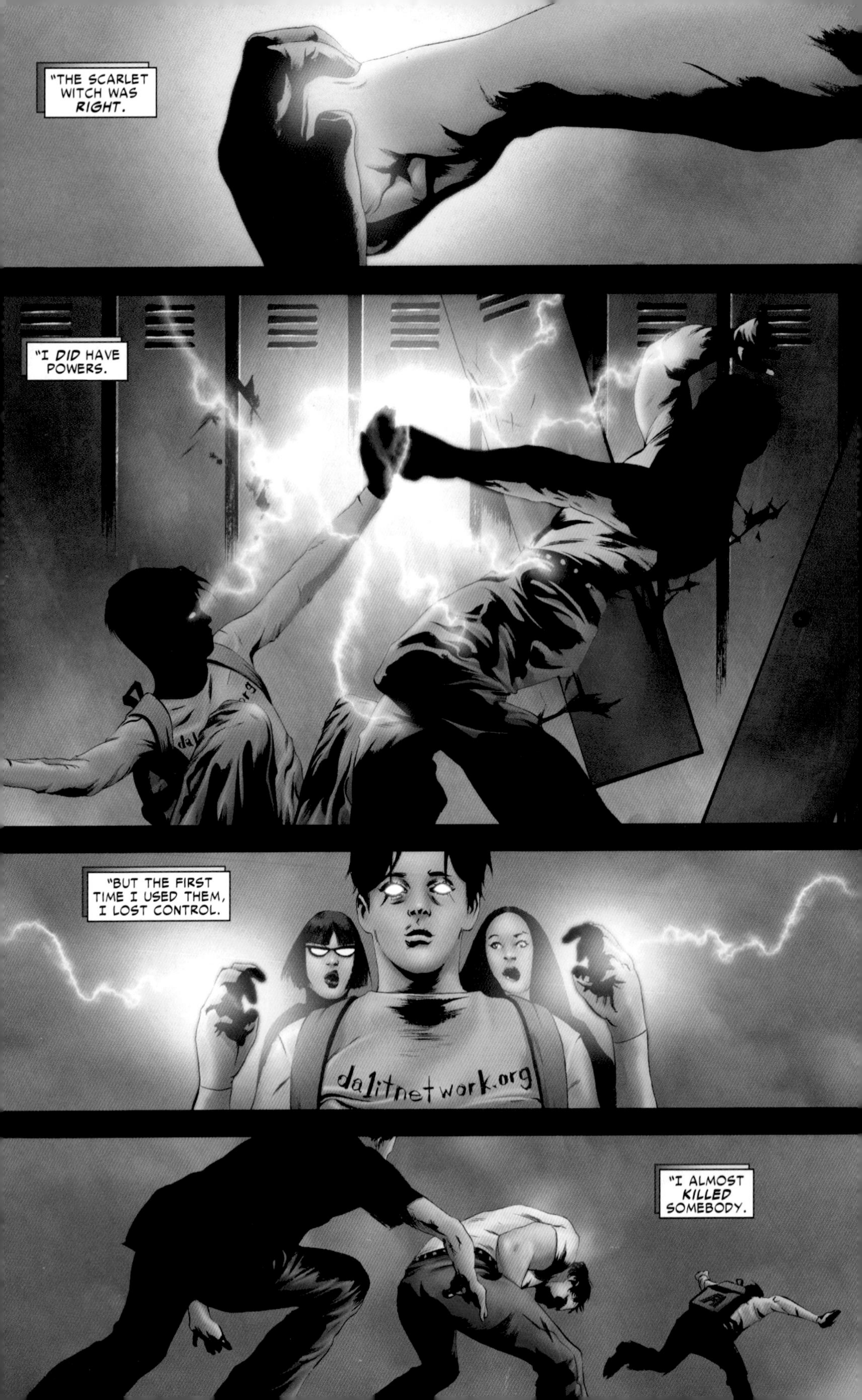
"THE SCARLET WITCH WAS RIGHT.
"I DID HAVE POWERS.
da1itnetwork.org
"BUT THE FIRST TIME I USED THEM, I LOST CONTROL.
"I ALMOST KILLED SOMEBODY.

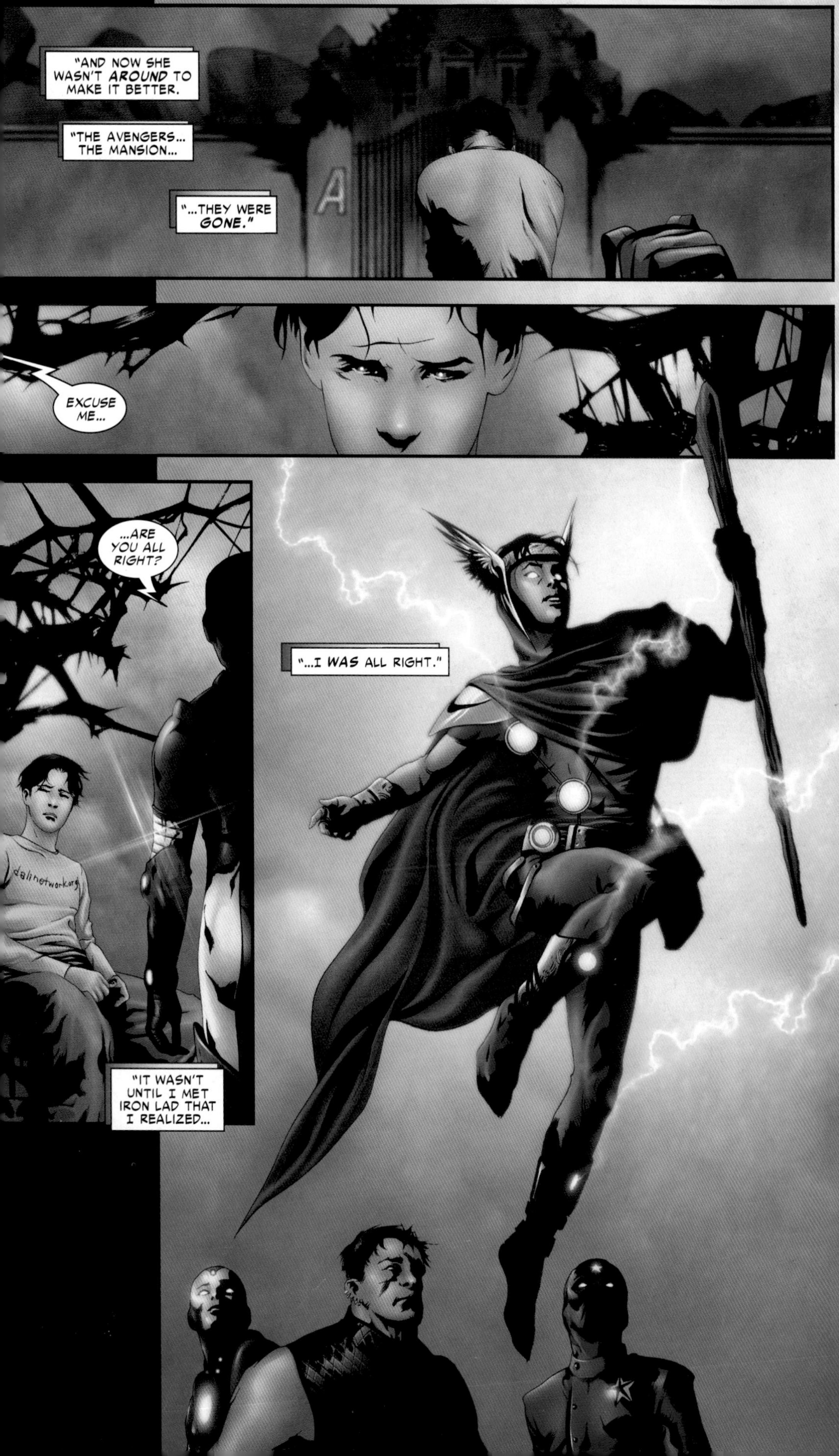
"AND NOW SHE WASN'T AROUND TO MAKE IT BETTER.
"THE AVENGERS... THE MANSION...
"...THEY WERE GONE."
EXCUSE ME...
...ARE YOU ALL RIGHT?
"...I WAS ALL RIGHT."
"IT WASN'T UNTIL I MET IRON LAD THAT I REALIZED...
dalinetwork.org

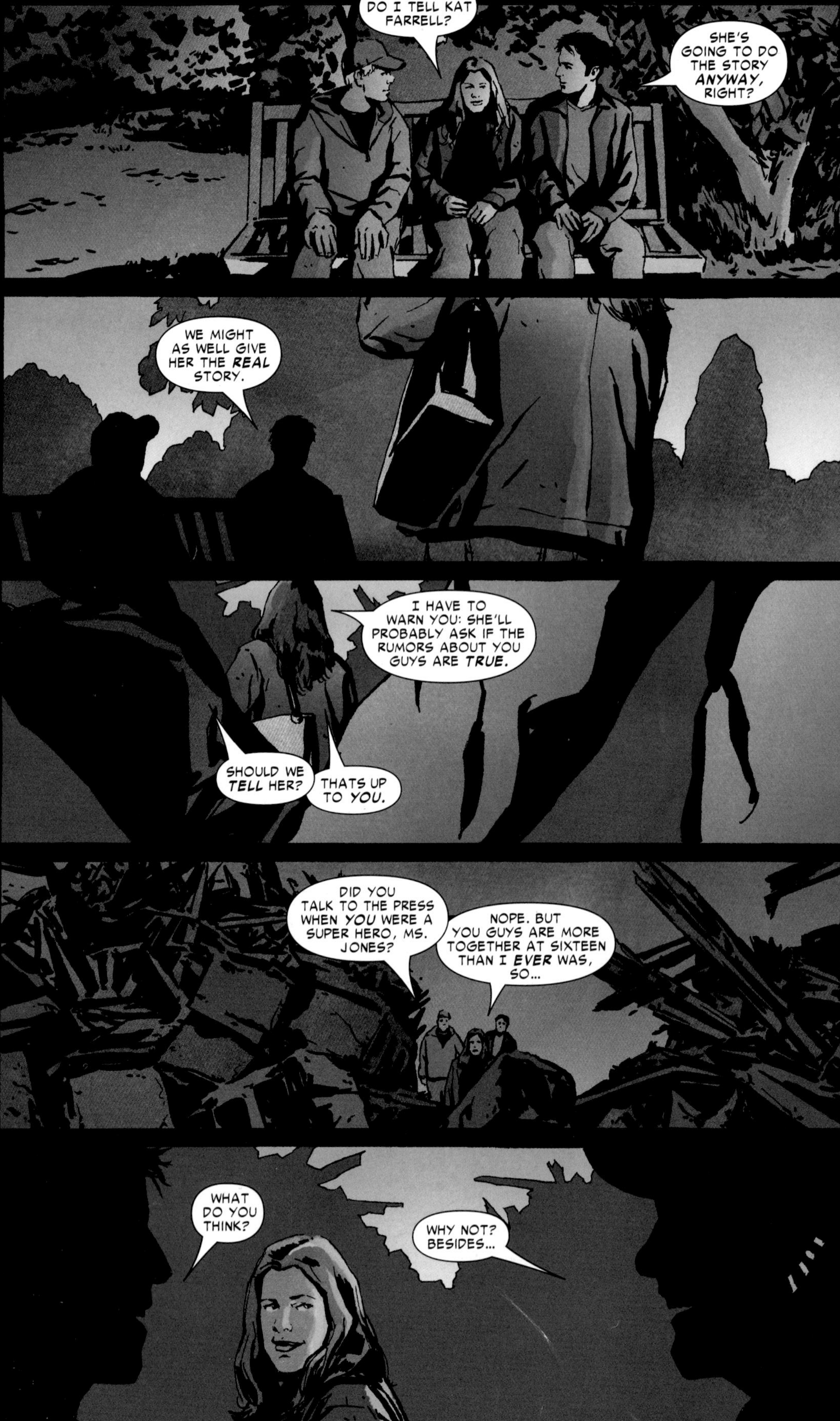
SO, WHAT DO I TELL KAT FARRELL?
SHE'S GOING TO DO THE STORY *ANYWAY*, RIGHT?
WE MIGHT AS WELL GIVE HER THE *REAL* STORY.
I HAVE TO WARN YOU: SHE'LL PROBABLY ASK IF THE RUMORS ABOUT YOU GUYS ARE *TRUE.*
SHOULD WE *TELL* HER?
THATS UP TO *YOU.*
DID YOU TALK TO THE PRESS WHEN *YOU* WERE A SUPER HERO, MS. JONES?
NOPE. BUT YOU GUYS ARE MORE TOGETHER AT SIXTEEN THAN I *EVER* WAS, SO...
WHAT DO YOU THINK?
WHY NOT? BESIDES...

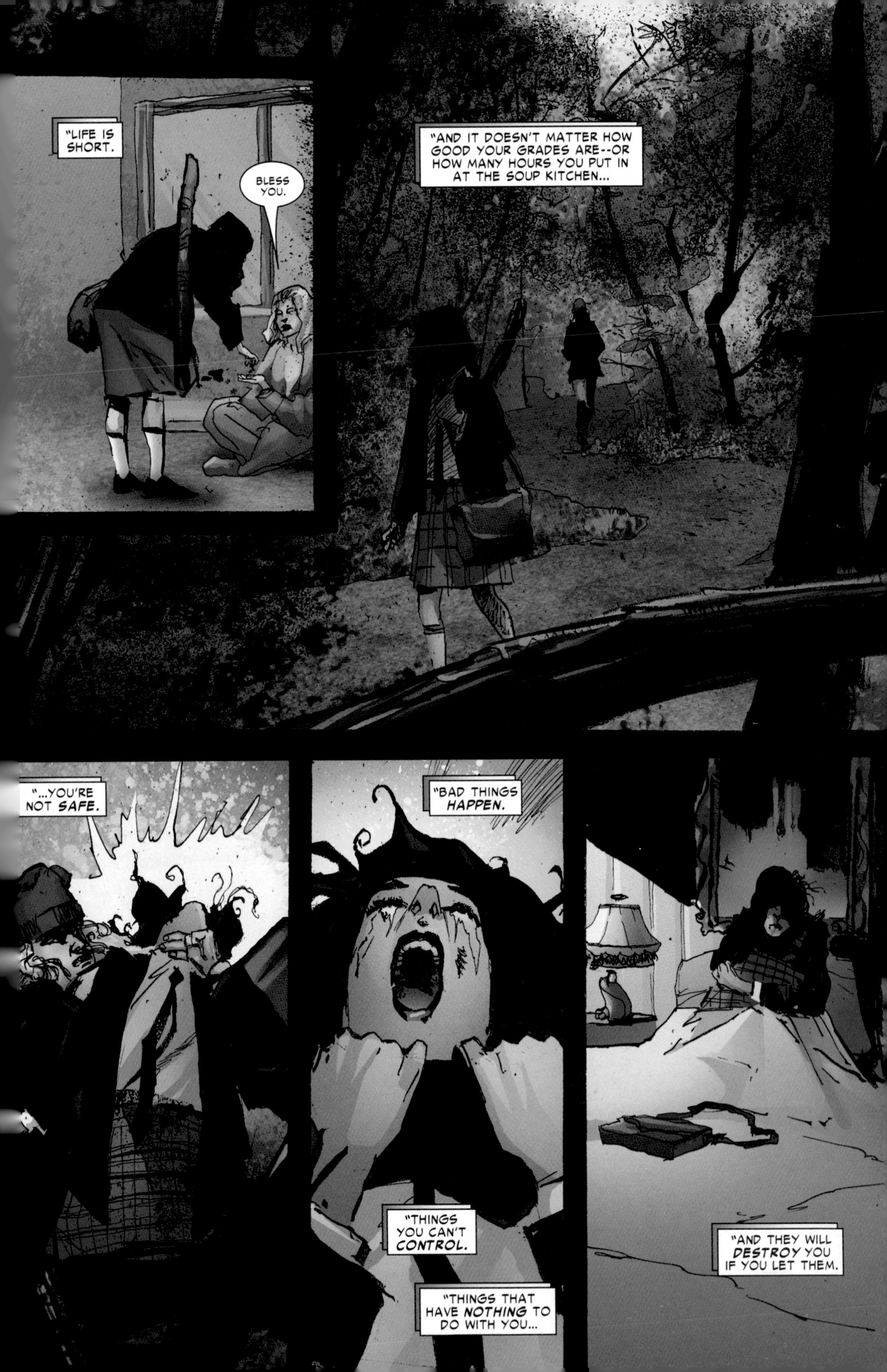
"LIFE IS SHORT.
BLESS YOU.
"AND IT DOESN'T MATTER HOW GOOD YOUR GRADES ARE--OR HOW MANY HOURS YOU PUT IN AT THE SOUP KITCHEN...
"...YOU'RE NOT SAFE.
"BAD THINGS HAPPEN.
"THINGS YOU CAN'T CONTROL.
"THINGS THAT HAVE NOTHING TO DO WITH YOU...
"AND THEY WILL DESTROY YOU IF YOU LET THEM.

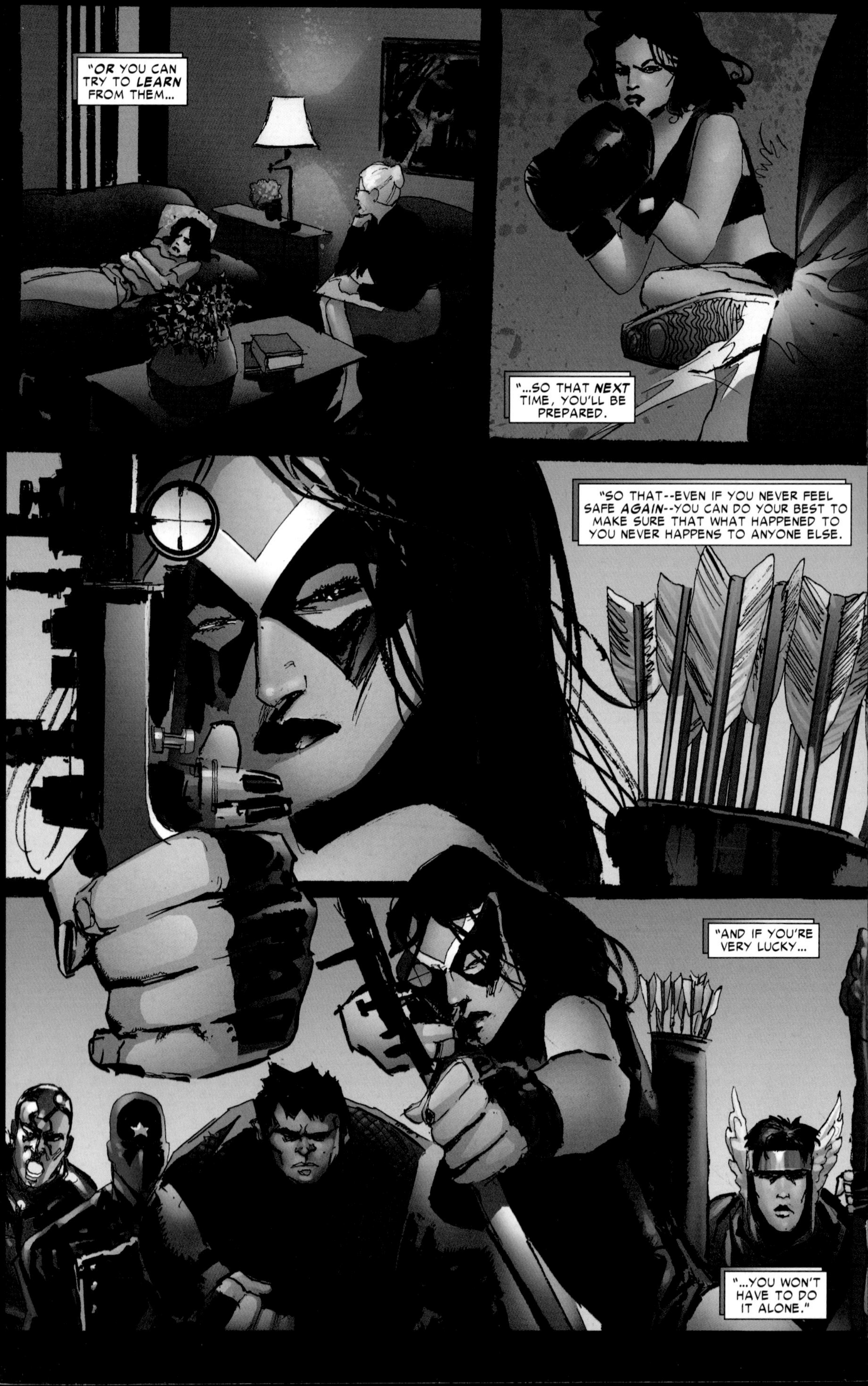
"OR YOU CAN TRY TO LEARN FROM THEM...
"...SO THAT NEXT TIME, YOU'LL BE PREPARED.
"SO THAT--EVEN IF YOU NEVER FEEL SAFE AGAIN--YOU CAN DO YOUR BEST TO MAKE SURE THAT WHAT HAPPENED TO YOU NEVER HAPPENS TO ANYONE ELSE.
"AND IF YOU'RE VERY LUCKY...
"...YOU WON'T HAVE TO DO IT ALONE."

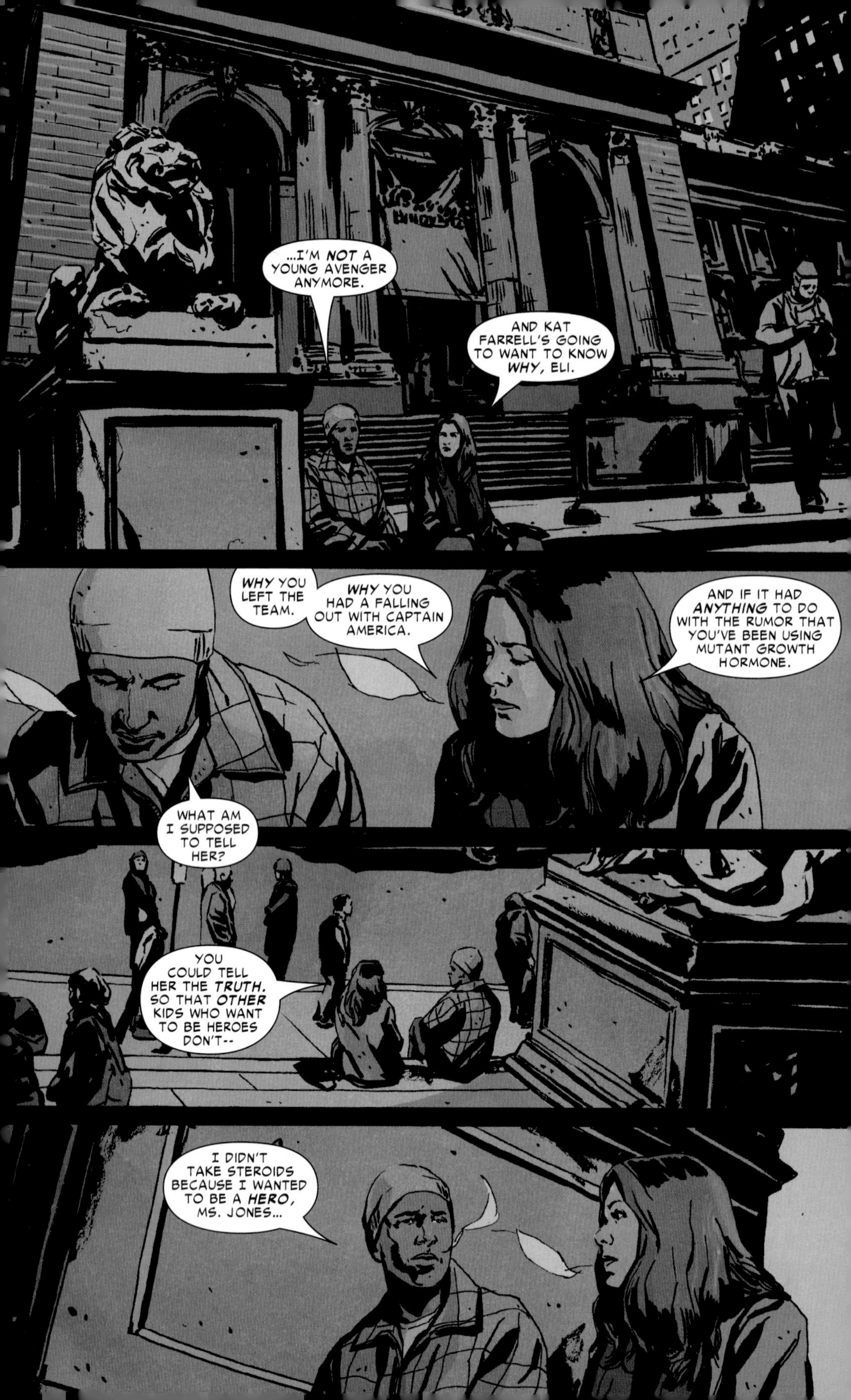
...I'M NOT A YOUNG AVENGER ANYMORE.
AND KAT FARRELL'S GOING TO WANT TO KNOW WHY, ELI.
WHY YOU LEFT THE TEAM.
WHY YOU HAD A FALLING OUT WITH CAPTAIN AMERICA.
AND IF IT HAD ANYTHING TO DO WITH THE RUMOR THAT YOU'VE BEEN USING MUTANT GROWTH HORMONE.
WHAT AM I SUPPOSED TO TELL HER?
YOU COULD TELL HER THE TRUTH. SO THAT OTHER KIDS WHO WANT TO BE HEROES DON'T--
I DIDN'T TAKE STEROIDS BECAUSE I WANTED TO BE A HERO, MS. JONES...

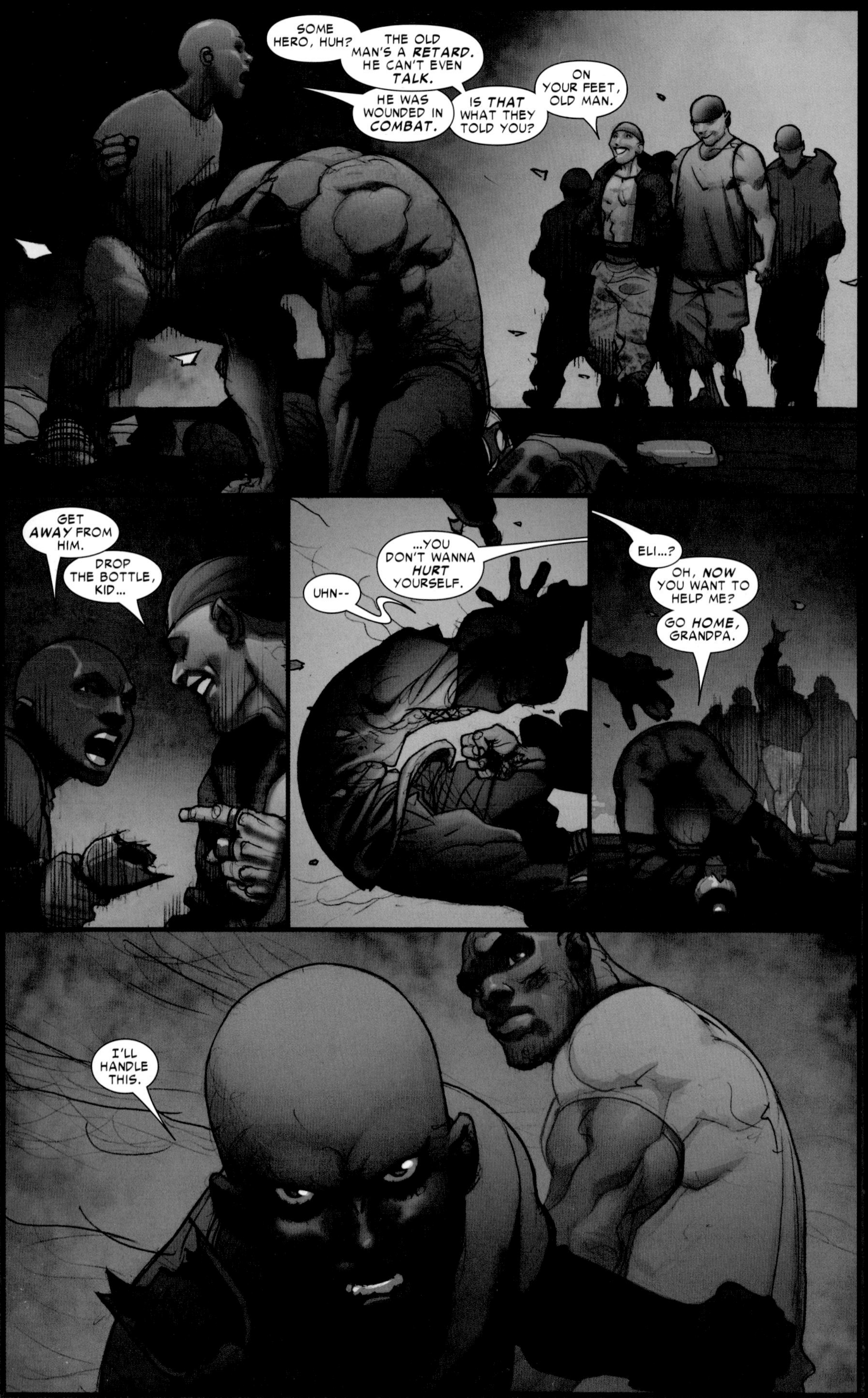
SOME HERO, HUH?
THE OLD MAN'S A *RETARD*. HE CAN'T EVEN *TALK*.
HE WAS WOUNDED IN *COMBAT*.
IS *THAT* WHAT THEY TOLD YOU?
ON YOUR FEET, OLD MAN.
GET *AWAY* FROM HIM.
DROP THE BOTTLE, KID...
...YOU DON'T WANNA *HURT* YOURSELF.
UHN--
ELI...?
OH, *NOW* YOU WANT TO HELP ME?
GO *HOME*, GRANDPA.
I'LL HANDLE THIS.

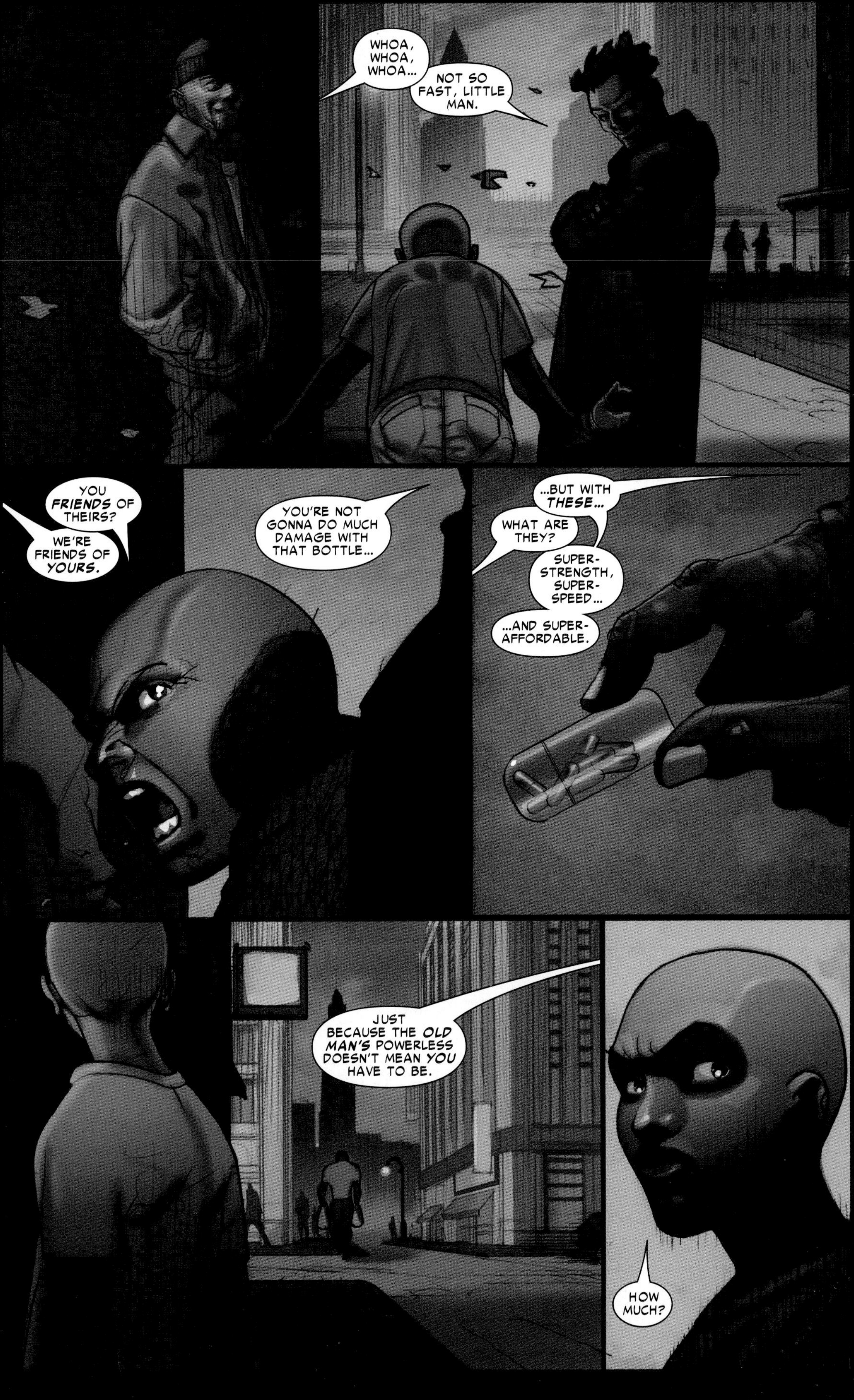
WHOA, WHOA, WHOA...
NOT SO FAST, LITTLE MAN.
YOU FRIENDS OF THEIRS?
WE'RE FRIENDS OF YOURS.
YOU'RE NOT GONNA DO MUCH DAMAGE WITH THAT BOTTLE...
...BUT WITH THESE...
WHAT ARE THEY?
SUPER-STRENGTH, SUPER-SPEED...
...AND SUPER-AFFORDABLE.
JUST BECAUSE THE OLD MAN'S POWERLESS DOESN'T MEAN YOU HAVE TO BE.
HOW MUCH?

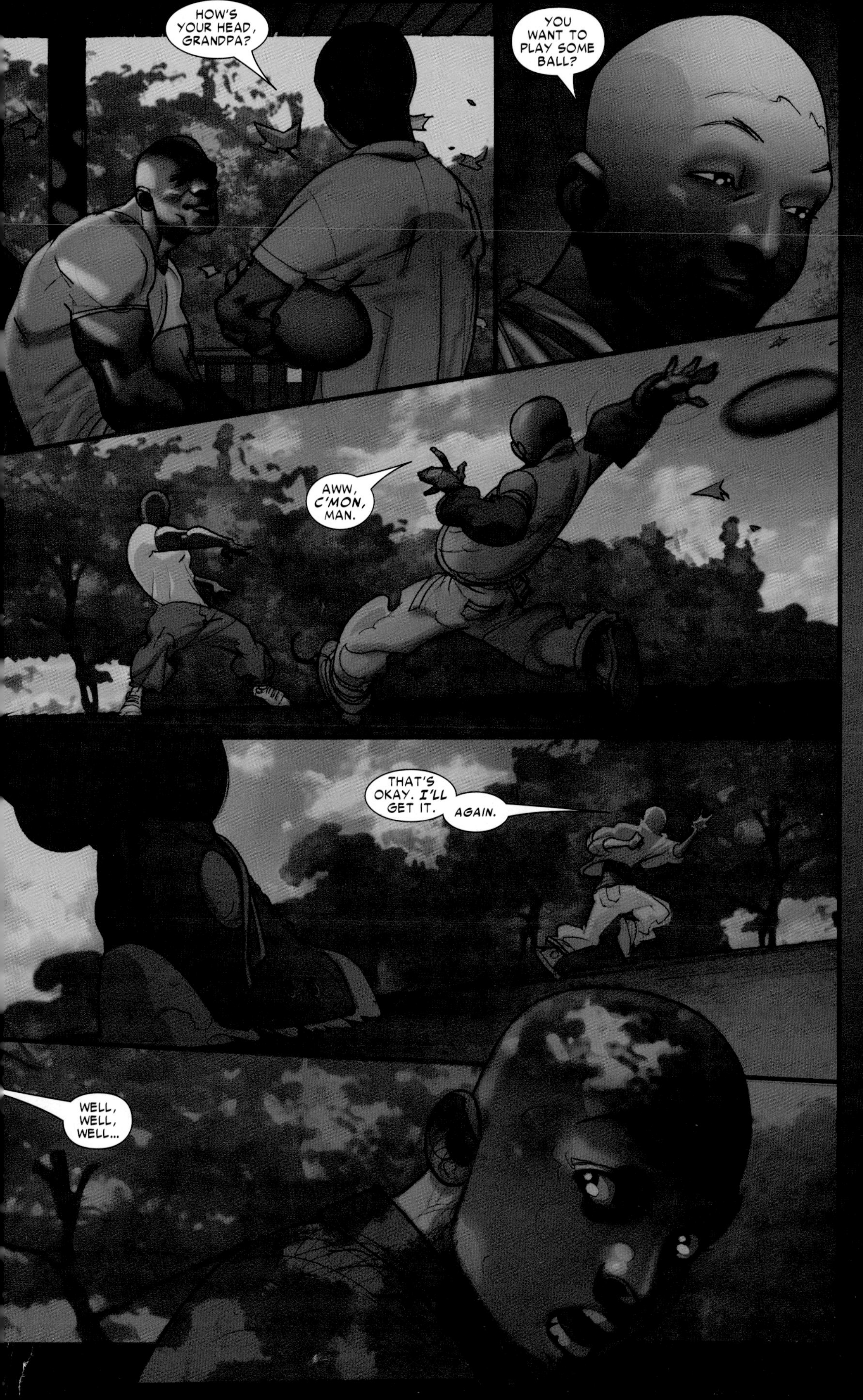
HOW'S YOUR HEAD, GRANDPA?
YOU WANT TO PLAY SOME BALL?
AWW, C'MON, MAN.
THAT'S OKAY. I'LL GET IT.
AGAIN.
WELL, WELL, WELL...

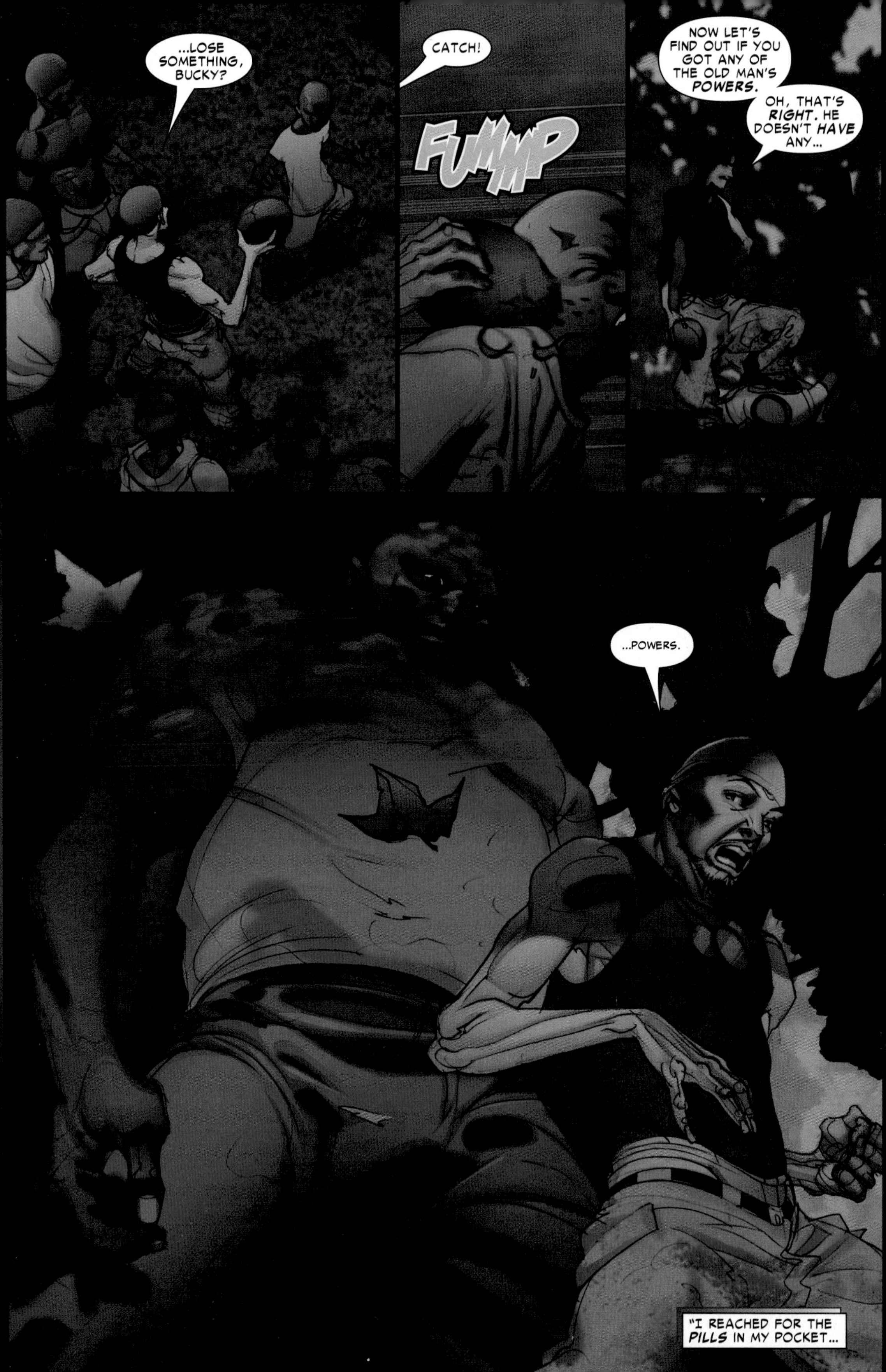
...LOSE SOMETHING, BUCKY?
CATCH!
FUMMP
NOW LET'S FIND OUT IF YOU GOT ANY OF THE OLD MAN'S POWERS.
OH, THAT'S RIGHT. HE DOESN'T HAVE ANY...
...POWERS.
"I REACHED FOR THE PILLS IN MY POCKET...

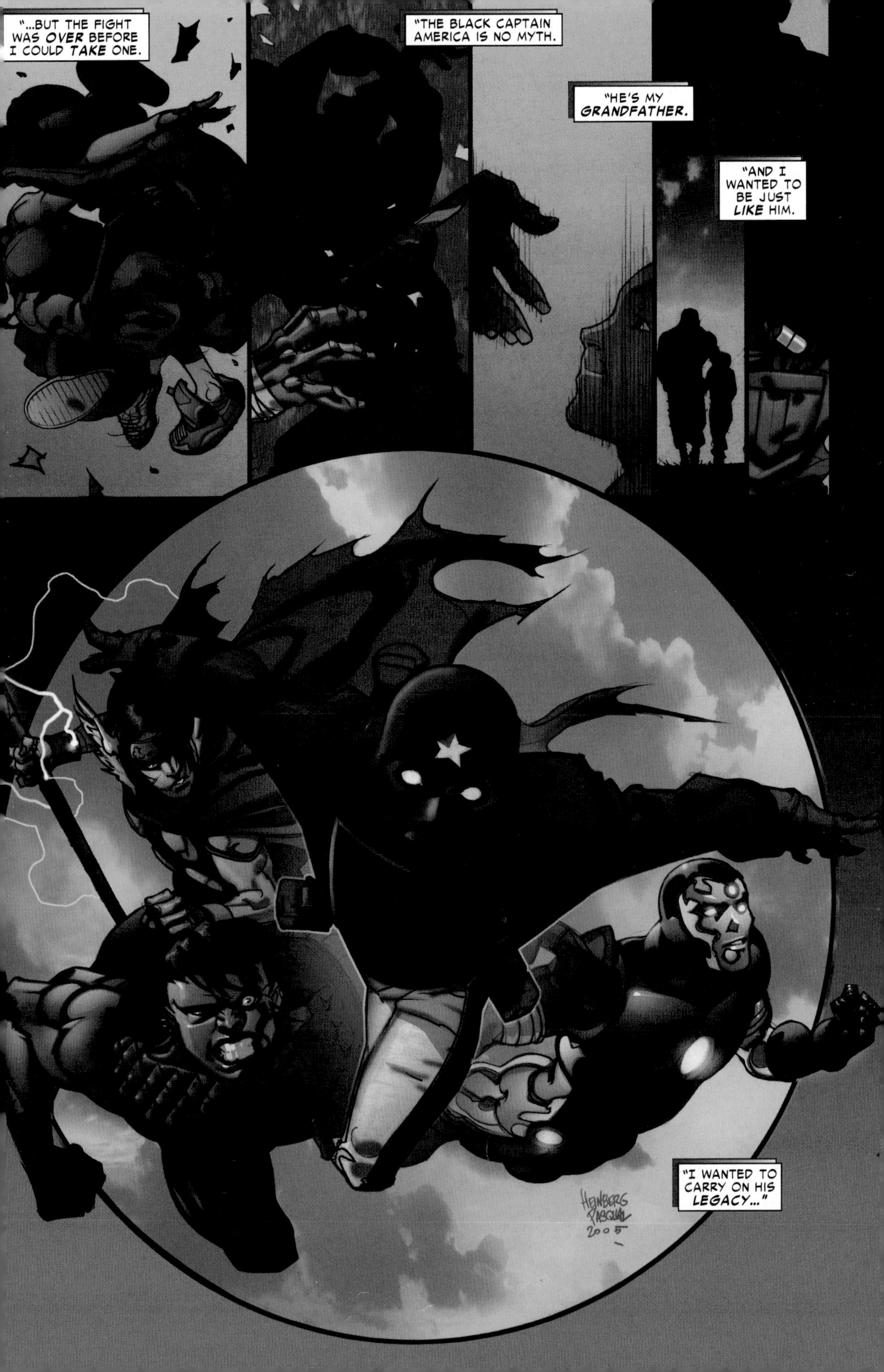
"...BUT THE FIGHT WAS OVER BEFORE I COULD TAKE ONE.
"THE BLACK CAPTAIN AMERICA IS NO MYTH.
"HE'S MY GRANDFATHER.
"AND I WANTED TO BE JUST LIKE HIM.
"I WANTED TO CARRY ON HIS LEGACY..."
HEINBERG PASQUAL 2005

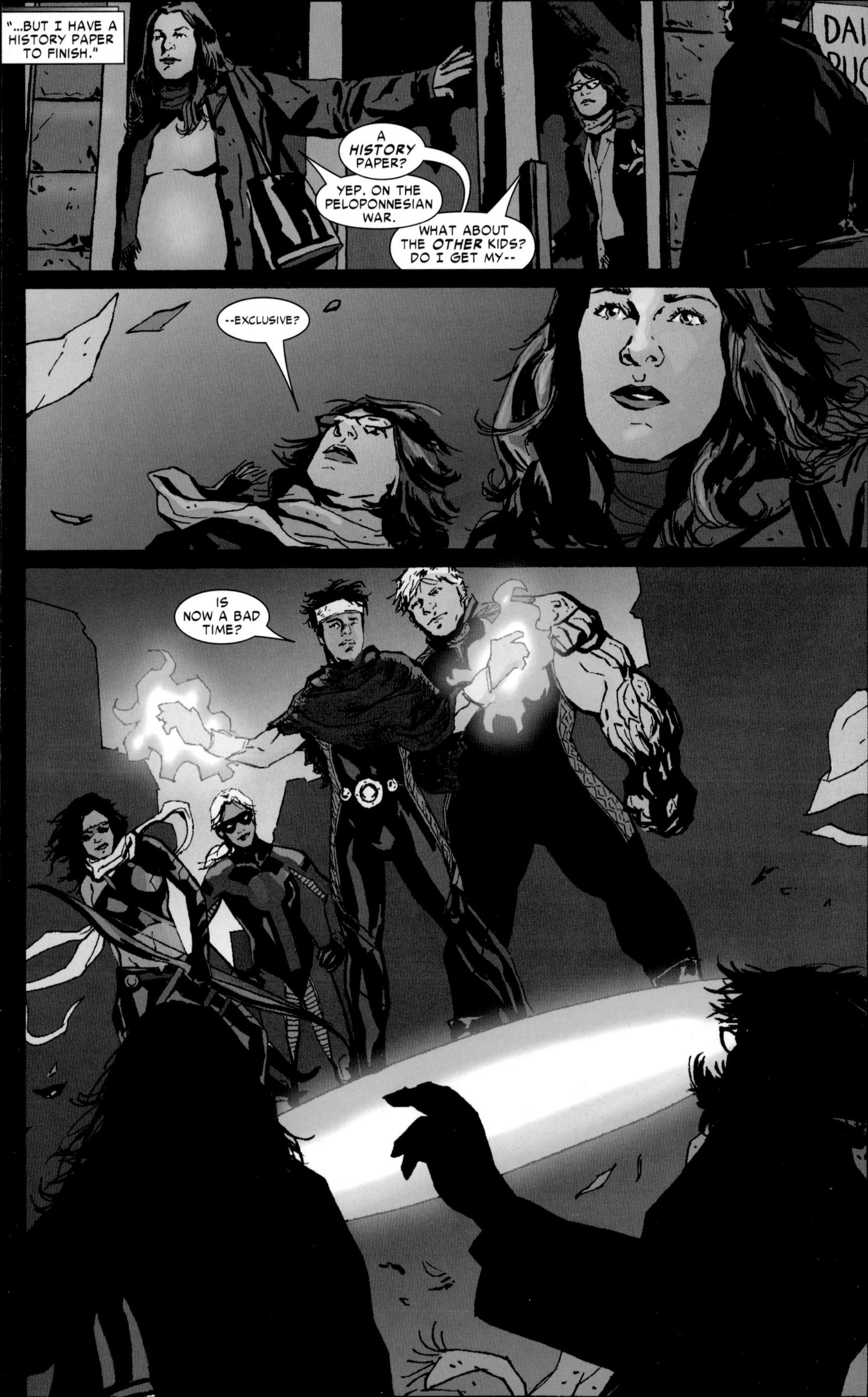
"...BUT I HAVE A HISTORY PAPER TO FINISH."
A HISTORY PAPER?
YEP. ON THE PELOPONNESIAN WAR.
WHAT ABOUT THE OTHER KIDS? DO I GET MY--
--EXCLUSIVE?
IS NOW A BAD TIME?

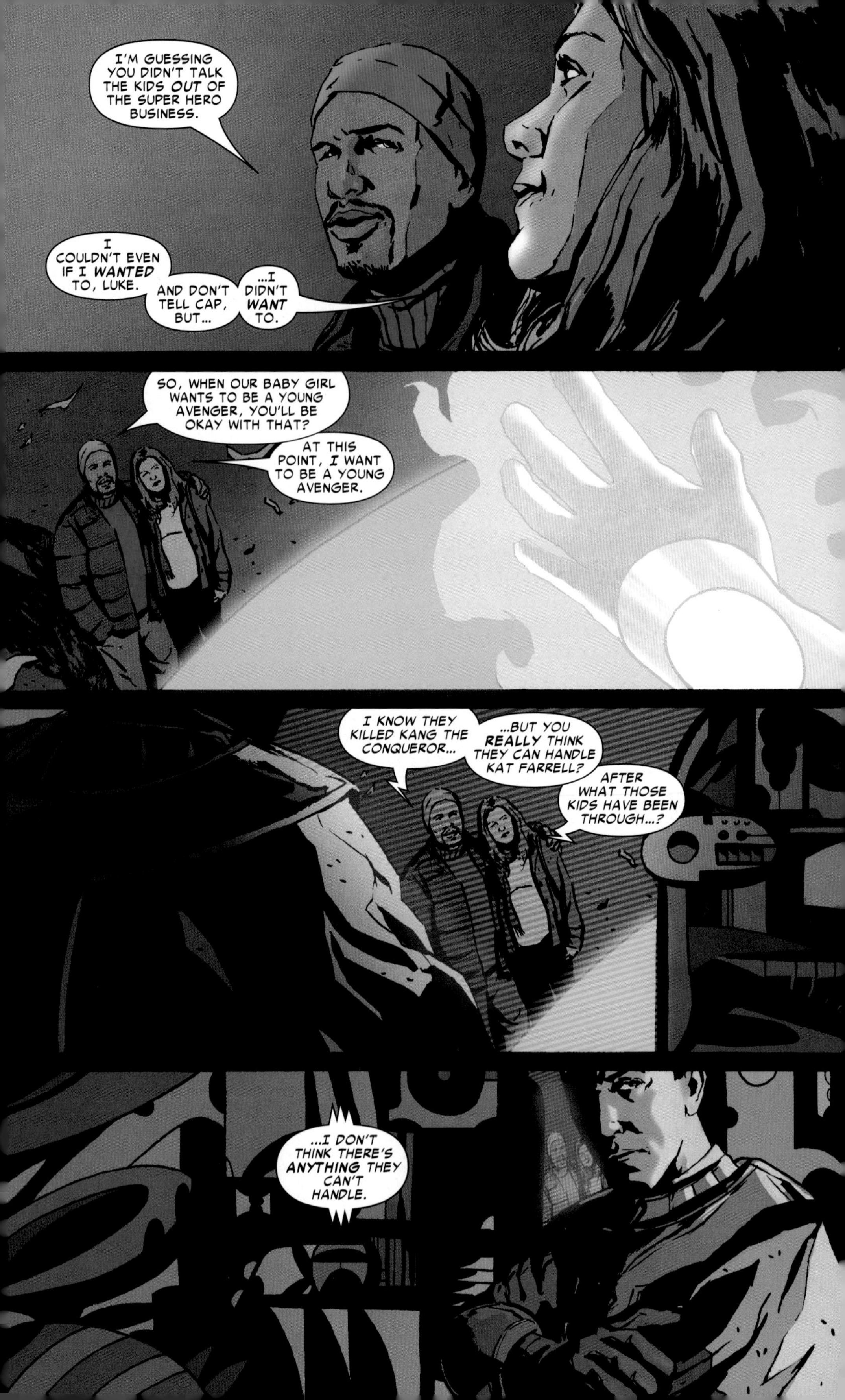
I'M GUESSING YOU DIDN'T TALK THE KIDS OUT OF THE SUPER HERO BUSINESS.
I COULDN'T EVEN IF I WANTED TO, LUKE.
AND DON'T TELL CAP, BUT...
...I DIDN'T WANT TO.
SO, WHEN OUR BABY GIRL WANTS TO BE A YOUNG AVENGER, YOU'LL BE OKAY WITH THAT?
AT THIS POINT, I WANT TO BE A YOUNG AVENGER.
I KNOW THEY KILLED KANG THE CONQUEROR...
...BUT YOU REALLY THINK THEY CAN HANDLE KAT FARRELL?
AFTER WHAT THOSE KIDS HAVE BEEN THROUGH...?
...I DON'T THINK THERE'S ANYTHING THEY CAN'T HANDLE.

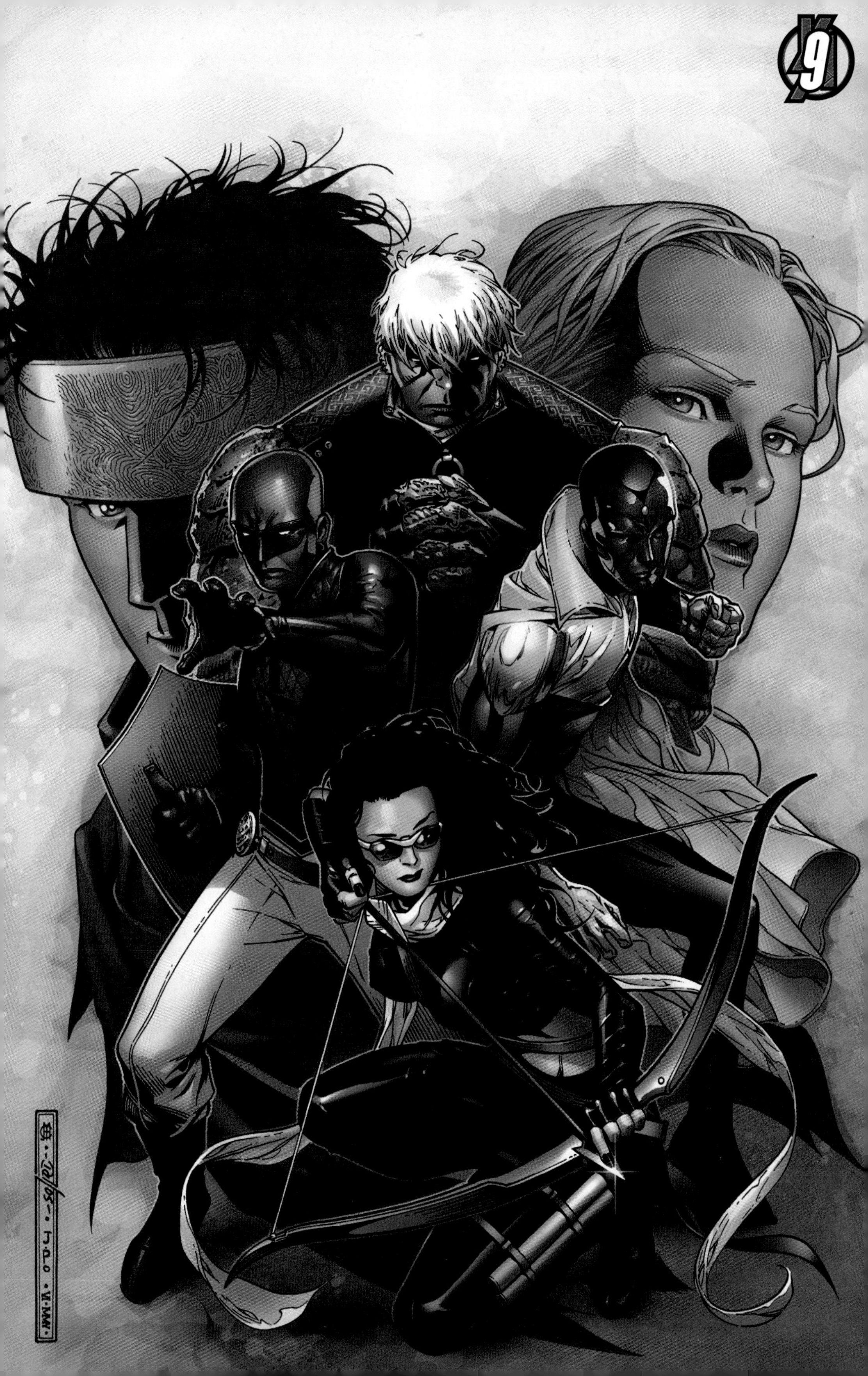
9

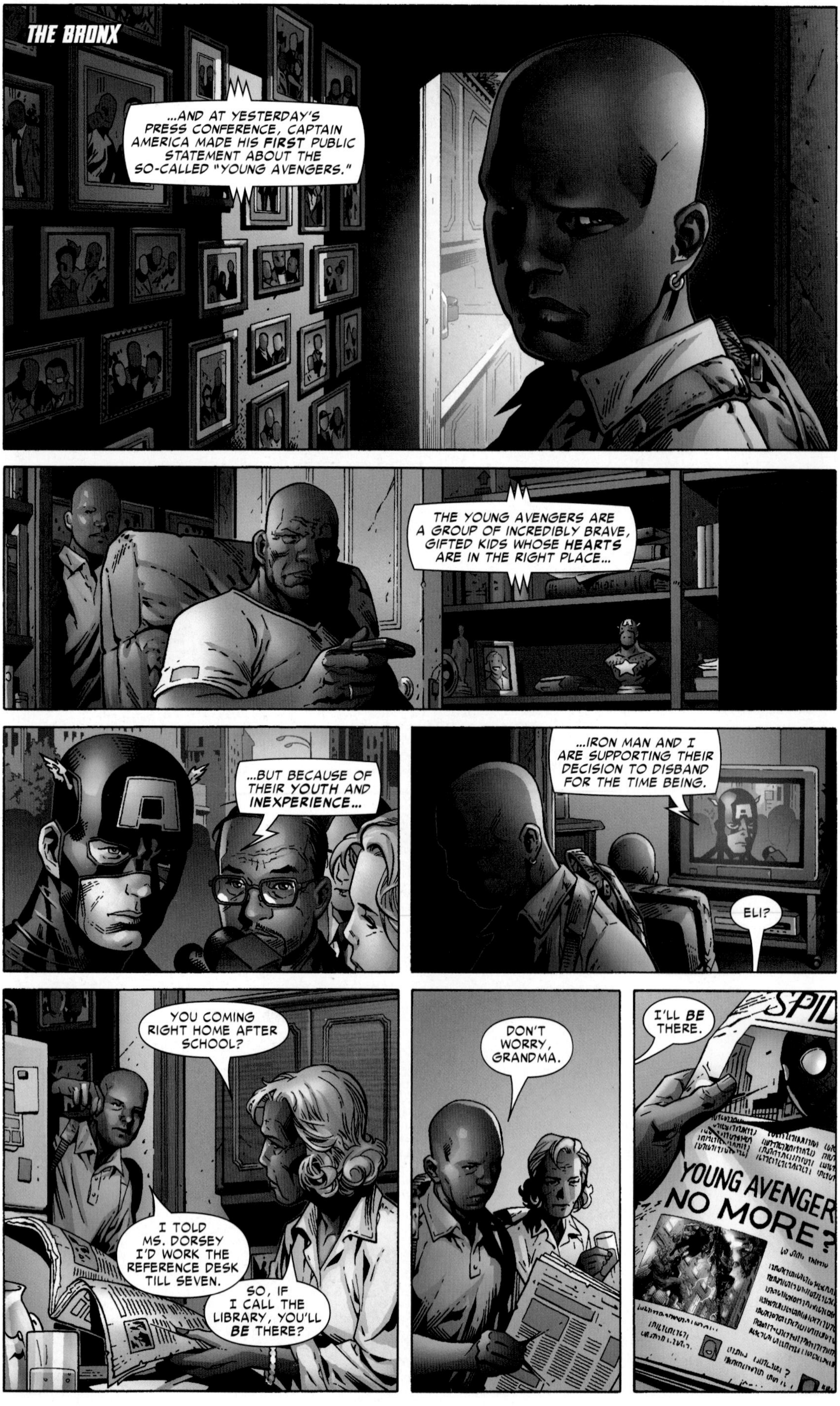
THE BRONX
...AND AT YESTERDAY'S PRESS CONFERENCE, CAPTAIN AMERICA MADE HIS FIRST PUBLIC STATEMENT ABOUT THE SO-CALLED "YOUNG AVENGERS."
THE YOUNG AVENGERS ARE A GROUP OF INCREDIBLY BRAVE, GIFTED KIDS WHOSE HEARTS ARE IN THE RIGHT PLACE...
...BUT BECAUSE OF THEIR YOUTH AND INEXPERIENCE...
...IRON MAN AND I ARE SUPPORTING THEIR DECISION TO DISBAND FOR THE TIME BEING.
ELI?
YOU COMING RIGHT HOME AFTER SCHOOL?
I TOLD MS. DORSEY I'D WORK THE REFERENCE DESK TILL SEVEN.
SO, IF I CALL THE LIBRARY, YOU'LL BE THERE?
DON'T WORRY, GRANDMA.
I'LL BE THERE.
YOUNG AVENGER NO MORE?

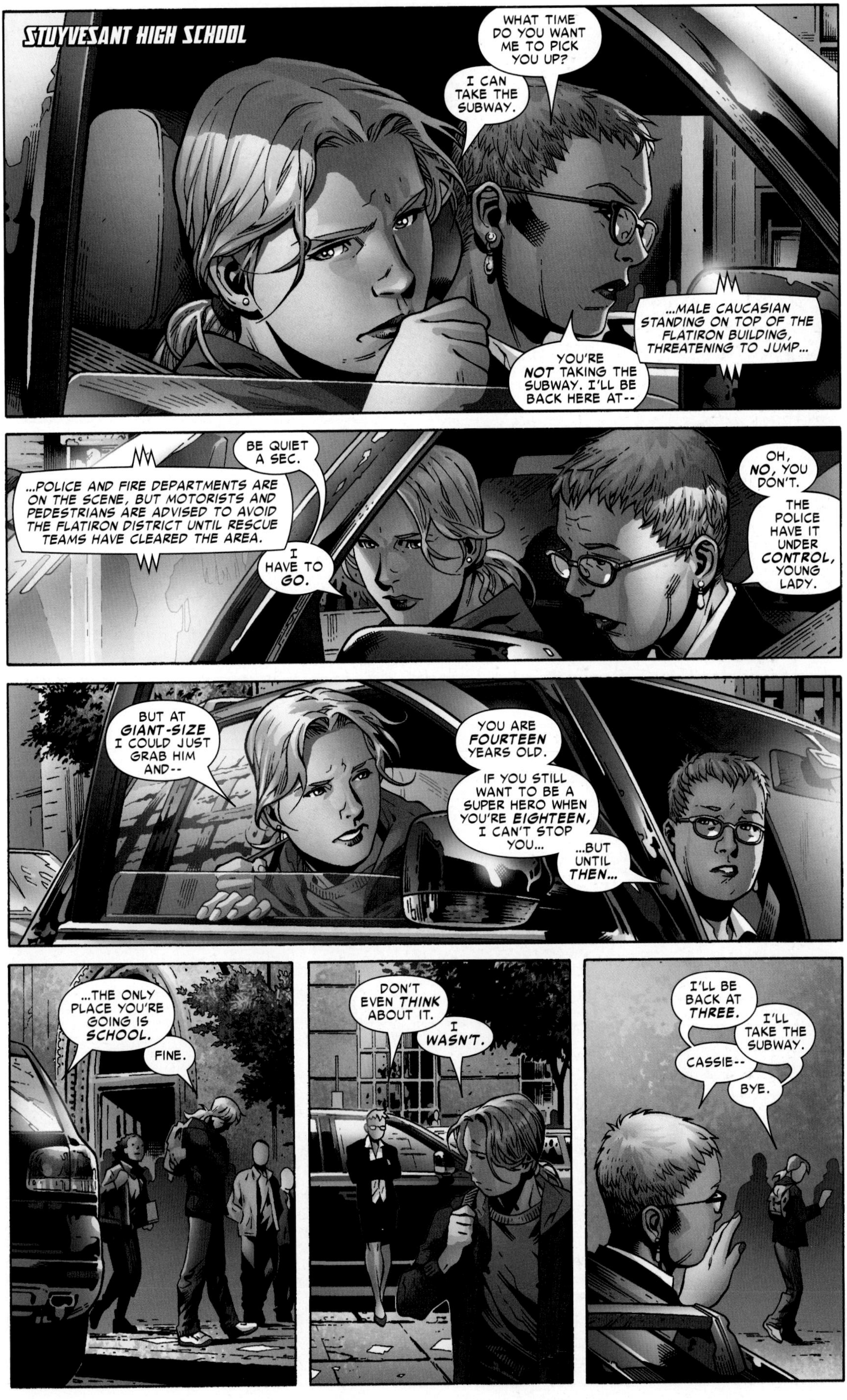
STUYVESANT HIGH SCHOOL
WHAT TIME DO YOU WANT ME TO PICK YOU UP?
I CAN TAKE THE SUBWAY.
...MALE CAUCASIAN STANDING ON TOP OF THE FLATIRON BUILDING, THREATENING TO JUMP...
YOU'RE NOT TAKING THE SUBWAY. I'LL BE BACK HERE AT--
...POLICE AND FIRE DEPARTMENTS ARE ON THE SCENE, BUT MOTORISTS AND PEDESTRIANS ARE ADVISED TO AVOID THE FLATIRON DISTRICT UNTIL RESCUE TEAMS HAVE CLEARED THE AREA.
BE QUIET A SEC.
I HAVE TO GO.
OH, NO, YOU DON'T.
THE POLICE HAVE IT UNDER CONTROL, YOUNG LADY.
BUT AT GIANT-SIZE I COULD JUST GRAB HIM AND--
YOU ARE FOURTEEN YEARS OLD.
IF YOU STILL WANT TO BE A SUPER HERO WHEN YOU'RE EIGHTEEN, I CAN'T STOP YOU...
...BUT UNTIL THEN...
...THE ONLY PLACE YOU'RE GOING IS SCHOOL.
FINE.
DON'T EVEN THINK ABOUT IT.
I WASN'T.
I'LL BE BACK AT THREE.
I'LL TAKE THE SUBWAY.
CASSIE--
BYE.

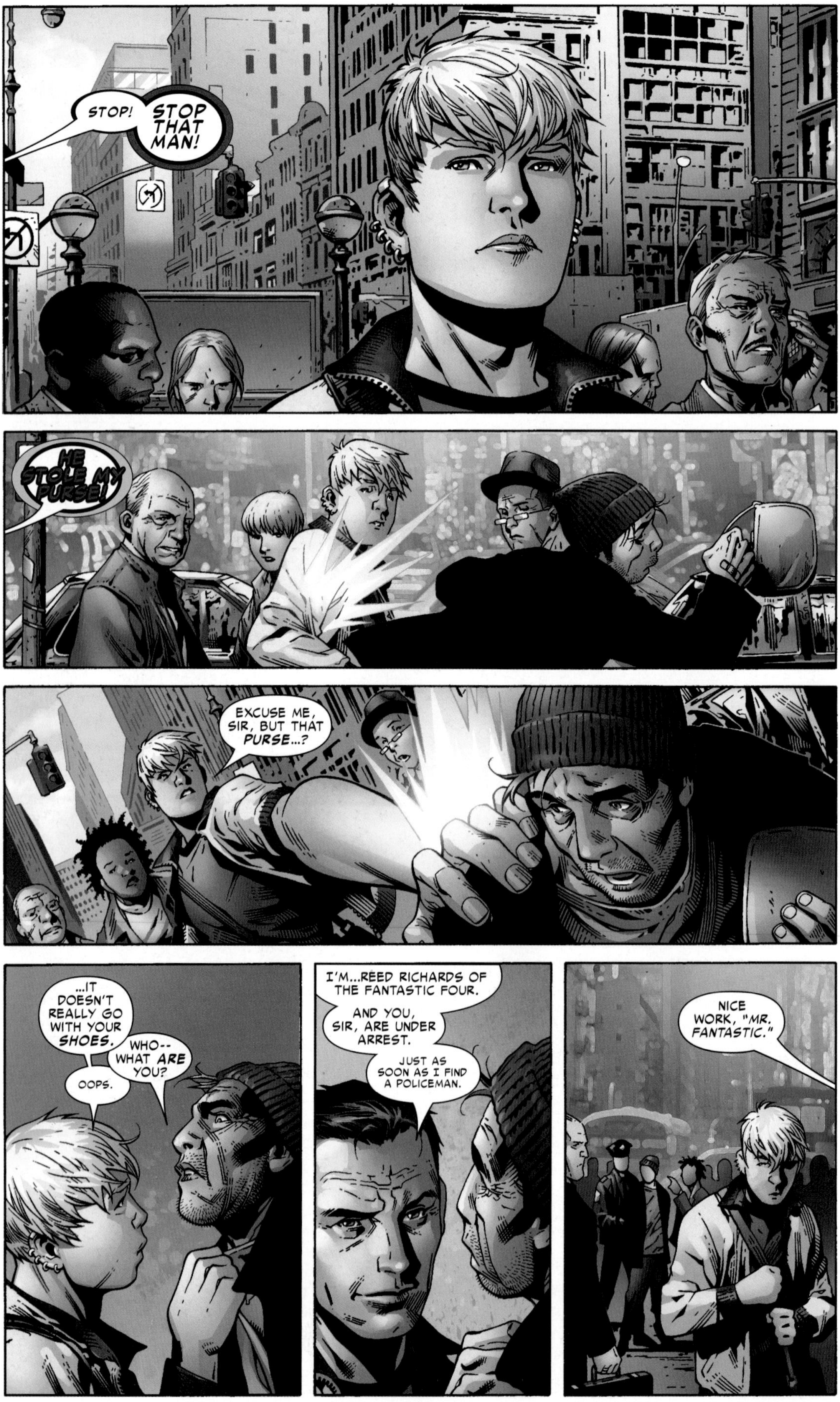
STOP!
STOP THAT MAN!
HE STOLE MY PURSE!
EXCUSE ME, SIR, BUT THAT PURSE...?
...IT DOESN'T REALLY GO WITH YOUR SHOES.
OOPS.
WHO-- WHAT ARE YOU?
I'M...REED RICHARDS OF THE FANTASTIC FOUR.
AND YOU, SIR, ARE UNDER ARREST.
JUST AS SOON AS I FIND A POLICEMAN.
NICE WORK, "MR. FANTASTIC."

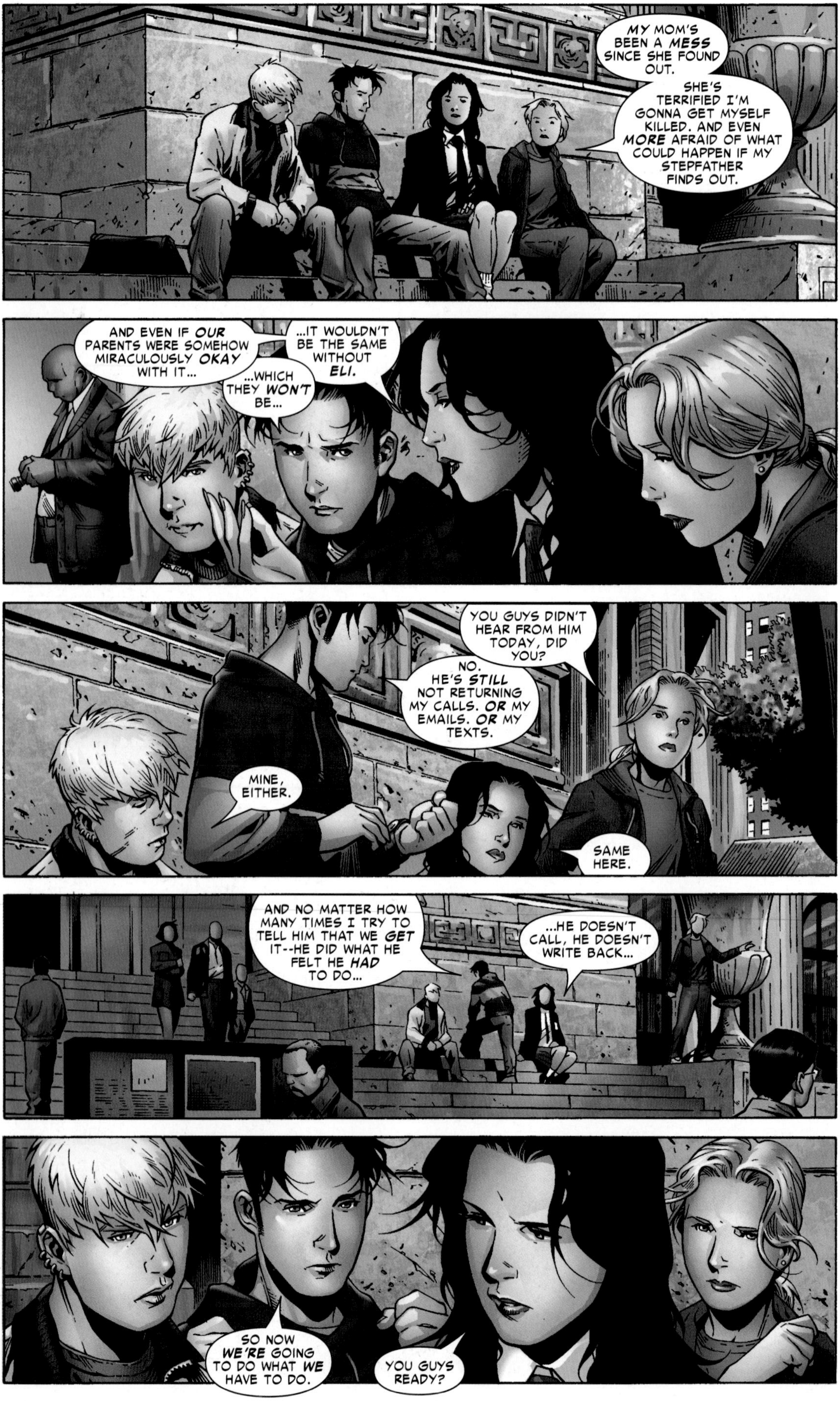
MY MOM'S BEEN A MESS SINCE SHE FOUND OUT.
SHE'S TERRIFIED I'M GONNA GET MYSELF KILLED. AND EVEN MORE AFRAID OF WHAT COULD HAPPEN IF MY STEPFATHER FINDS OUT.
AND EVEN IF OUR PARENTS WERE SOMEHOW MIRACULOUSLY OKAY WITH IT...
...WHICH THEY WON'T BE...
...IT WOULDN'T BE THE SAME WITHOUT ELI.
YOU GUYS DIDN'T HEAR FROM HIM TODAY, DID YOU?
NO. HE'S STILL NOT RETURNING MY CALLS. OR MY EMAILS. OR MY TEXTS.
MINE, EITHER.
SAME HERE.
AND NO MATTER HOW MANY TIMES I TRY TO TELL HIM THAT WE GET IT--HE DID WHAT HE FELT HE HAD TO DO...
...HE DOESN'T CALL, HE DOESN'T WRITE BACK...
SO NOW WE'RE GOING TO DO WHAT WE HAVE TO DO.
YOU GUYS READY?

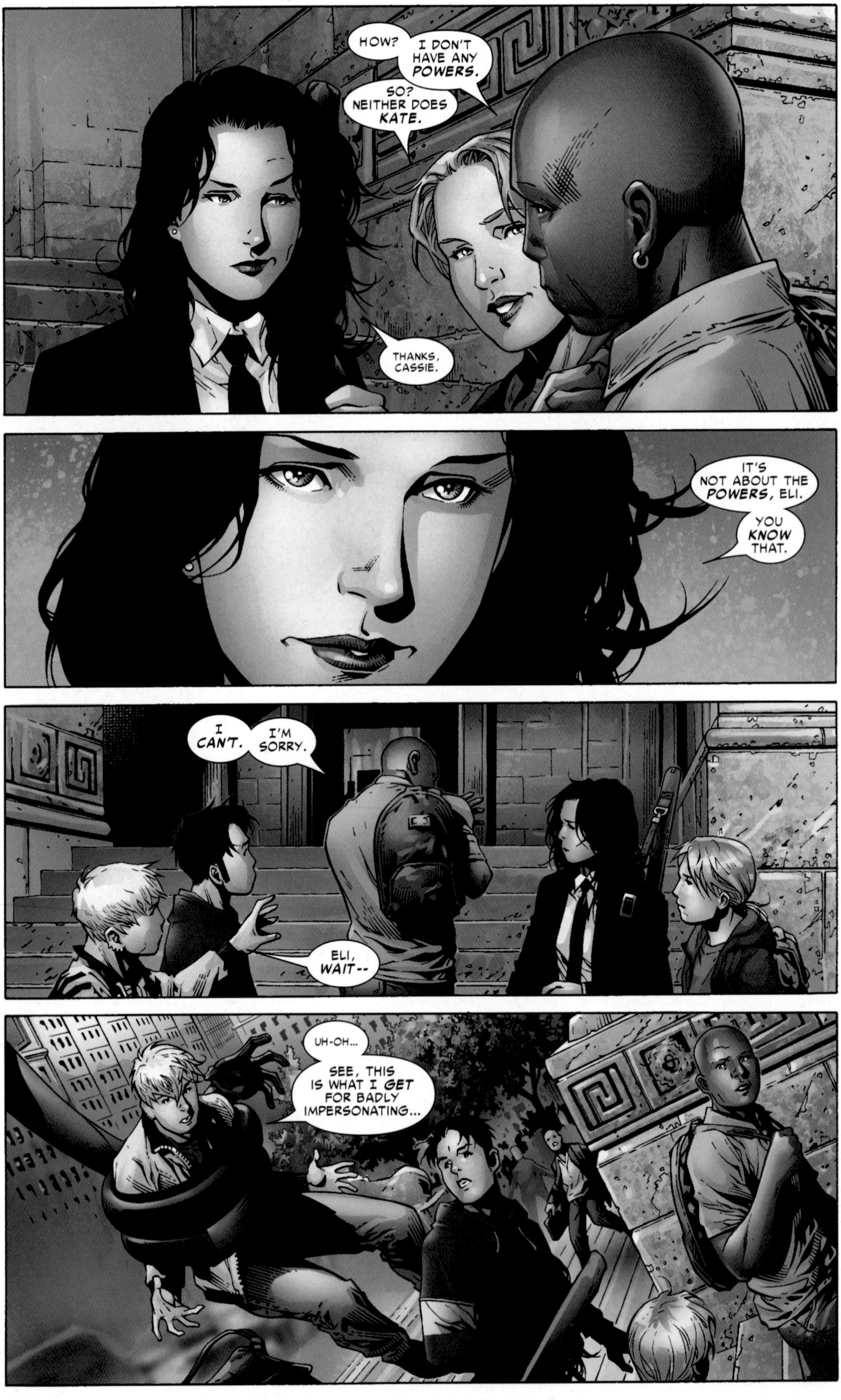
HOW?
I DON'T HAVE ANY POWERS.
SO? NEITHER DOES KATE.
THANKS, CASSIE.
IT'S NOT ABOUT THE POWERS, ELI.
YOU KNOW THAT.
I CAN'T.
I'M SORRY.
ELI, WAIT--
UH-OH...
SEE, THIS IS WHAT I GET FOR BADLY IMPERSONATING...

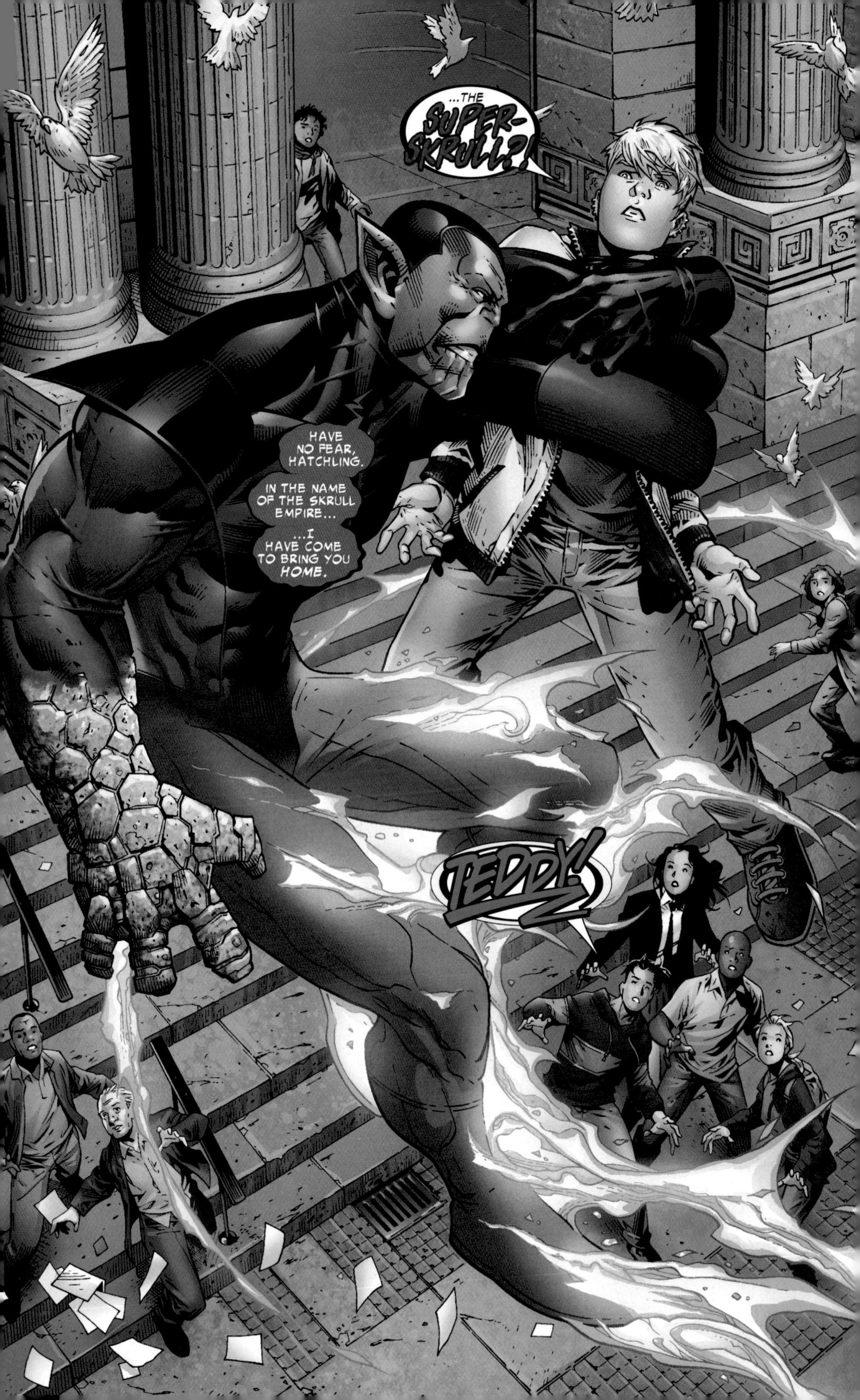
...THE SUPER-SKRULL?!
HAVE NO FEAR, HATCHLING.
IN THE NAME OF THE SKRULL EMPIRE...
...I HAVE COME TO BRING YOU HOME.
TEDDY!

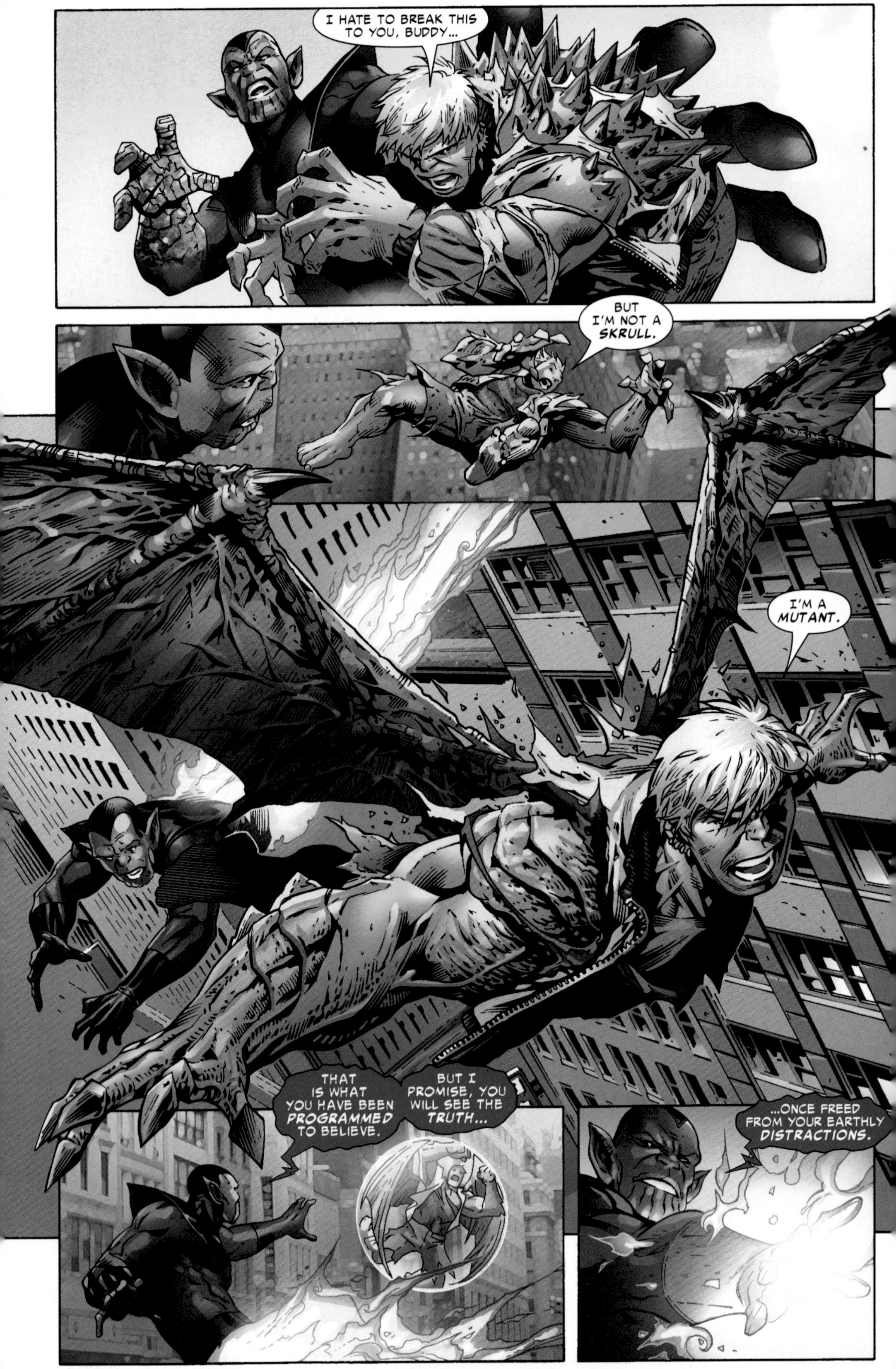
I HATE TO BREAK THIS TO YOU, BUDDY...
BUT I'M NOT A SKRULL.
I'M A MUTANT.
THAT IS WHAT YOU HAVE BEEN PROGRAMMED TO BELIEVE.
BUT I PROMISE, YOU WILL SEE THE TRUTH...
...ONCE FREED FROM YOUR EARTHLY DISTRACTIONS.

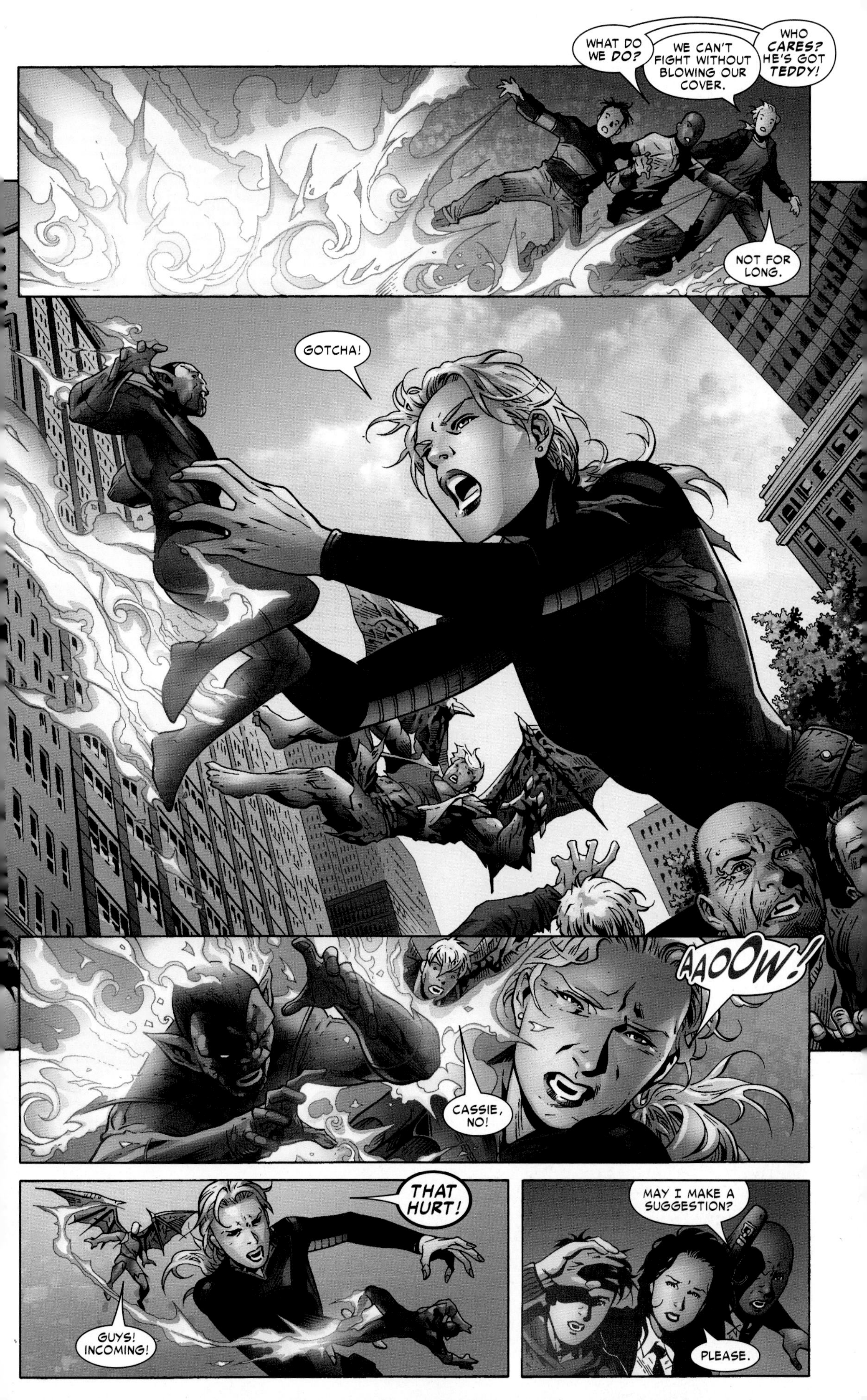
WHAT DO WE DO?
WE CAN'T FIGHT WITHOUT BLOWING OUR COVER.
WHO CARES? HE'S GOT TEDDY!
NOT FOR LONG.
GOTCHA!
AAOOW!
CASSIE, NO!
THAT HURT!
GUYS! INCOMING!
MAY I MAKE A SUGGESTION?
PLEASE.

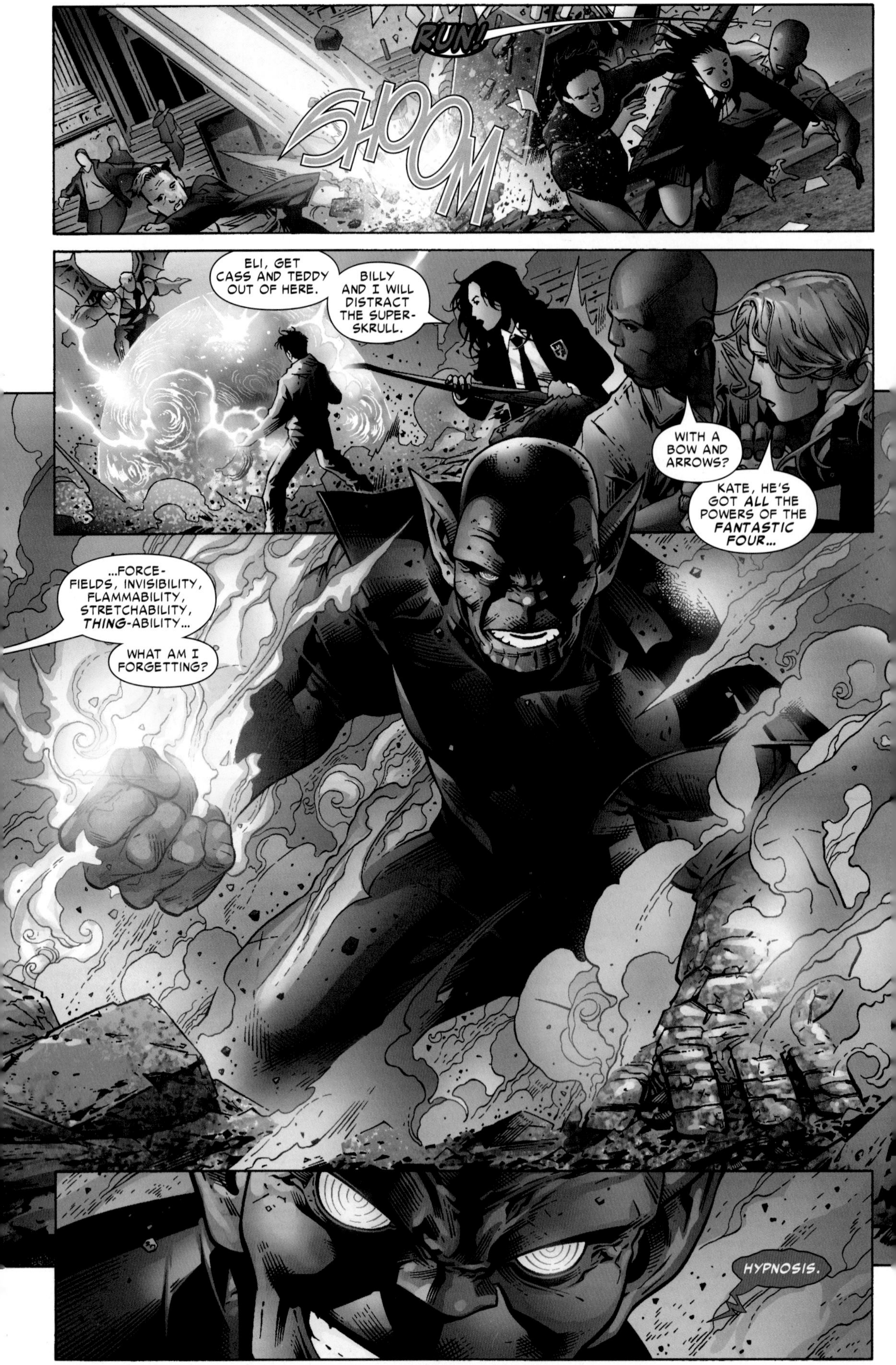
RUN!
SHOOM
ELI, GET CASS AND TEDDY OUT OF HERE.
BILLY AND I WILL DISTRACT THE SUPER-SKRULL.
WITH A BOW AND ARROWS?
KATE, HE'S GOT ALL THE POWERS OF THE FANTASTIC FOUR...
...FORCE-FIELDS, INVISIBILITY, FLAMMABILITY, STRETCHABILITY, THING-ABILITY...
WHAT AM I FORGETTING?
HYPNOSIS.

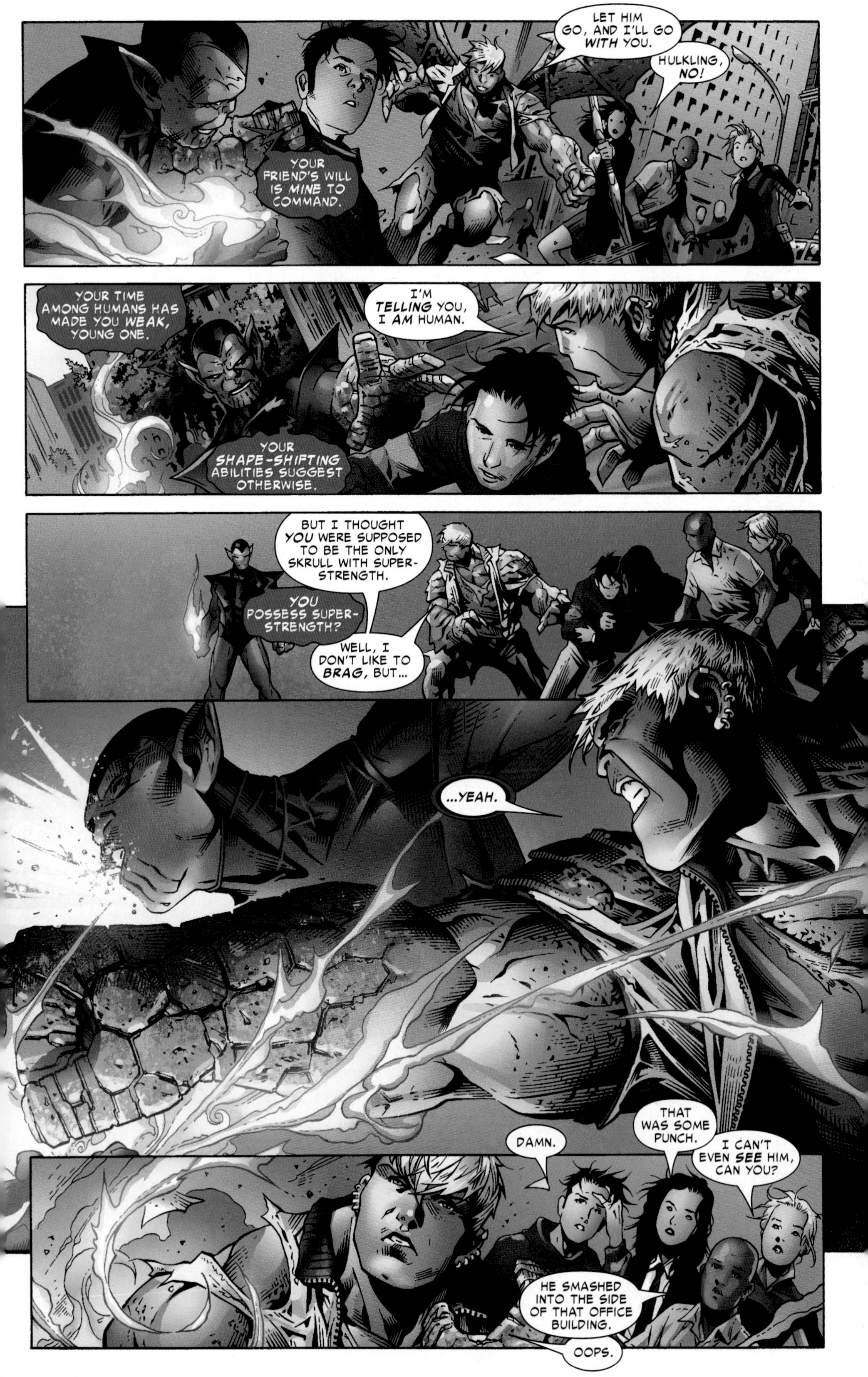
LET HIM GO, AND I'LL GO WITH YOU.
HULKLING, NO!
YOUR FRIEND'S WILL IS MINE TO COMMAND.
YOUR TIME AMONG HUMANS HAS MADE YOU WEAK, YOUNG ONE.
I'M TELLING YOU, I AM HUMAN.
YOUR SHAPE-SHIFTING ABILITIES SUGGEST OTHERWISE.
BUT I THOUGHT YOU WERE SUPPOSED TO BE THE ONLY SKRULL WITH SUPER-STRENGTH.
YOU POSSESS SUPER-STRENGTH?
WELL, I DON'T LIKE TO BRAG, BUT...
...YEAH.
DAMN.
THAT WAS SOME PUNCH.
I CAN'T EVEN SEE HIM, CAN YOU?
HE SMASHED INTO THE SIDE OF THAT OFFICE BUILDING.
OOPS.

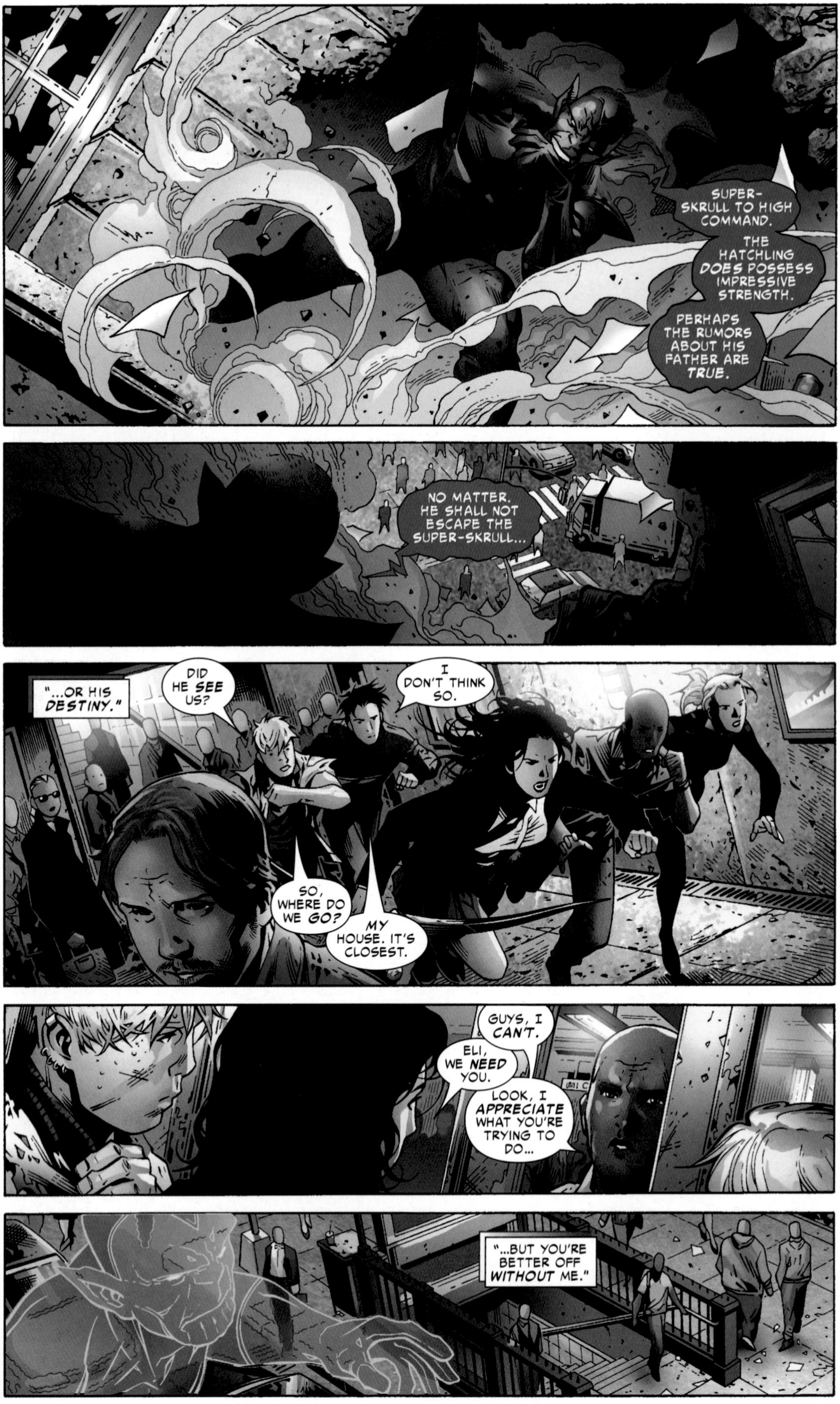
SUPER-SKRULL TO HIGH COMMAND.
THE HATCHLING DOES POSSESS IMPRESSIVE STRENGTH.
PERHAPS THE RUMORS ABOUT HIS FATHER ARE TRUE.
NO MATTER. HE SHALL NOT ESCAPE THE SUPER-SKRULL...
"...OR HIS DESTINY."
DID HE SEE US?
I DON'T THINK SO.
SO, WHERE DO WE GO?
MY HOUSE. IT'S CLOSEST.
GUYS, I CAN'T.
ELI, WE NEED YOU.
LOOK, I APPRECIATE WHAT YOU'RE TRYING TO DO...
"...BUT YOU'RE BETTER OFF WITHOUT ME."

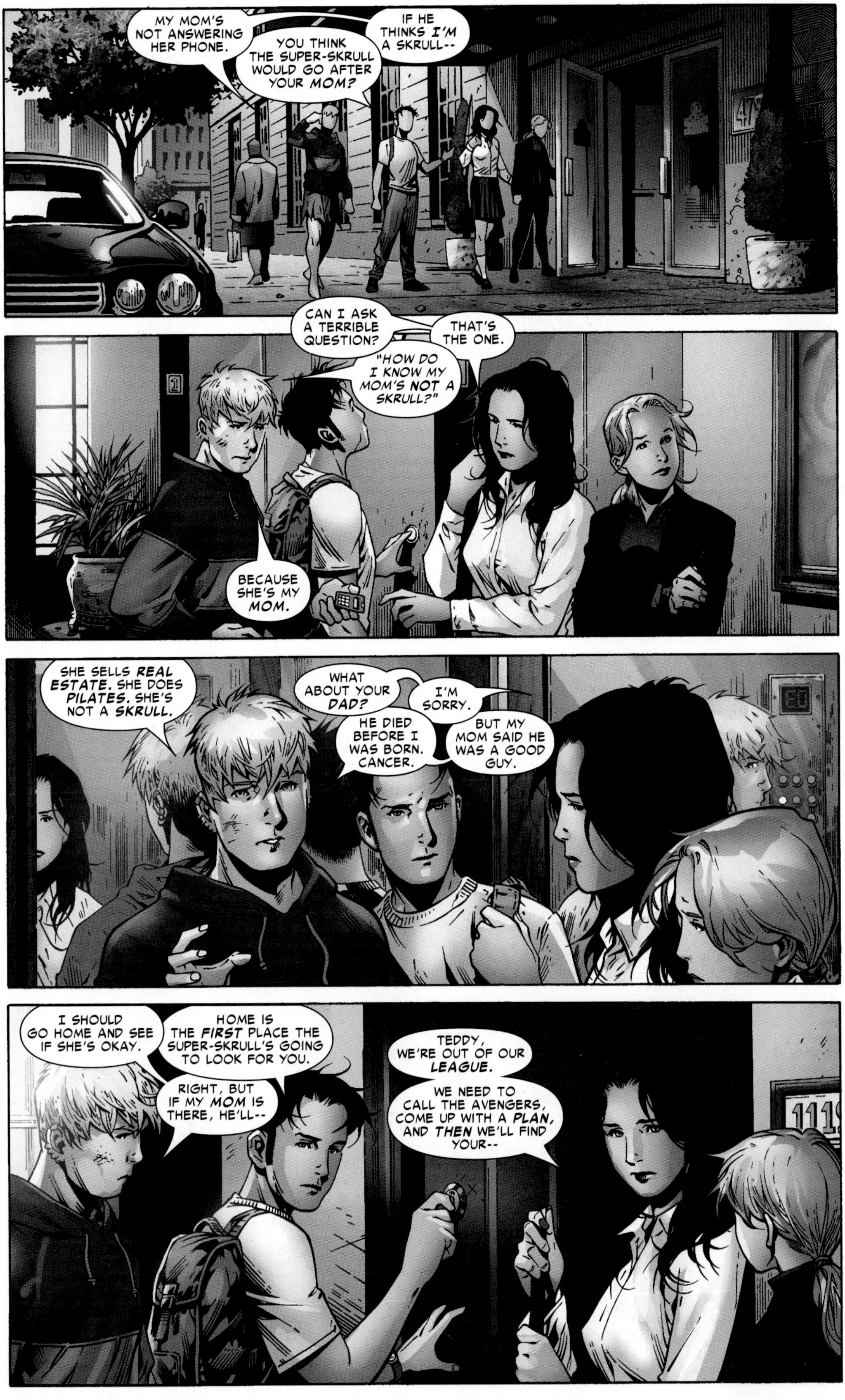
MY MOM'S NOT ANSWERING HER PHONE.
YOU THINK THE SUPER-SKRULL WOULD GO AFTER YOUR *MOM?*
IF HE THINKS *I'M* A SKRULL--
CAN I ASK A TERRIBLE QUESTION?
"HOW DO I KNOW MY MOM'S *NOT* A SKRULL?"
THAT'S THE ONE.
BECAUSE SHE'S MY *MOM.*
SHE SELLS *REAL ESTATE.* SHE DOES *PILATES.* SHE'S NOT A *SKRULL.*
WHAT ABOUT YOUR *DAD?*
HE DIED BEFORE I WAS BORN. CANCER.
I'M SORRY.
BUT MY MOM SAID HE WAS A GOOD GUY.
I SHOULD GO HOME AND SEE IF SHE'S OKAY.
HOME IS THE *FIRST* PLACE THE SUPER-SKRULL'S GOING TO LOOK FOR YOU.
RIGHT, BUT IF MY *MOM* IS THERE, HE'LL--
TEDDY, WE'RE OUT OF OUR *LEAGUE.*
WE NEED TO CALL THE AVENGERS, COME UP WITH A *PLAN,* AND *THEN* WE'LL FIND YOUR--

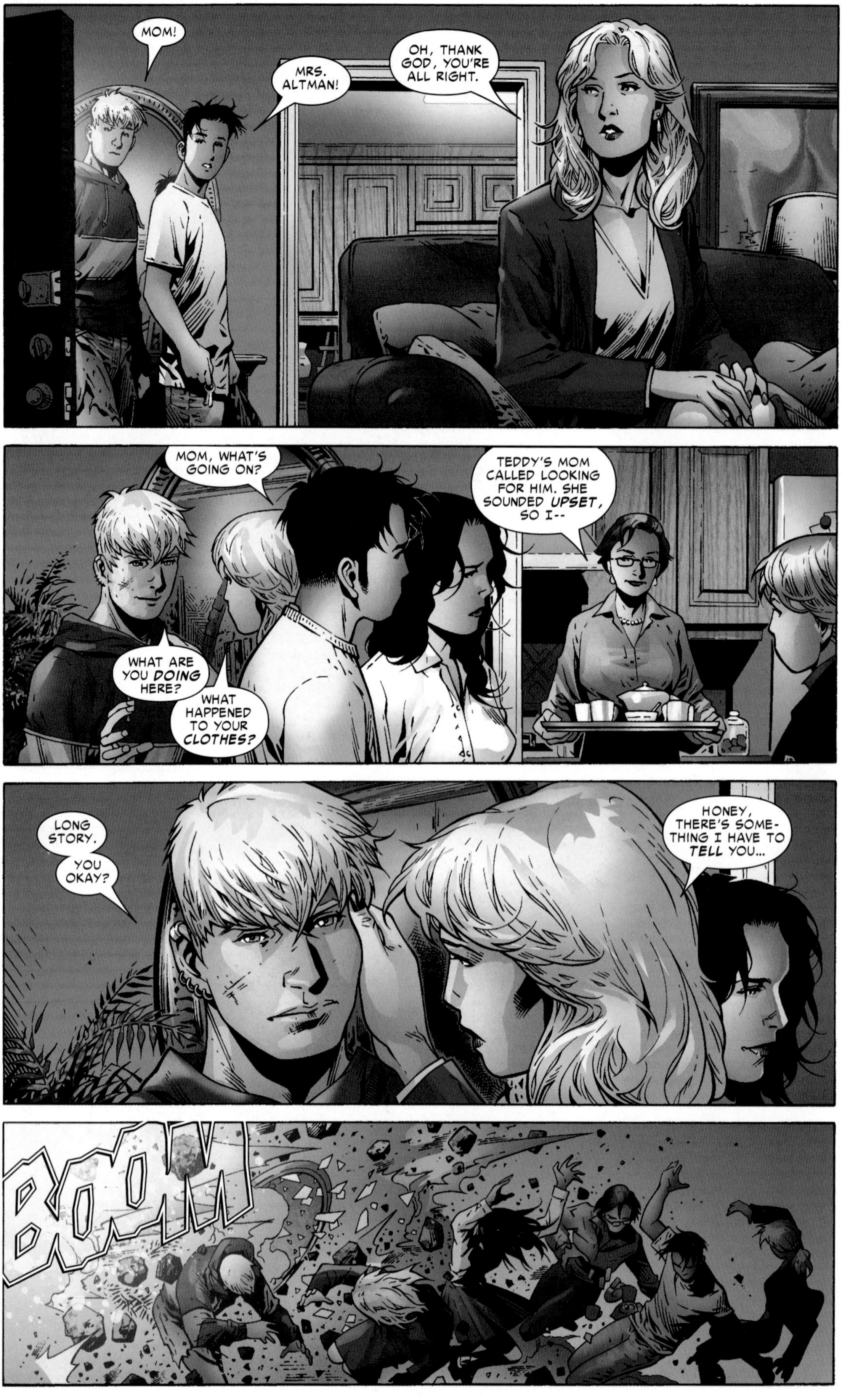
MOM!
MRS. ALTMAN!
OH, THANK GOD, YOU'RE ALL RIGHT.
MOM, WHAT'S GOING ON?
TEDDY'S MOM CALLED LOOKING FOR HIM. SHE SOUNDED *UPSET*, SO I--
WHAT ARE YOU *DOING* HERE?
WHAT HAPPENED TO YOUR *CLOTHES?*
LONG STORY.
YOU OKAY?
HONEY, THERE'S SOME-THING I HAVE TO *TELL* YOU...
BOOM

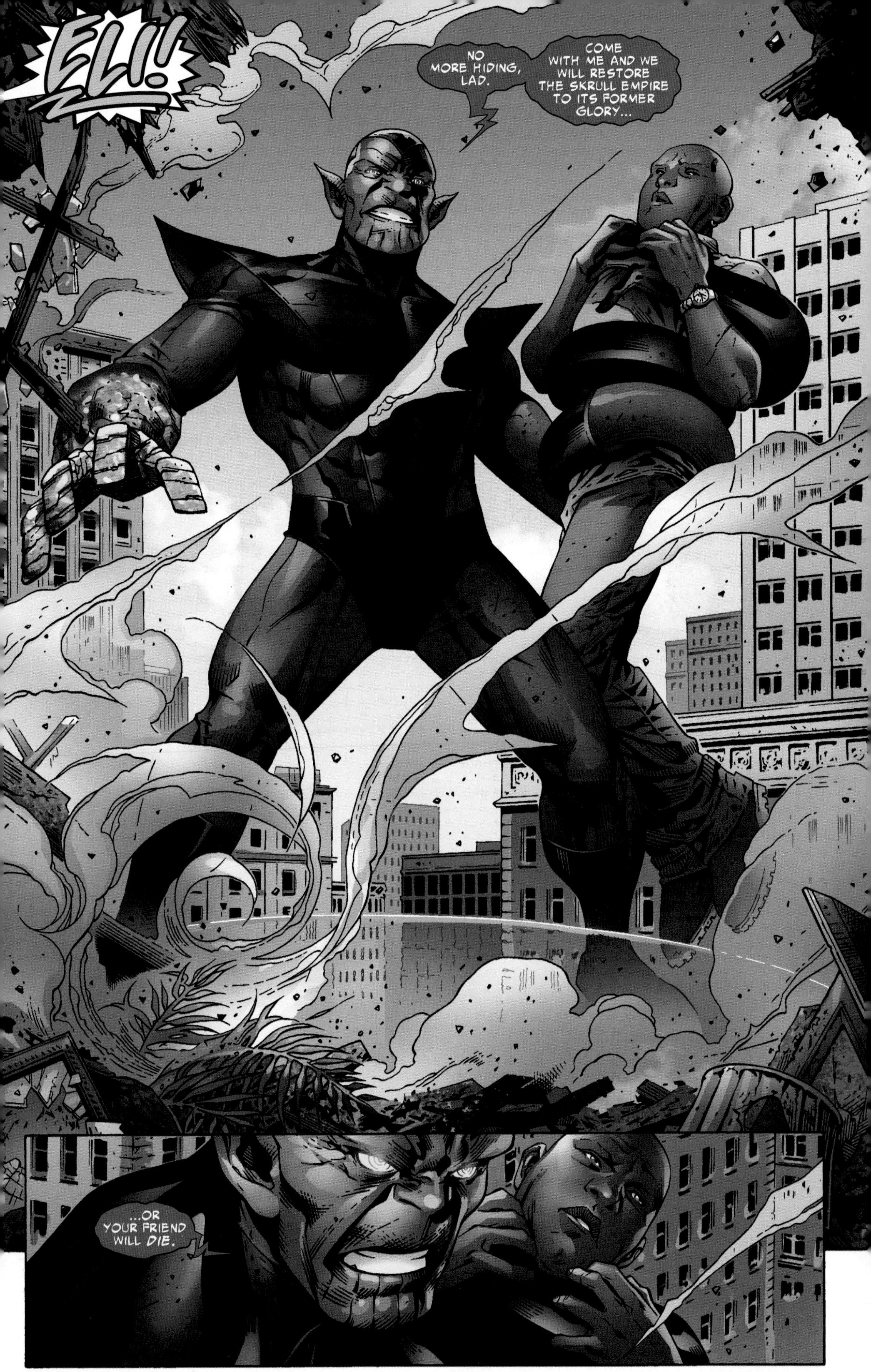
ELI!
NO MORE HIDING, LAD.
COME WITH ME AND WE WILL RESTORE THE SKRULL EMPIRE TO ITS FORMER GLORY...
...OR YOUR FRIEND WILL DIE.

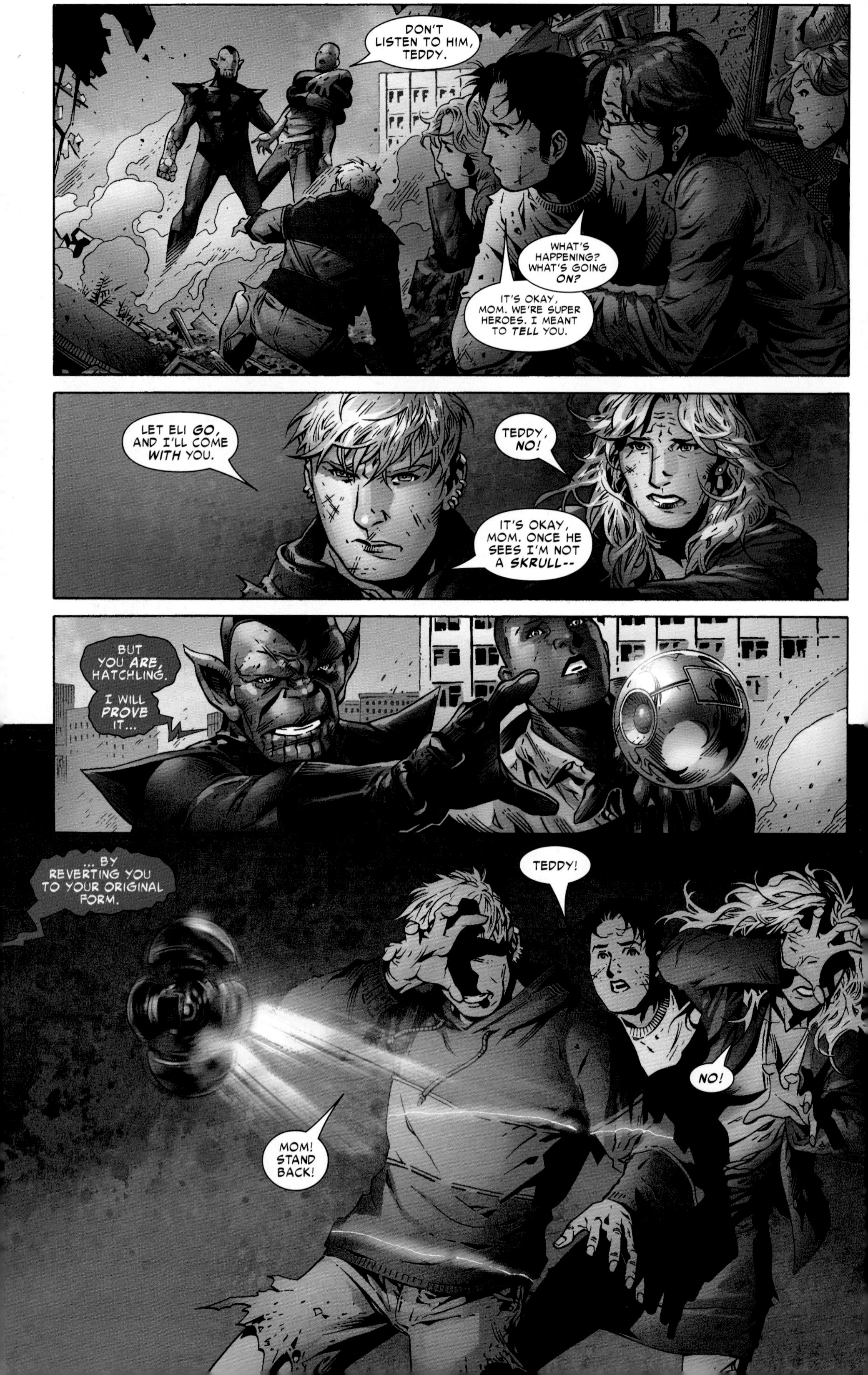
DON'T LISTEN TO HIM, TEDDY.
WHAT'S HAPPENING? WHAT'S GOING ON?
IT'S OKAY, MOM. WE'RE SUPER HEROES. I MEANT TO TELL YOU.
LET ELI GO, AND I'LL COME WITH YOU.
TEDDY, NO!
IT'S OKAY, MOM. ONCE HE SEES I'M NOT A SKRULL--
BUT YOU ARE, HATCHLING.
I WILL PROVE IT...
... BY REVERTING YOU TO YOUR ORIGINAL FORM.
TEDDY!
NO!
MOM! STAND BACK!

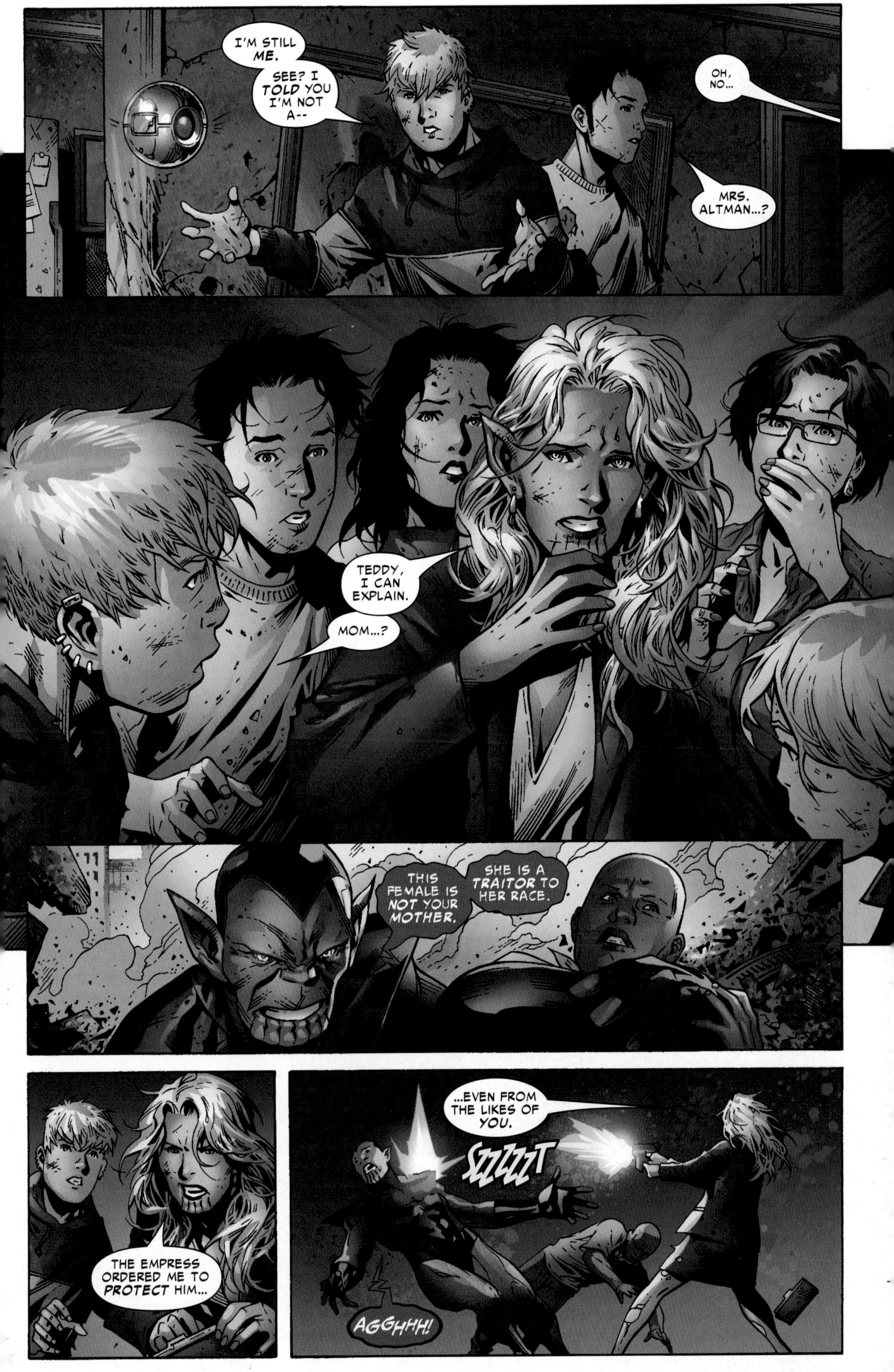
I'M STILL ME.
SEE? I TOLD YOU I'M NOT A--
OH, NO...
MRS. ALTMAN...?
TEDDY, I CAN EXPLAIN.
MOM...?
THIS FEMALE IS NOT YOUR MOTHER.
SHE IS A TRAITOR TO HER RACE.
THE EMPRESS ORDERED ME TO PROTECT HIM...
...EVEN FROM THE LIKES OF YOU.
SZZZZZT
AGGHHH!

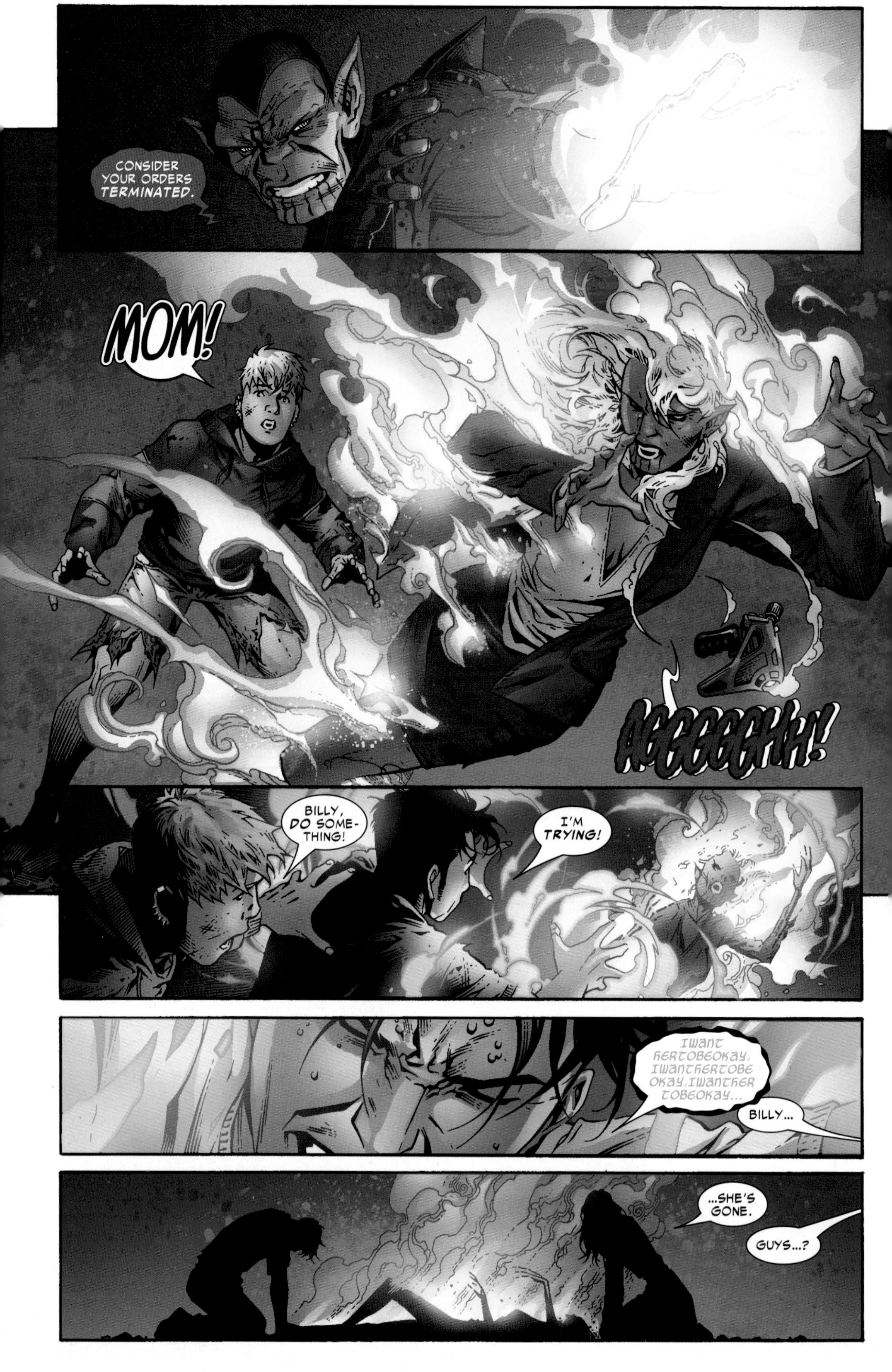

CONSIDER YOUR ORDERS TERMINATED.
MOM!
AGGGGGHH!
BILLY, DO SOME-THING!
I'M TRYING!
IWANT HERTOBEOKAY, IWANTHERTOBE OKAY, IWANTHER TOBEOKAY...
BILLY...
...SHE'S GONE.
GUYS...?

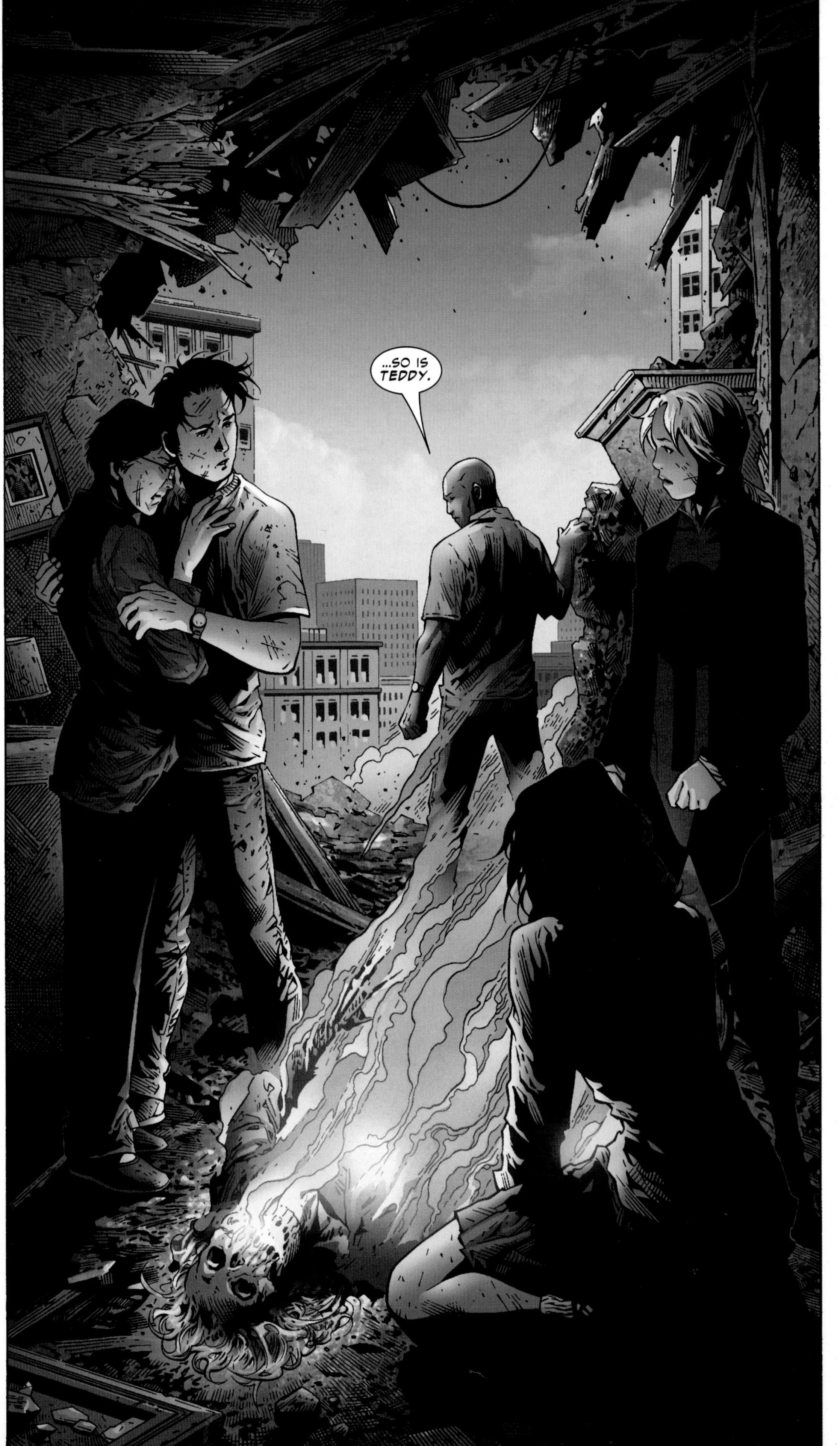
...SO IS TEDDY.

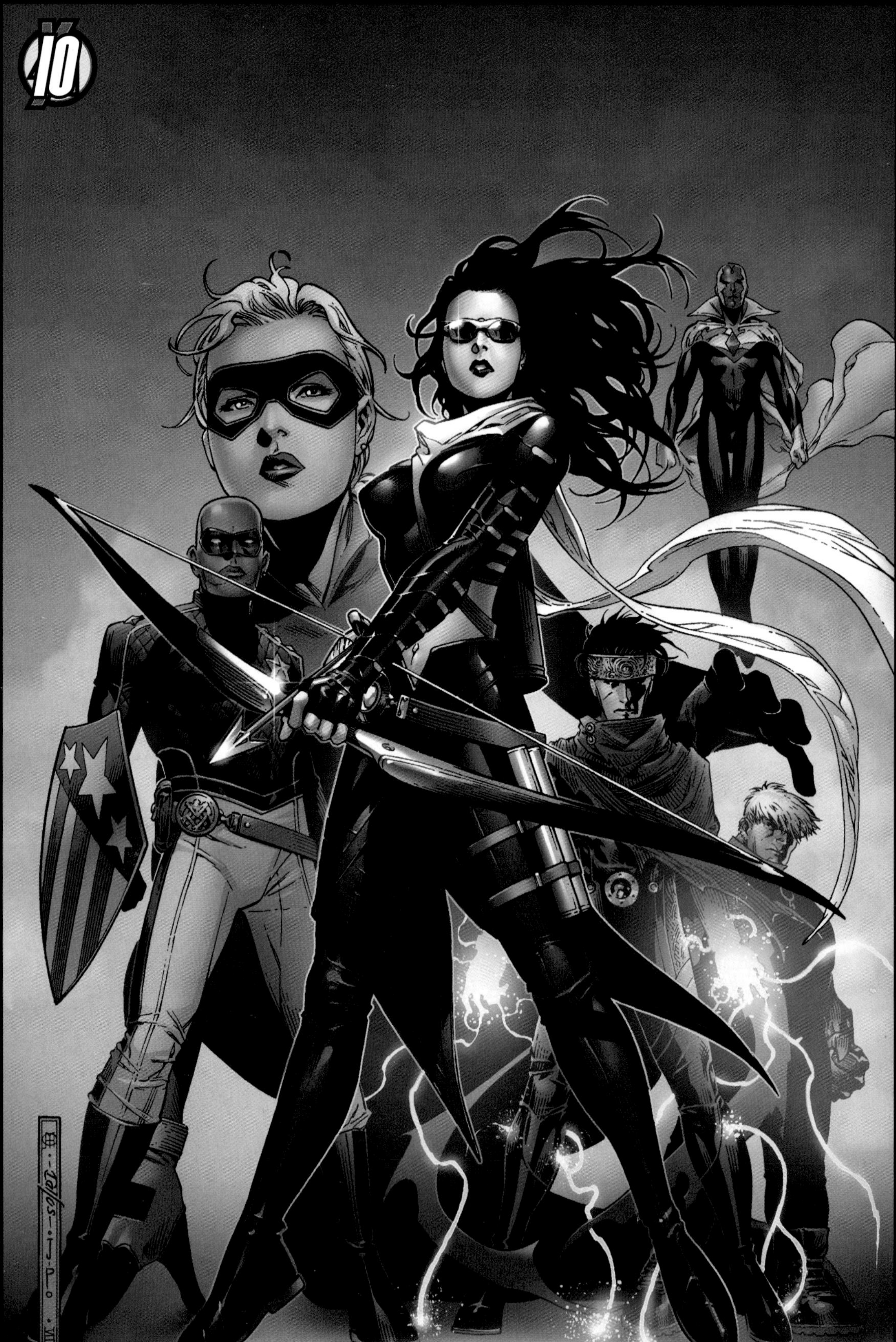

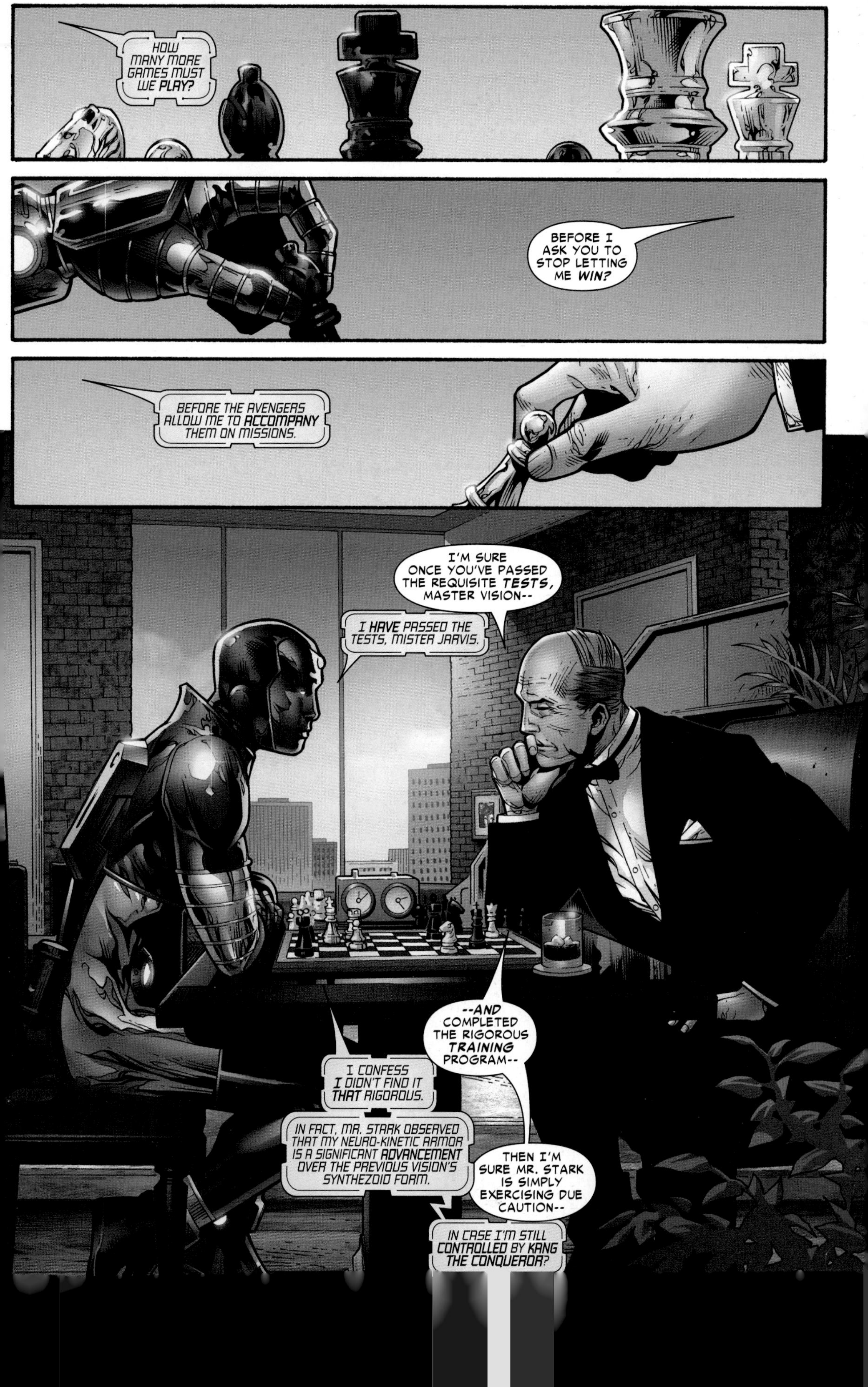
HOW MANY MORE GAMES MUST WE PLAY?
BEFORE I ASK YOU TO STOP LETTING ME WIN?
BEFORE THE AVENGERS ALLOW ME TO ACCOMPANY THEM ON MISSIONS.
I'M SURE ONCE YOU'VE PASSED THE REQUISITE TESTS, MASTER VISION--
I HAVE PASSED THE TESTS, MISTER JARVIS.
--AND COMPLETED THE RIGOROUS TRAINING PROGRAM--
I CONFESS I DIDN'T FIND IT THAT RIGOROUS.
IN FACT, MR. STARK OBSERVED THAT MY NEURO-KINETIC ARMOR IS A SIGNIFICANT ADVANCEMENT OVER THE PREVIOUS VISION'S SYNTHEZOID FORM.
THEN I'M SURE MR. STARK IS SIMPLY EXERCISING DUE CAUTION--
IN CASE I'M STILL CONTROLLED BY KANG THE CONQUEROR?

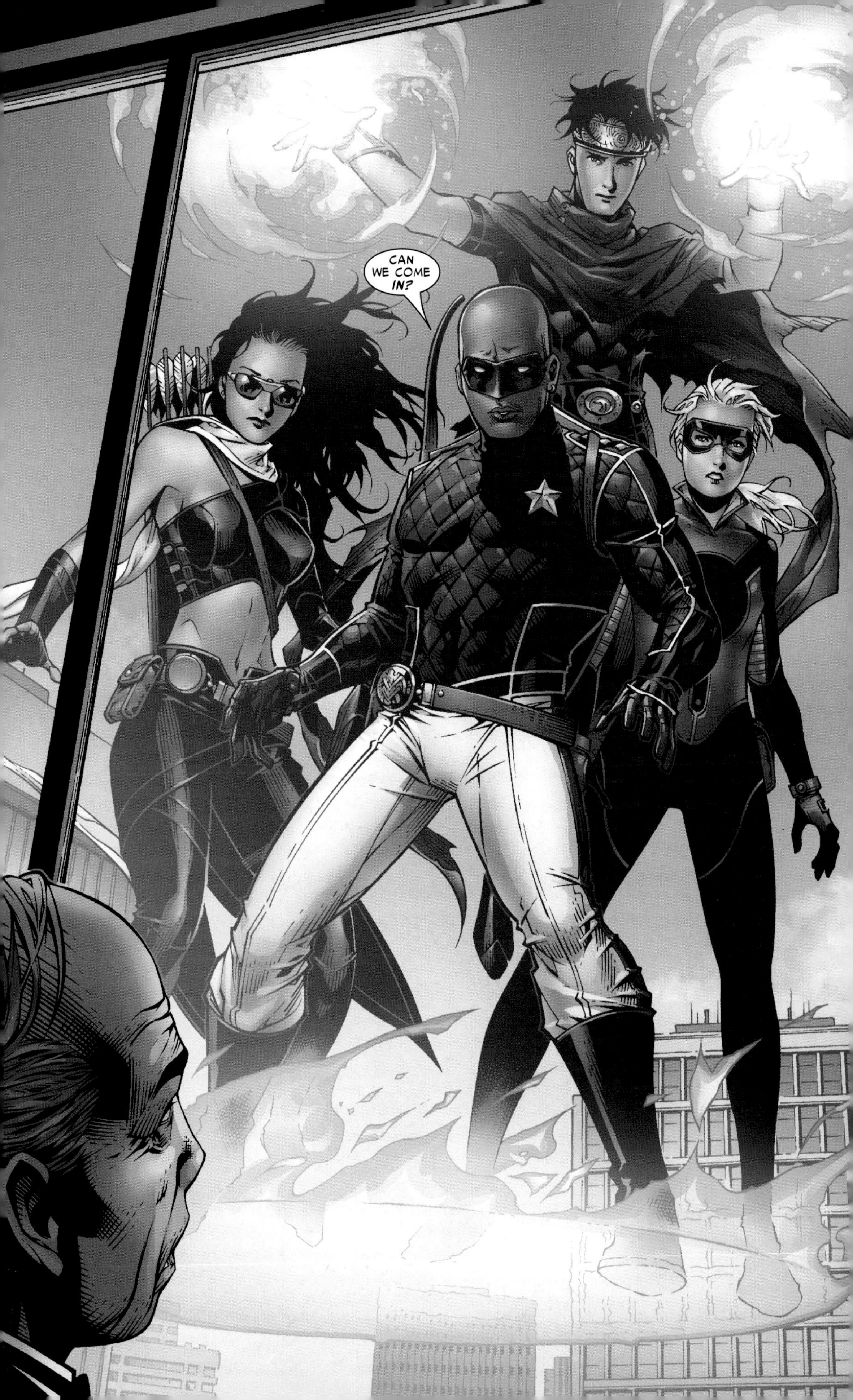
CAN WE COME IN?

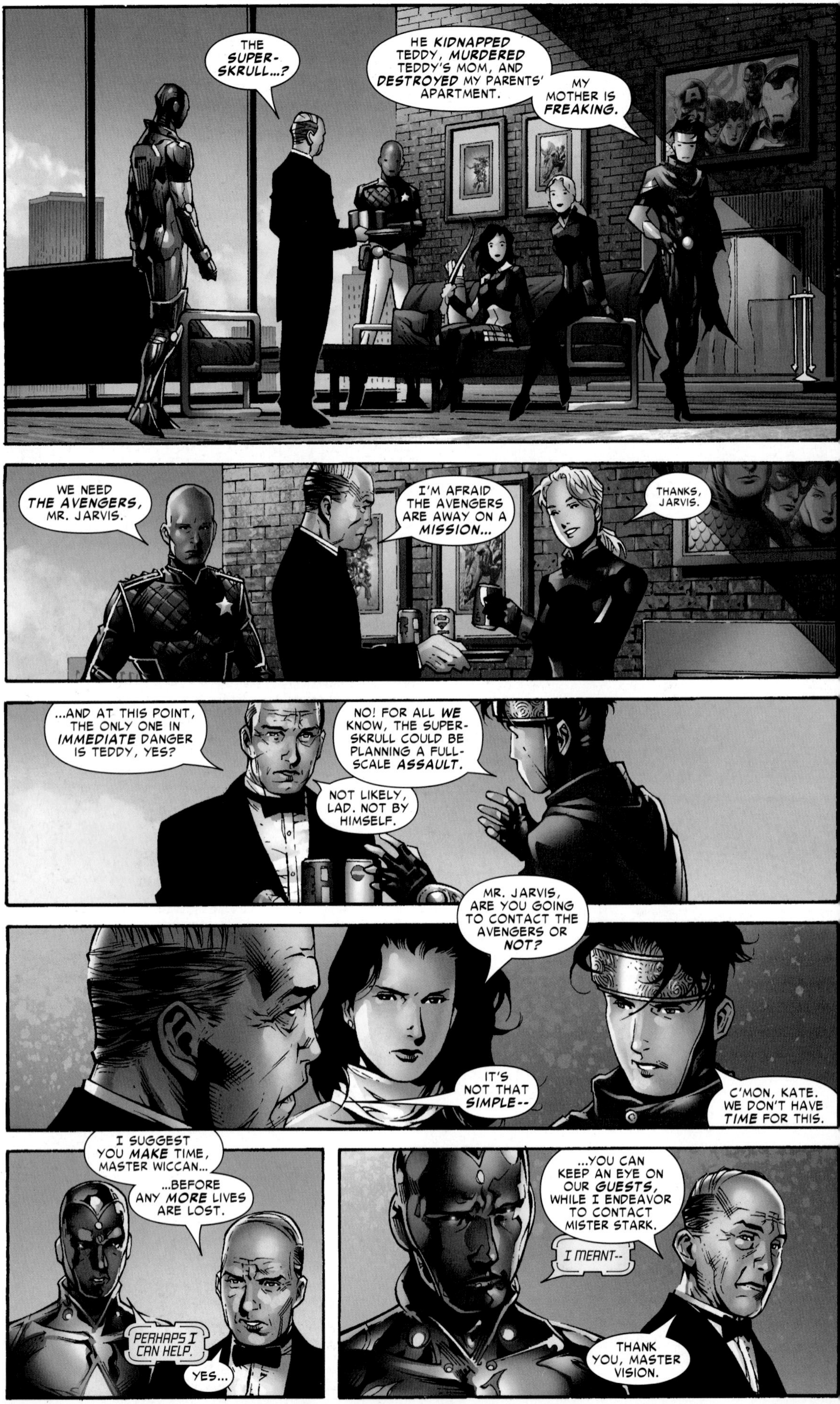
THE SUPER-SKRULL...?
HE KIDNAPPED TEDDY, MURDERED TEDDY'S MOM, AND DESTROYED MY PARENTS' APARTMENT.
MY MOTHER IS FREAKING.
WE NEED THE AVENGERS, MR. JARVIS.
I'M AFRAID THE AVENGERS ARE AWAY ON A MISSION...
THANKS, JARVIS.
...AND AT THIS POINT, THE ONLY ONE IN IMMEDIATE DANGER IS TEDDY, YES?
NO! FOR ALL WE KNOW, THE SUPER-SKRULL COULD BE PLANNING A FULL-SCALE ASSAULT.
NOT LIKELY, LAD. NOT BY HIMSELF.
MR. JARVIS, ARE YOU GOING TO CONTACT THE AVENGERS OR NOT?
IT'S NOT THAT SIMPLE--
C'MON, KATE. WE DON'T HAVE TIME FOR THIS.
I SUGGEST YOU MAKE TIME, MASTER WICCAN...
...BEFORE ANY MORE LIVES ARE LOST.
PERHAPS I CAN HELP.
YES...
...YOU CAN KEEP AN EYE ON OUR GUESTS, WHILE I ENDEAVOR TO CONTACT MISTER STARK.
I MEANT--
THANK YOU, MASTER VISION.

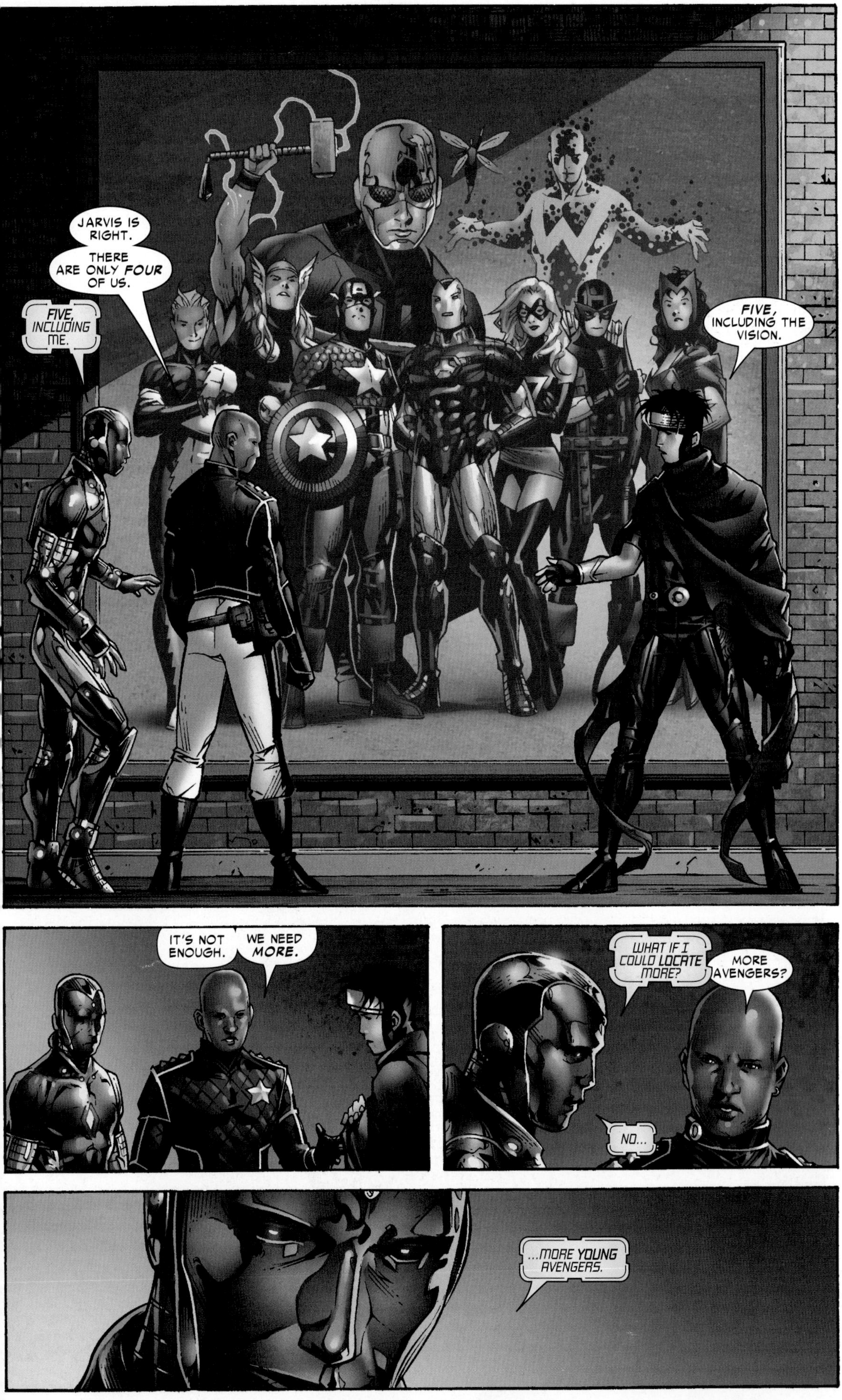
JARVIS IS RIGHT.
THERE ARE ONLY FOUR OF US.
FIVE, INCLUDING ME.
FIVE, INCLUDING THE VISION.
IT'S NOT ENOUGH.
WE NEED MORE.
WHAT IF I COULD LOCATE MORE?
MORE AVENGERS?
NO...
...MORE YOUNG AVENGERS.

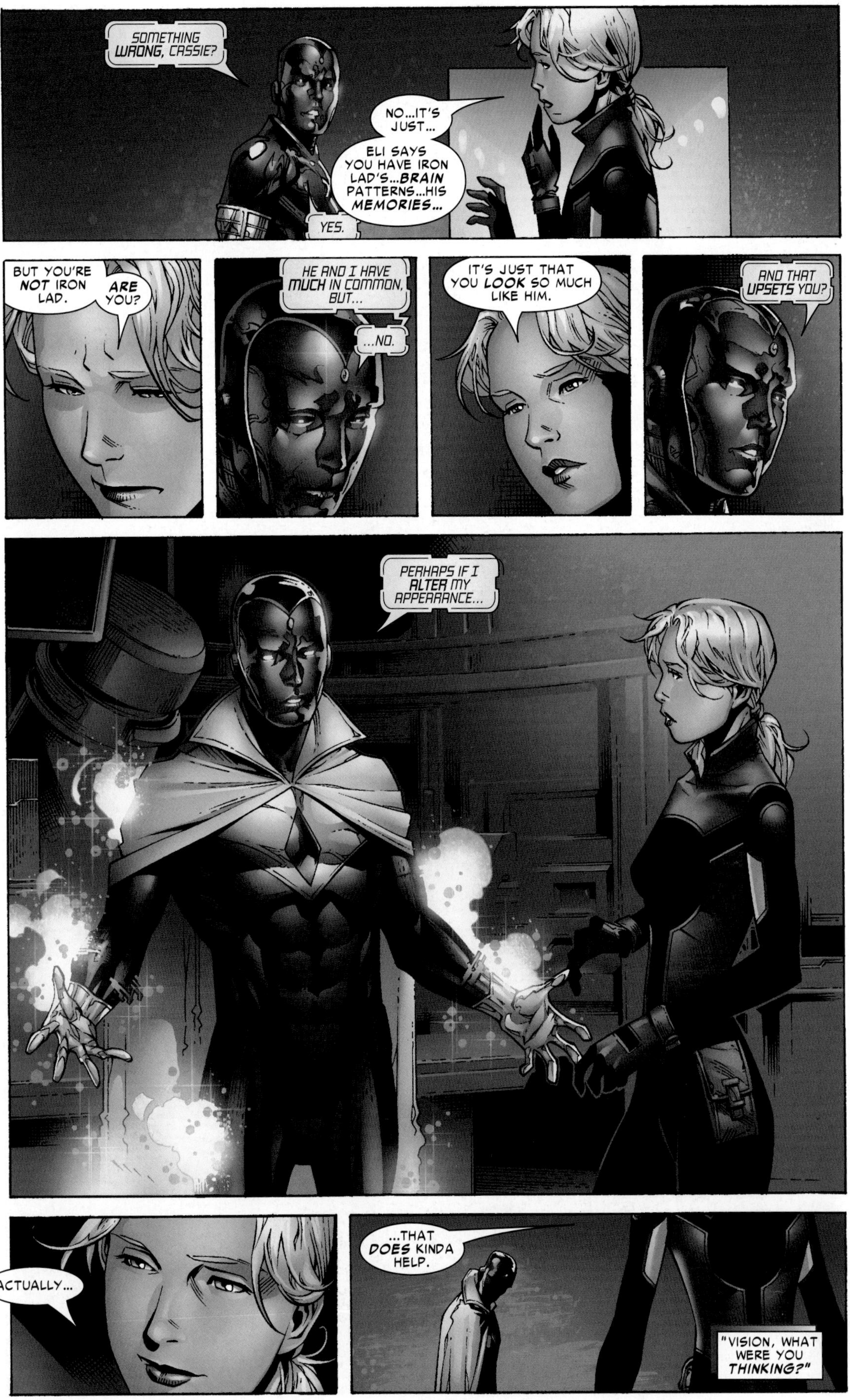
SOMETHING WRONG, CASSIE?
NO...IT'S JUST...
ELI SAYS YOU HAVE IRON LAD'S...BRAIN PATTERNS...HIS MEMORIES...
YES.
BUT YOU'RE NOT IRON LAD.
ARE YOU?
HE AND I HAVE MUCH IN COMMON, BUT...
...NO.
IT'S JUST THAT YOU LOOK SO MUCH LIKE HIM.
AND THAT UPSETS YOU?
PERHAPS IF I ALTER MY APPEARANCE...
ACTUALLY...
...THAT DOES KINDA HELP.
"VISION, WHAT WERE YOU THINKING?"

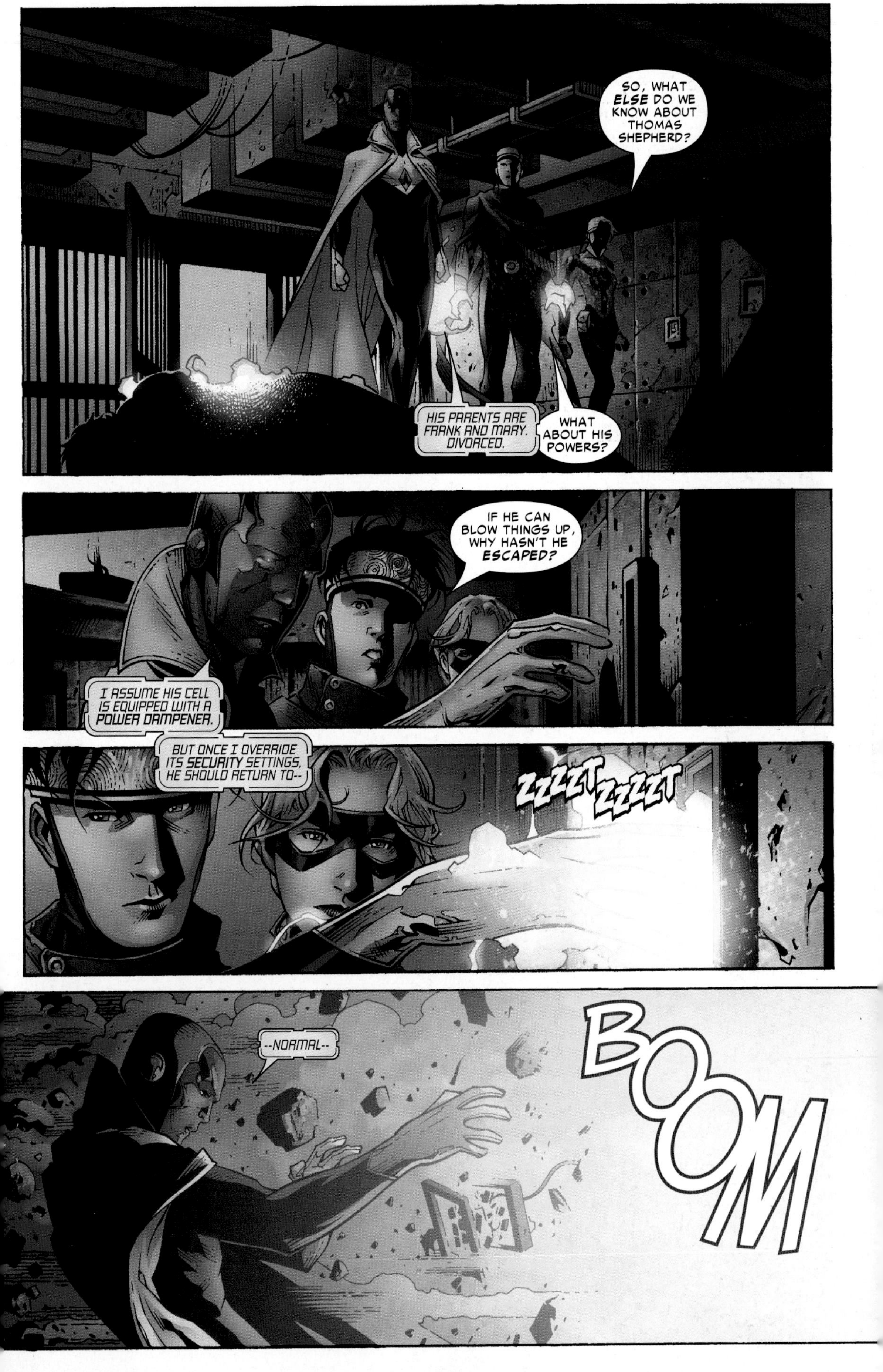
SO, WHAT ELSE DO WE KNOW ABOUT THOMAS SHEPHERD?
HIS PARENTS ARE FRANK AND MARY. DIVORCED.
WHAT ABOUT HIS POWERS?
IF HE CAN BLOW THINGS UP, WHY HASN'T HE ESCAPED?
I ASSUME HIS CELL IS EQUIPPED WITH A POWER DAMPENER.
BUT ONCE I OVERRIDE ITS SECURITY SETTINGS, HE SHOULD RETURN TO--
ZZZZT ZZZZT
--NORMAL--
BOOM

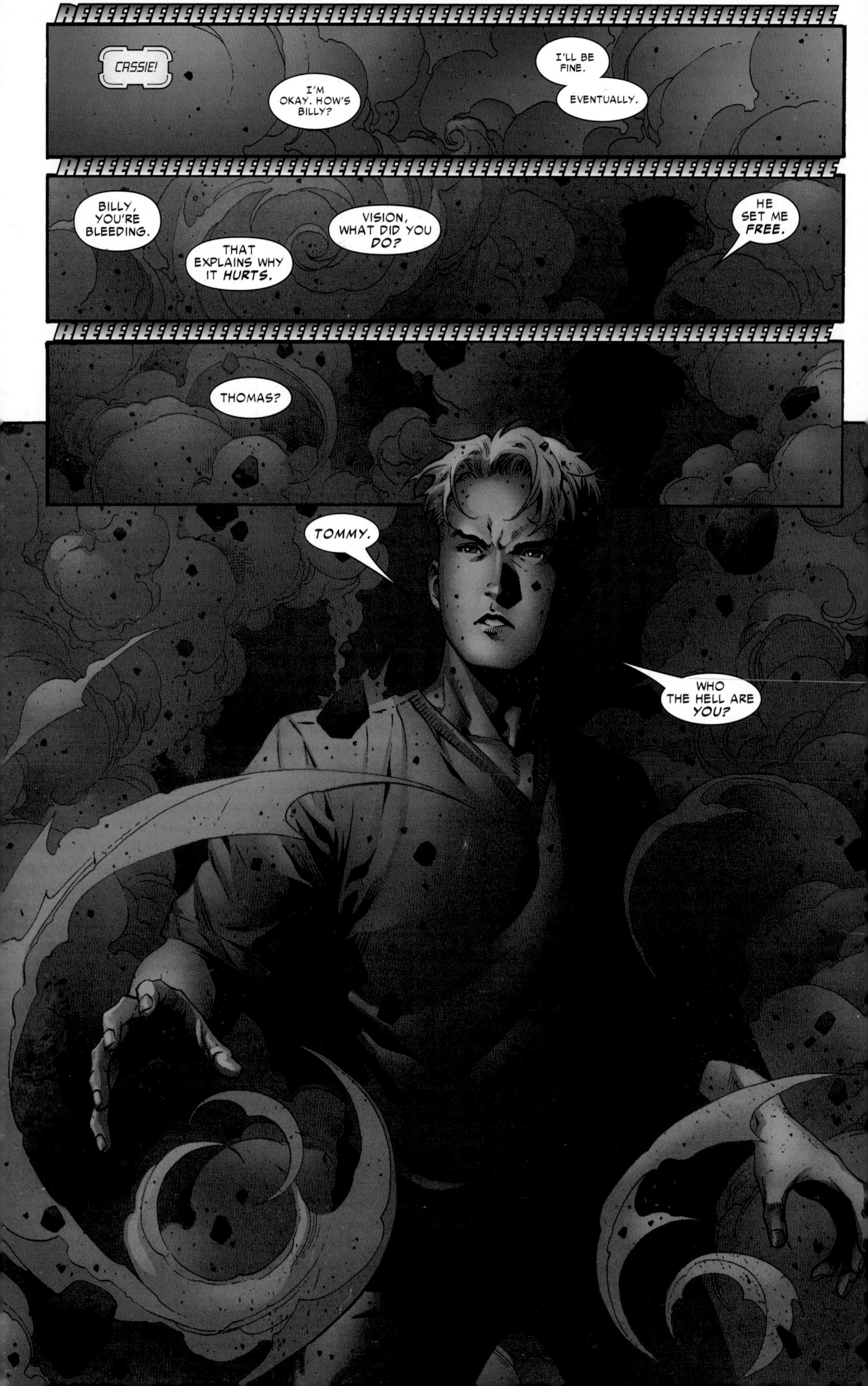
AEEEEEEEEEEEEEEEEEEEEEEEEEEEEEEEEEEEEEEEEEEEEEEEEEEEEEEEEEEEEEEEEEEEEEEES
CASSIE!
I'M OKAY. HOW'S BILLY?
I'LL BE FINE.
EVENTUALLY.
AEEEEEEEEEEEEEEEEEEEEEEEEEEEEEEEEEEEEEEEEEEEEEEEEEEEEEEEEEEEEEEEEEEEEEEES
BILLY, YOU'RE BLEEDING.
THAT EXPLAINS WHY IT HURTS.
VISION, WHAT DID YOU DO?
HE SET ME FREE.
AEEEEEEEEEEEEEEEEEEEEEEEEEEEEEEEEEEEEEEEEEEEEEEEEEEEEEEEEEEEEEEEEEEEEEEEE
THOMAS?
TOMMY.
WHO THE HELL ARE YOU?

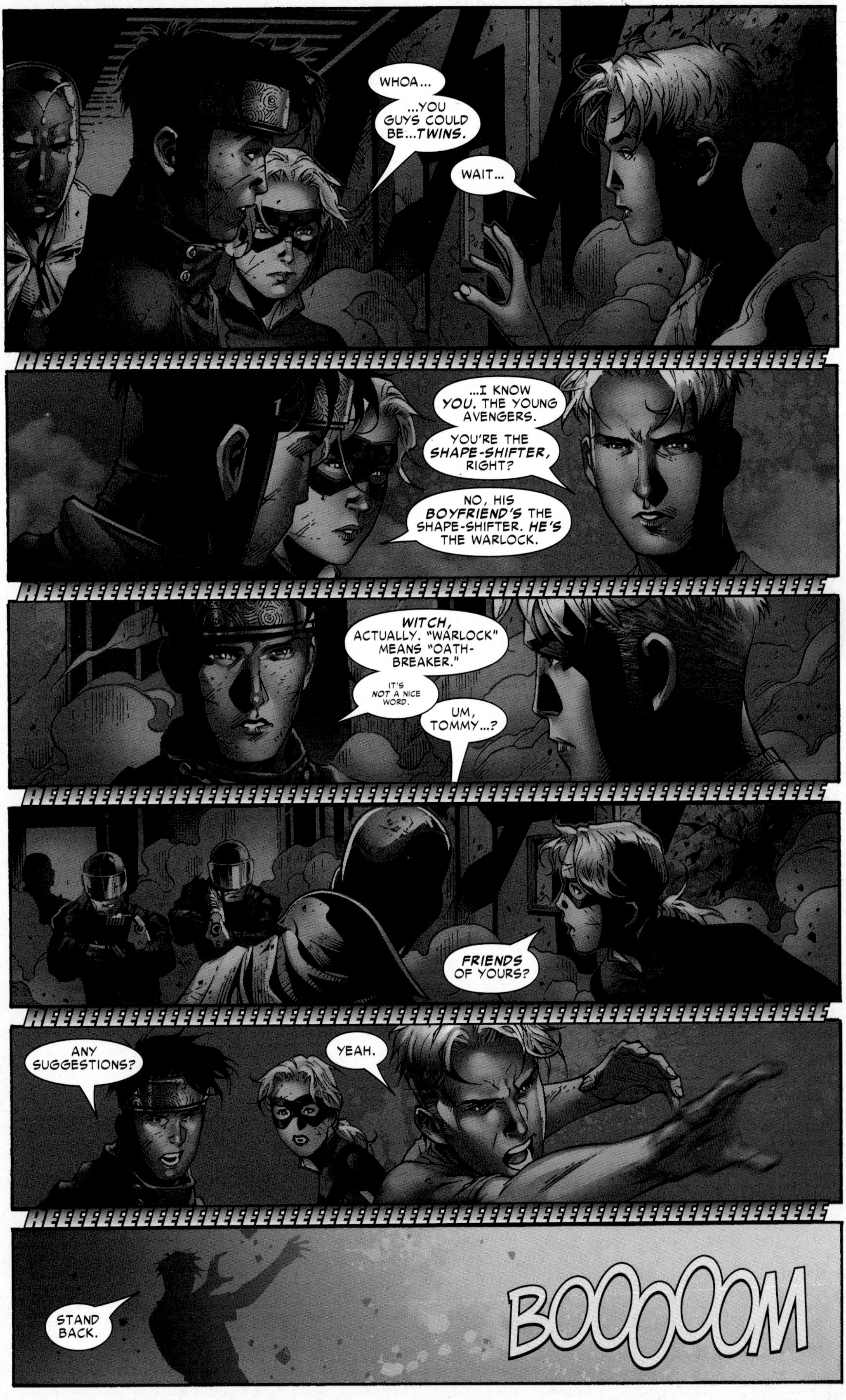
WHOA...
...YOU GUYS COULD BE...TWINS.
WAIT...
...I KNOW YOU. THE YOUNG AVENGERS.
YOU'RE THE SHAPE-SHIFTER, RIGHT?
NO, HIS BOYFRIEND'S THE SHAPE-SHIFTER. HE'S THE WARLOCK.
WITCH, ACTUALLY. "WARLOCK" MEANS "OATH-BREAKER."
IT'S NOT A NICE WORD.
UM, TOMMY...?
FRIENDS OF YOURS?
ANY SUGGESTIONS?
YEAH.
STAND BACK.
BOOOOOM

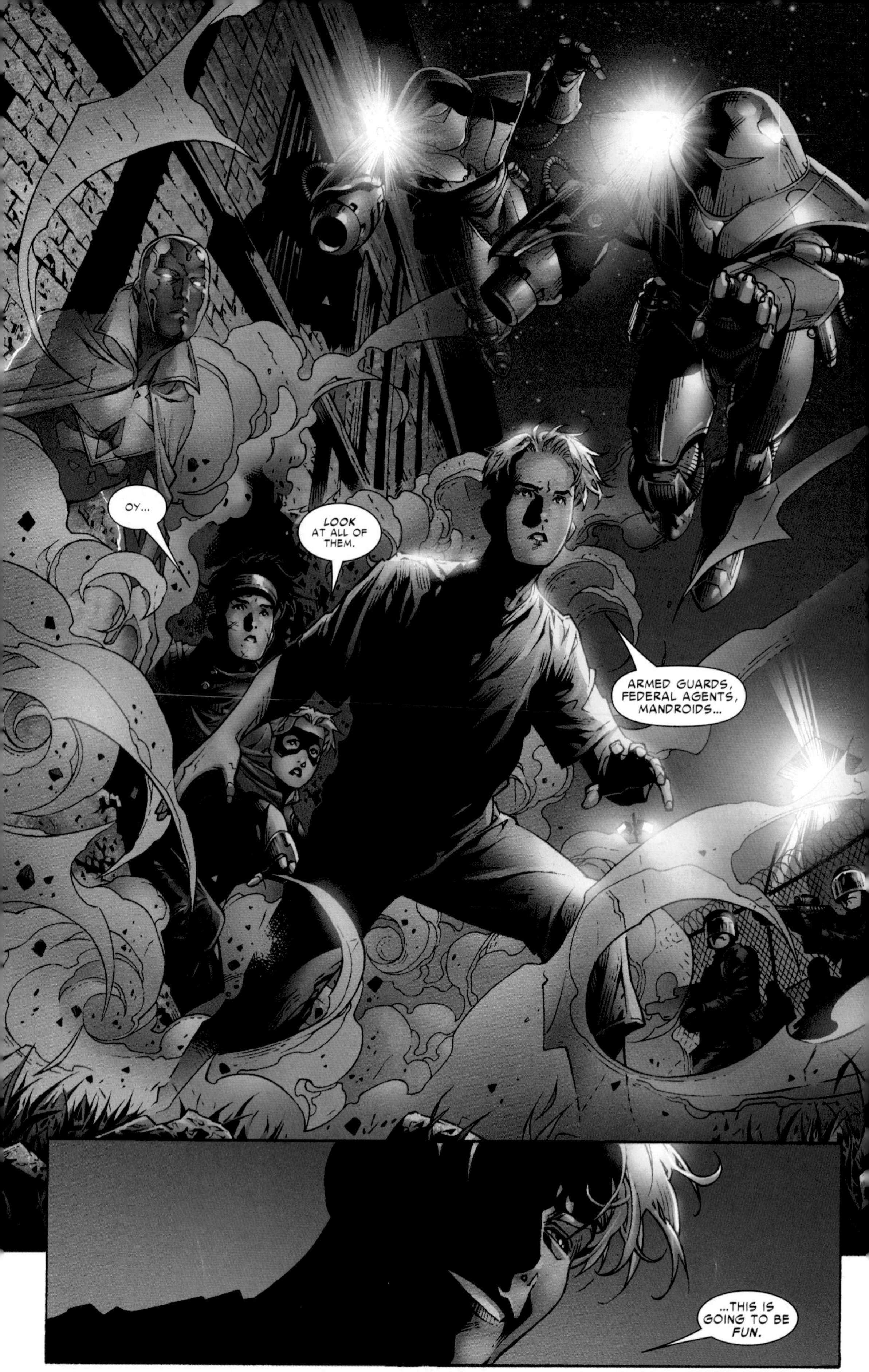
OY...
LOOK AT ALL OF THEM.
ARMED GUARDS, FEDERAL AGENTS, MANDROIDS...
...THIS IS GOING TO BE FUN.

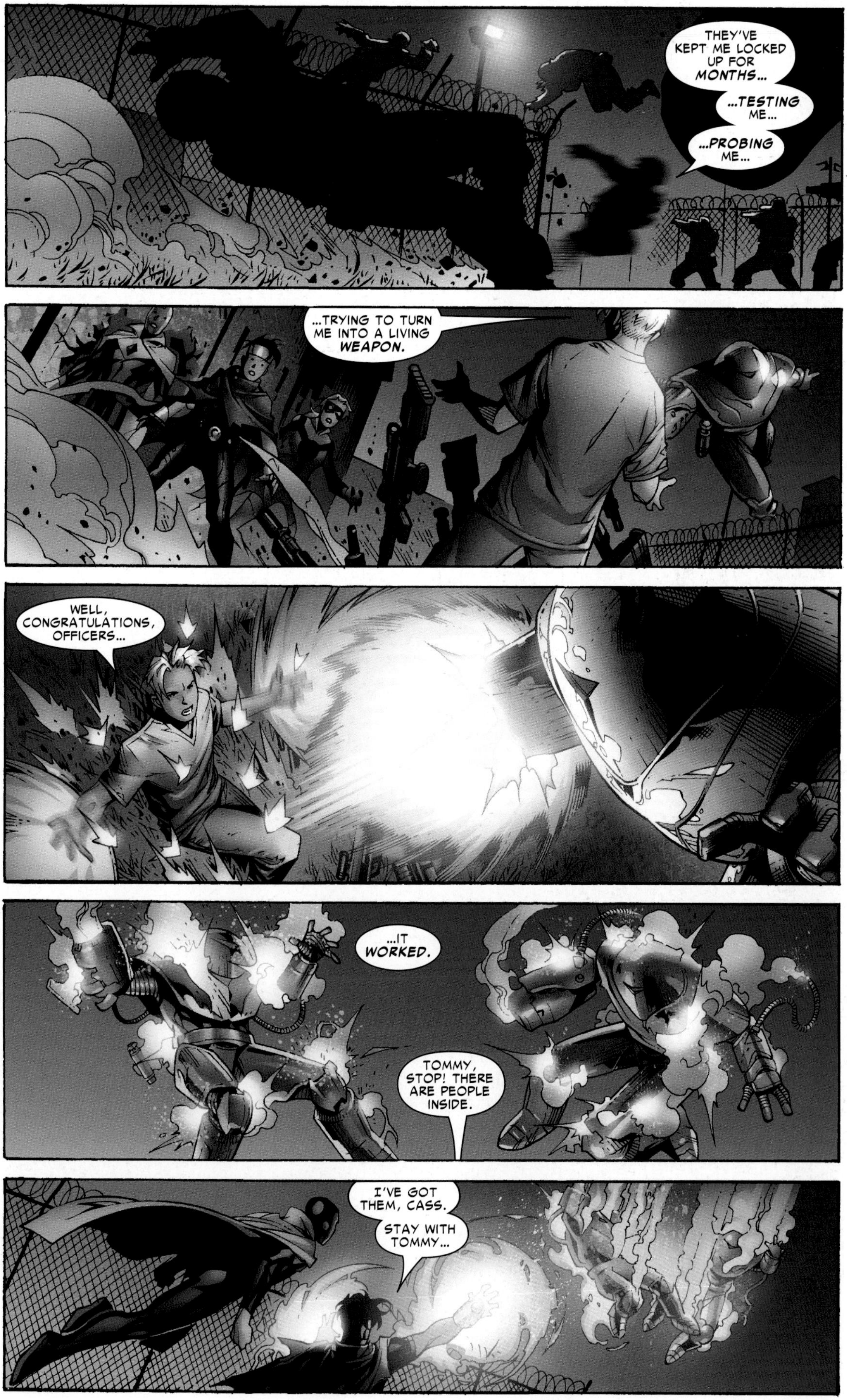
THEY'VE KEPT ME LOCKED UP FOR MONTHS...
...TESTING ME...
...PROBING ME...
...TRYING TO TURN ME INTO A LIVING WEAPON.
WELL, CONGRATULATIONS, OFFICERS...
...IT WORKED.
TOMMY, STOP! THERE ARE PEOPLE INSIDE.
I'VE GOT THEM, CASS.
STAY WITH TOMMY...

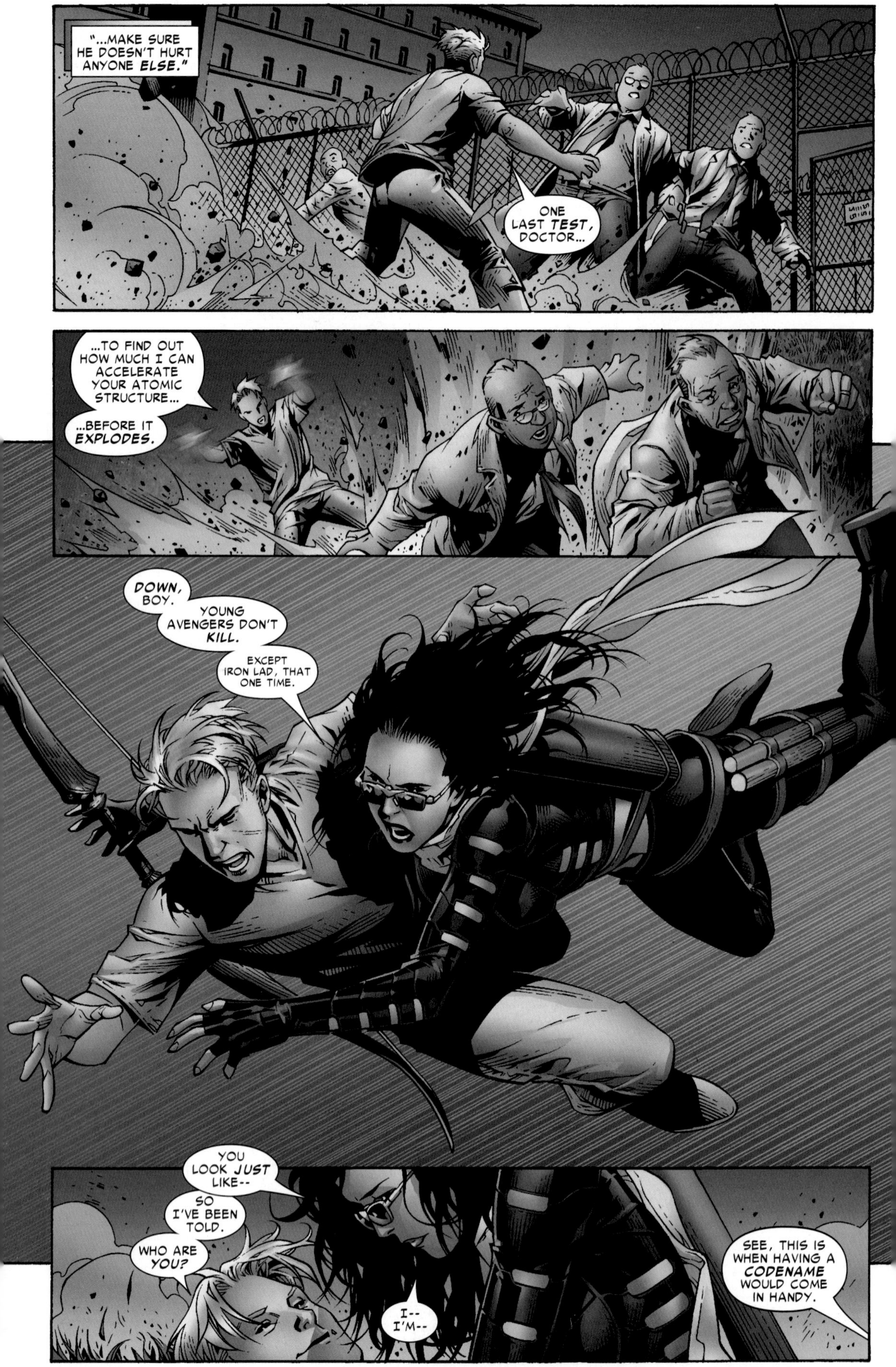
"...MAKE SURE HE DOESN'T HURT ANYONE ELSE."
ONE LAST TEST, DOCTOR...
...TO FIND OUT HOW MUCH I CAN ACCELERATE YOUR ATOMIC STRUCTURE...
...BEFORE IT EXPLODES.
DOWN, BOY.
YOUNG AVENGERS DON'T KILL.
EXCEPT IRON LAD, THAT ONE TIME.
YOU LOOK JUST LIKE--
SO I'VE BEEN TOLD.
WHO ARE YOU?
I-- I'M--
SEE, THIS IS WHEN HAVING A CODENAME WOULD COME IN HANDY.

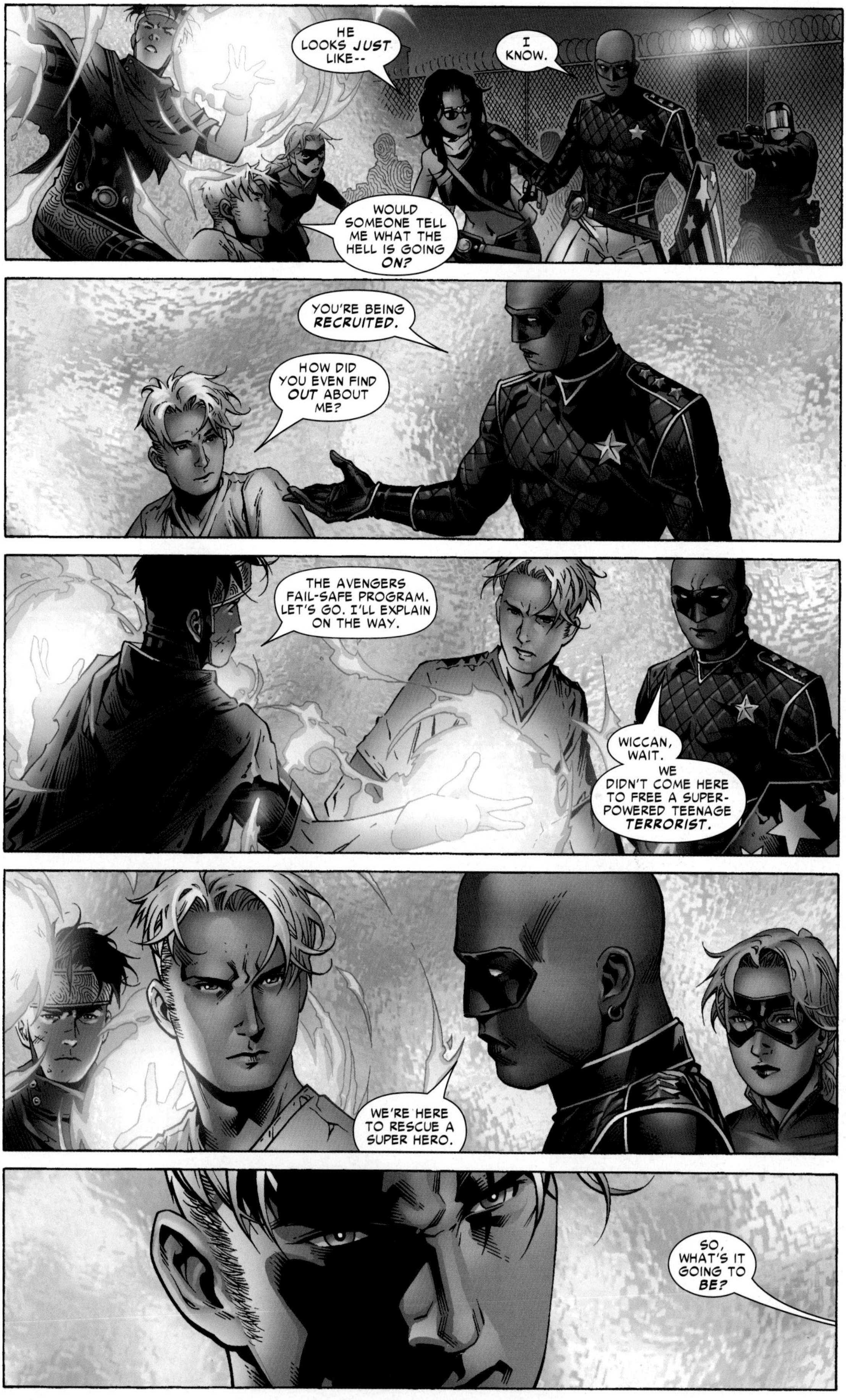
HE LOOKS JUST LIKE--
I KNOW.
WOULD SOMEONE TELL ME WHAT THE HELL IS GOING ON?
YOU'RE BEING RECRUITED.
HOW DID YOU EVEN FIND OUT ABOUT ME?
THE AVENGERS FAIL-SAFE PROGRAM. LET'S GO. I'LL EXPLAIN ON THE WAY.
WICCAN, WAIT.
WE DIDN'T COME HERE TO FREE A SUPER-POWERED TEENAGE TERRORIST.
WE'RE HERE TO RESCUE A SUPER HERO.
SO, WHAT'S IT GOING TO BE?

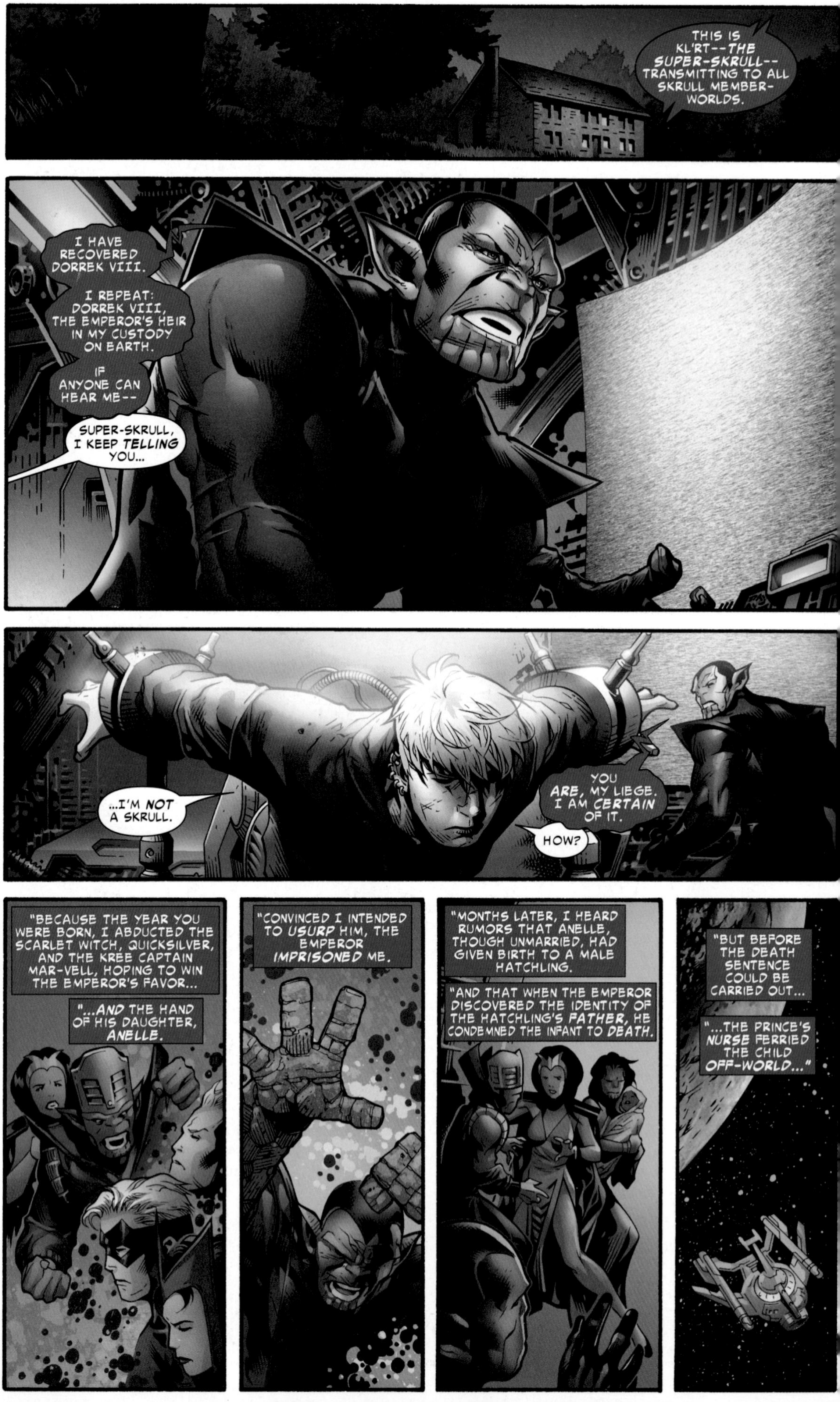
THIS IS KL'RT--THE SUPER-SKRULL--TRANSMITTING TO ALL SKRULL MEMBER-WORLDS.
I HAVE RECOVERED DORREK VIII.
I REPEAT: DORREK VIII, THE EMPEROR'S HEIR IN MY CUSTODY ON EARTH.
IF ANYONE CAN HEAR ME--
SUPER-SKRULL, I KEEP TELLING YOU...
...I'M NOT A SKRULL.
YOU ARE, MY LIEGE. I AM CERTAIN OF IT.
HOW?
"BECAUSE THE YEAR YOU WERE BORN, I ABDUCTED THE SCARLET WITCH, QUICKSILVER, AND THE KREE CAPTAIN MAR-VELL, HOPING TO WIN THE EMPEROR'S FAVOR...
"...AND THE HAND OF HIS DAUGHTER, ANELLE.
"CONVINCED I INTENDED TO USURP HIM, THE EMPEROR IMPRISONED ME.
"MONTHS LATER, I HEARD RUMORS THAT ANELLE, THOUGH UNMARRIED, HAD GIVEN BIRTH TO A MALE HATCHLING.
"AND THAT WHEN THE EMPEROR DISCOVERED THE IDENTITY OF THE HATCHLING'S FATHER, HE CONDEMNED THE INFANT TO DEATH.
"BUT BEFORE THE DEATH SENTENCE COULD BE CARRIED OUT...
"...THE PRINCE'S NURSE FERRIED THE CHILD OFF-WORLD..."

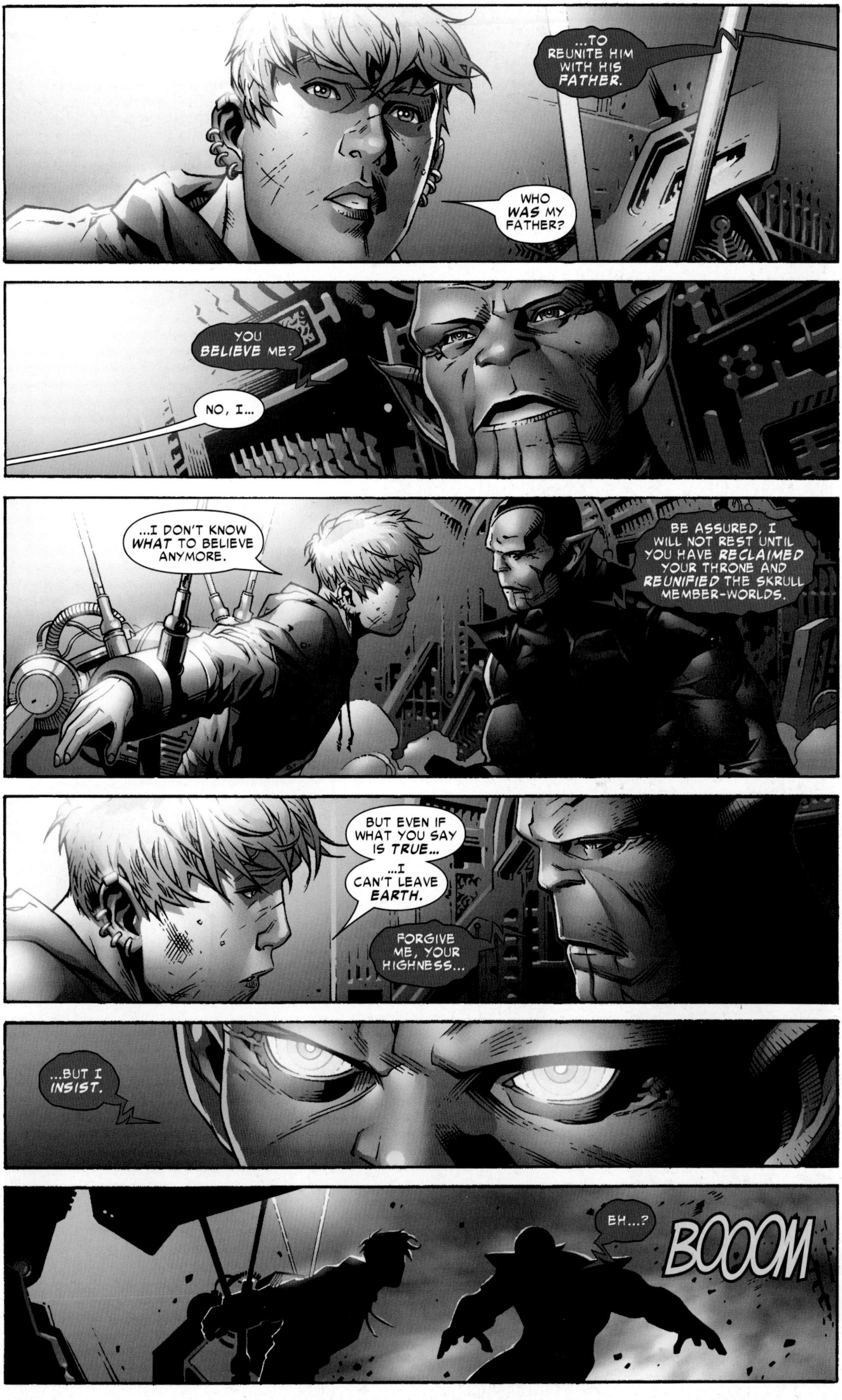
...TO REUNITE HIM WITH HIS FATHER.
WHO WAS MY FATHER?
YOU BELIEVE ME?
NO, I...
...I DON'T KNOW WHAT TO BELIEVE ANYMORE.
BE ASSURED, I WILL NOT REST UNTIL YOU HAVE RECLAIMED YOUR THRONE AND REUNIFIED THE SKRULL MEMBER-WORLDS.
BUT EVEN IF WHAT YOU SAY IS TRUE...
...I CAN'T LEAVE EARTH.
FORGIVE ME, YOUR HIGHNESS...
...BUT I INSIST.
EH...?
BOOOM

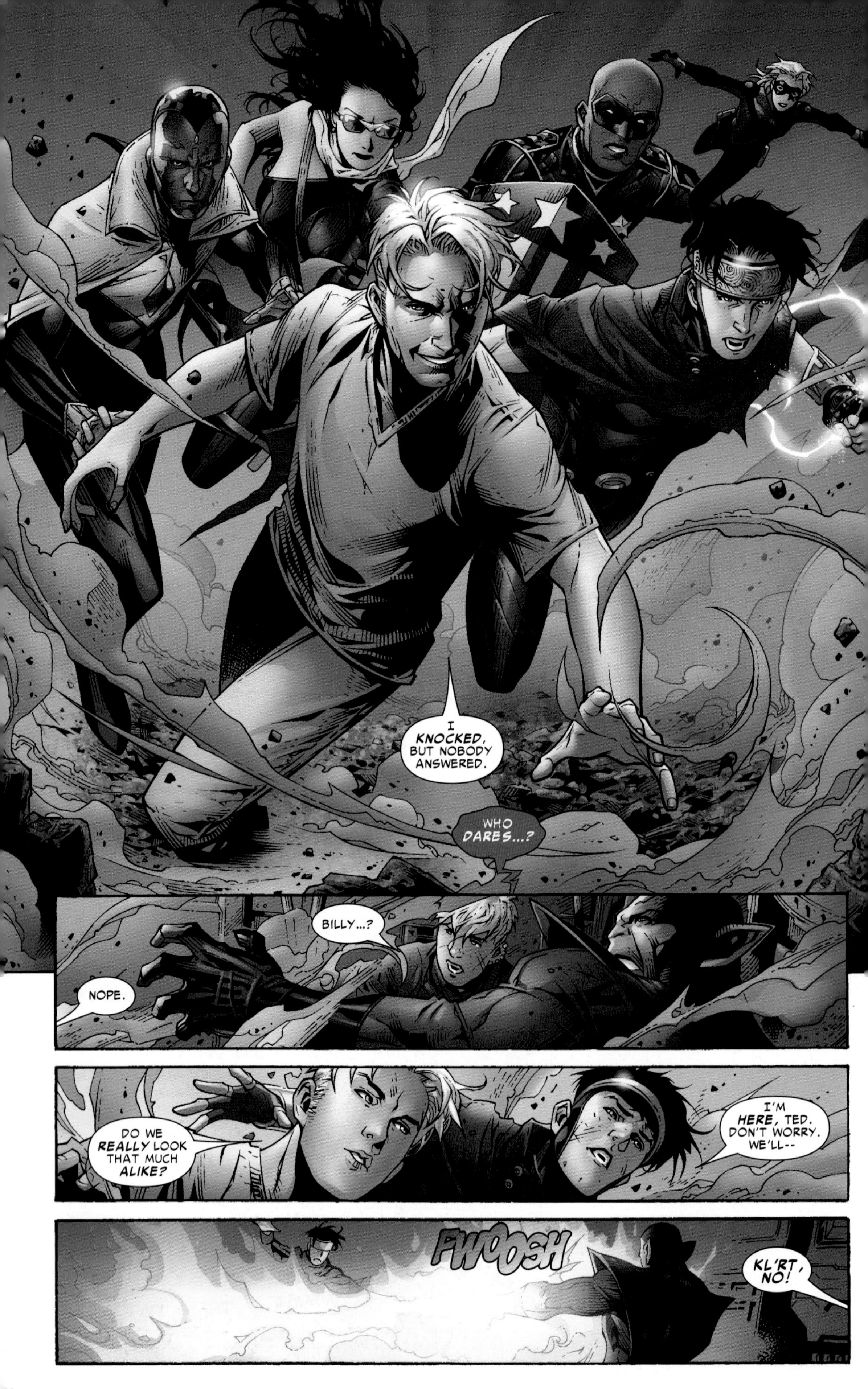
I KNOCKED, BUT NOBODY ANSWERED.
WHO DARES...?
BILLY...?
NOPE.
DO WE REALLY LOOK THAT MUCH ALIKE?
I'M HERE, TED. DON'T WORRY. WE'LL--
FWOOSH
KL'RT, NO!

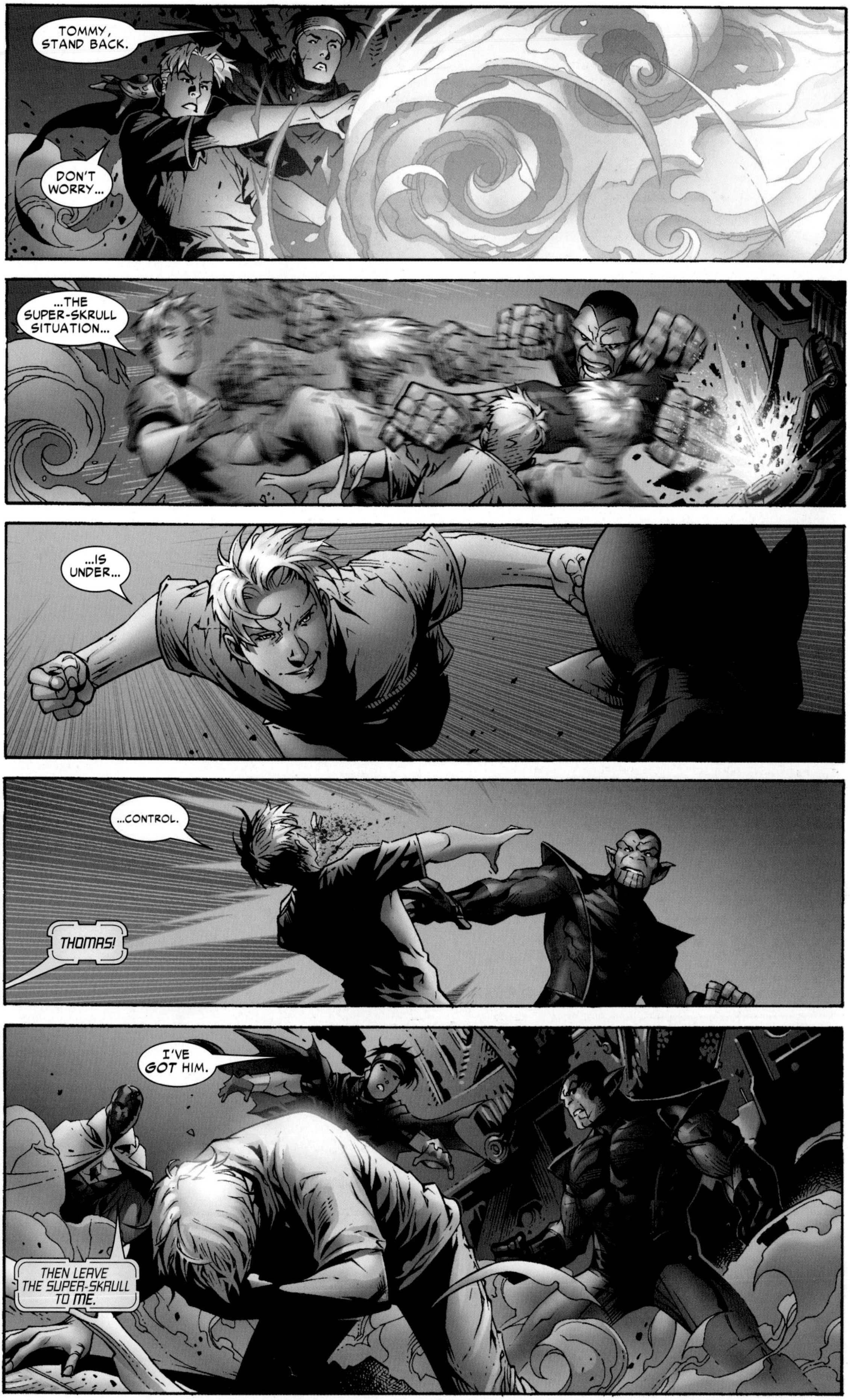
TOMMY, STAND BACK.
DON'T WORRY...
...THE SUPER-SKRULL SITUATION...
...IS UNDER...
...CONTROL.
THOMAS!
I'VE GOT HIM.
THEN LEAVE THE SUPER-SKRULL TO ME.

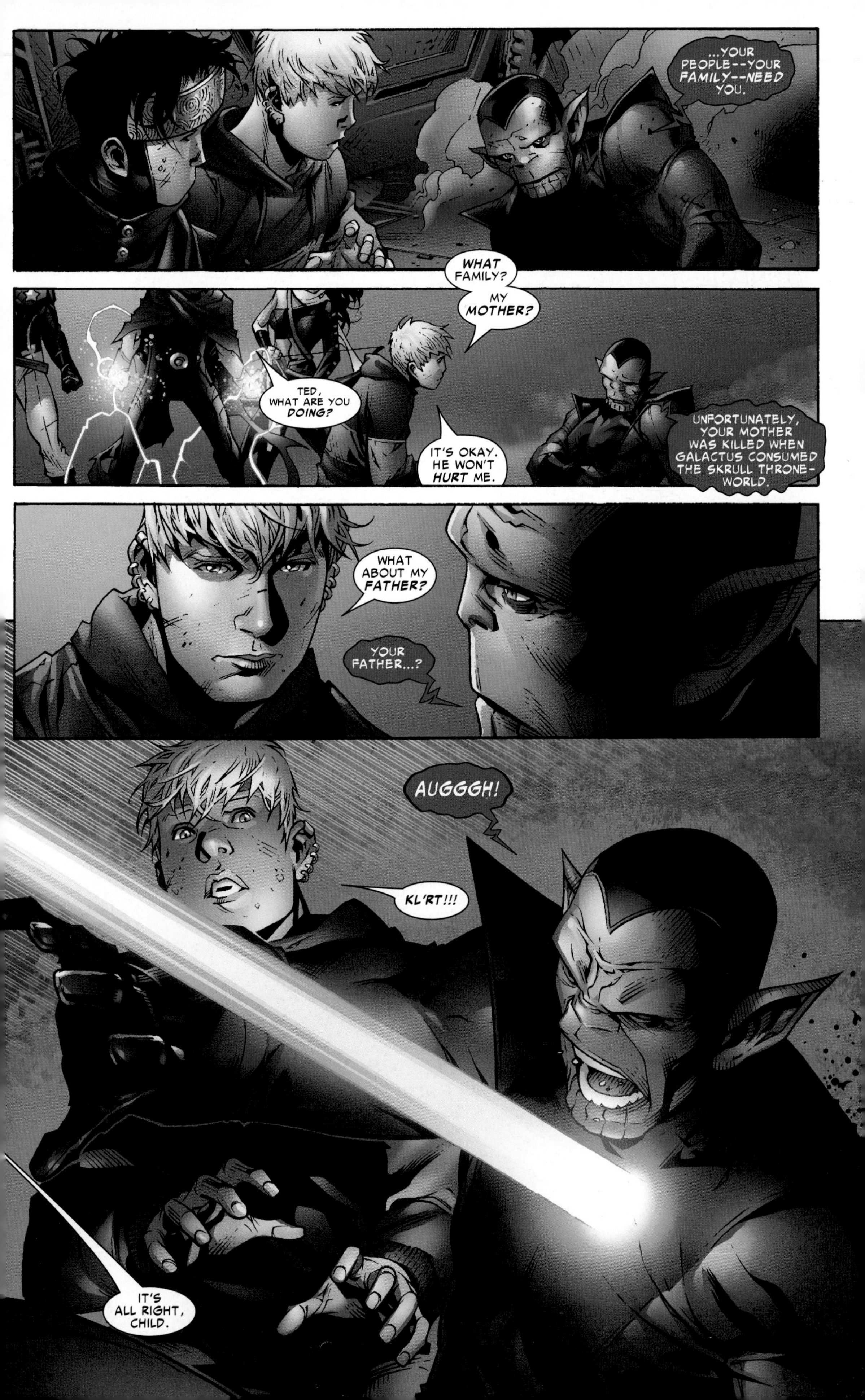
...YOUR PEOPLE--YOUR FAMILY--NEED YOU.
WHAT FAMILY?
MY MOTHER?
TED, WHAT ARE YOU DOING?
IT'S OKAY. HE WON'T HURT ME.
UNFORTUNATELY, YOUR MOTHER WAS KILLED WHEN GALACTUS CONSUMED THE SKRULL THRONE-WORLD.
WHAT ABOUT MY FATHER?
YOUR FATHER...?
AUGGGH!
KL'RT!!!
IT'S ALL RIGHT, CHILD.

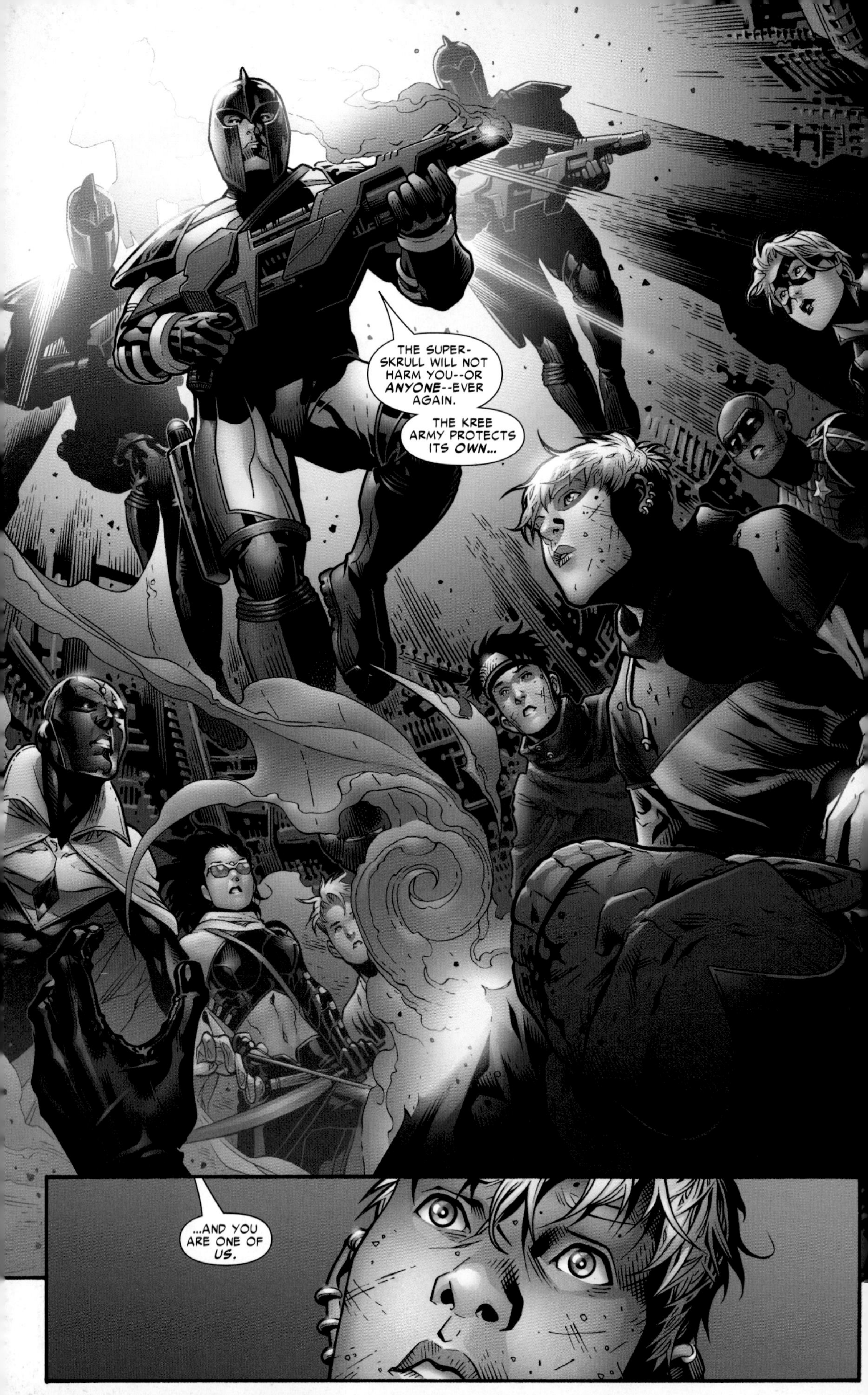
THE SUPER-SKRULL WILL NOT HARM YOU--OR ANYONE--EVER AGAIN.
THE KREE ARMY PROTECTS ITS OWN...
...AND YOU ARE ONE OF US.

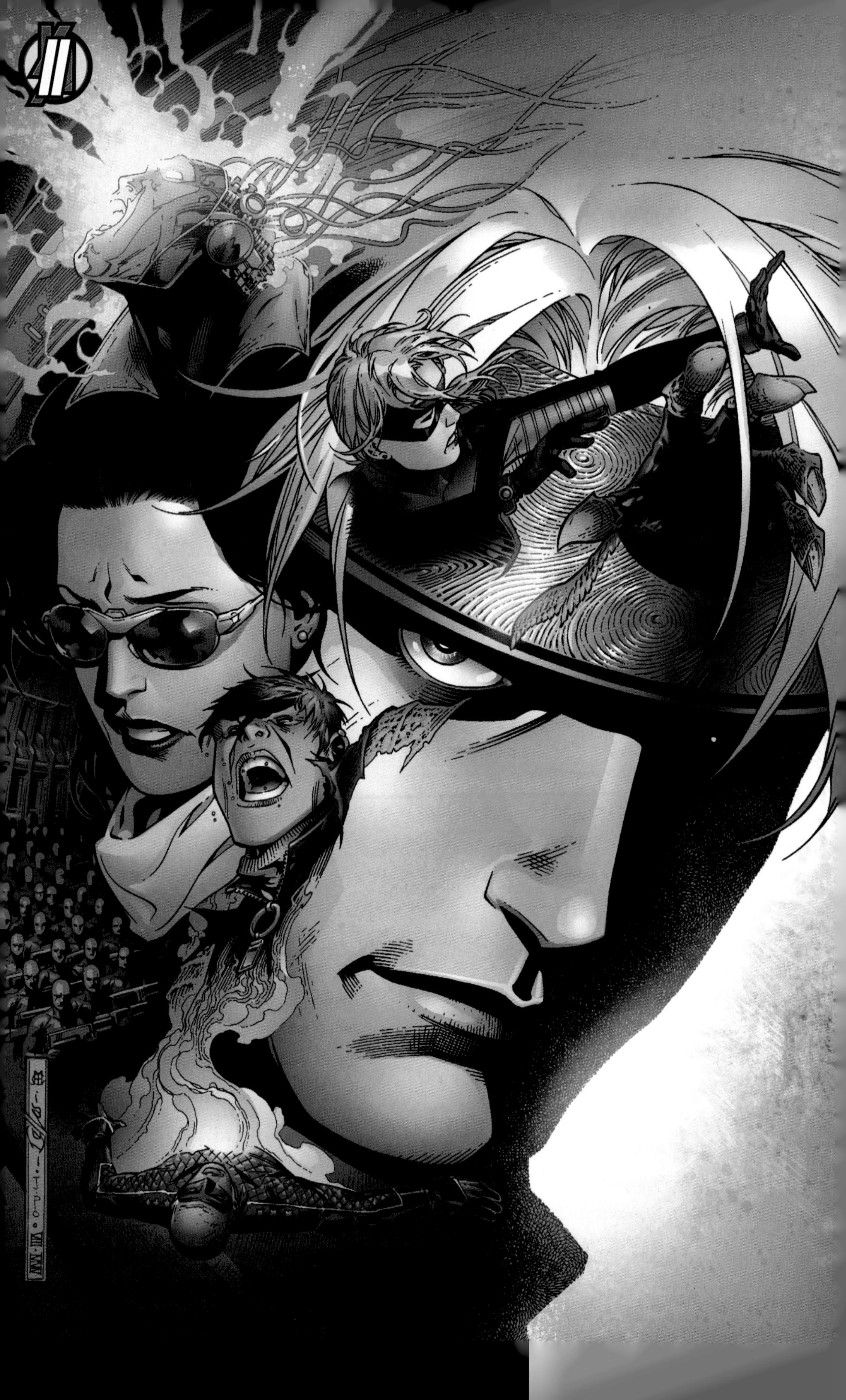

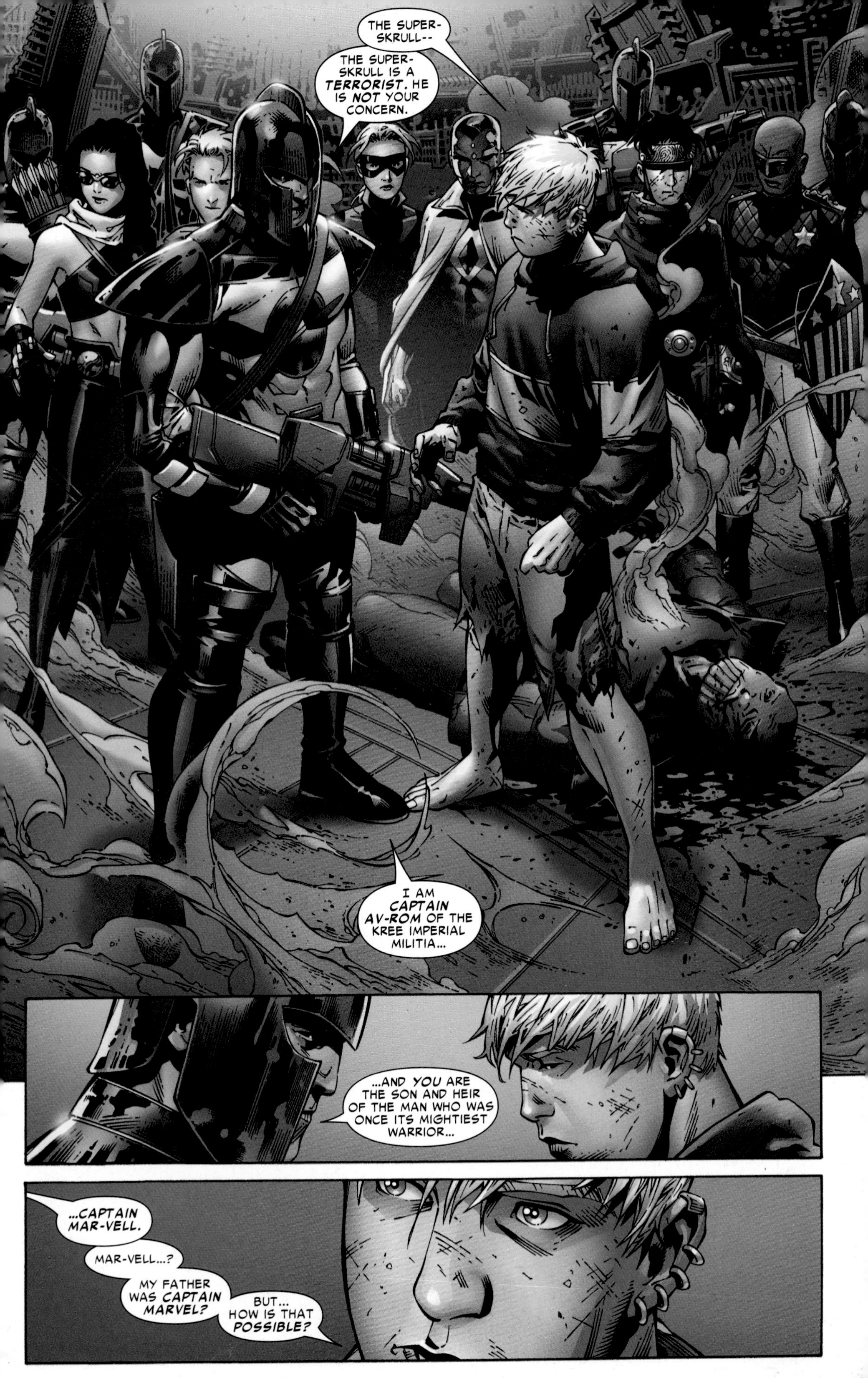
THE SUPER-SKRULL--
THE SUPER-SKRULL IS A TERRORIST. HE IS NOT YOUR CONCERN.
I AM CAPTAIN AV-ROM OF THE KREE IMPERIAL MILITIA...
...AND YOU ARE THE SON AND HEIR OF THE MAN WHO WAS ONCE ITS MIGHTIEST WARRIOR...
...CAPTAIN MAR-VELL.
MAR-VELL...?
MY FATHER WAS CAPTAIN MARVEL?
BUT... HOW IS THAT POSSIBLE?

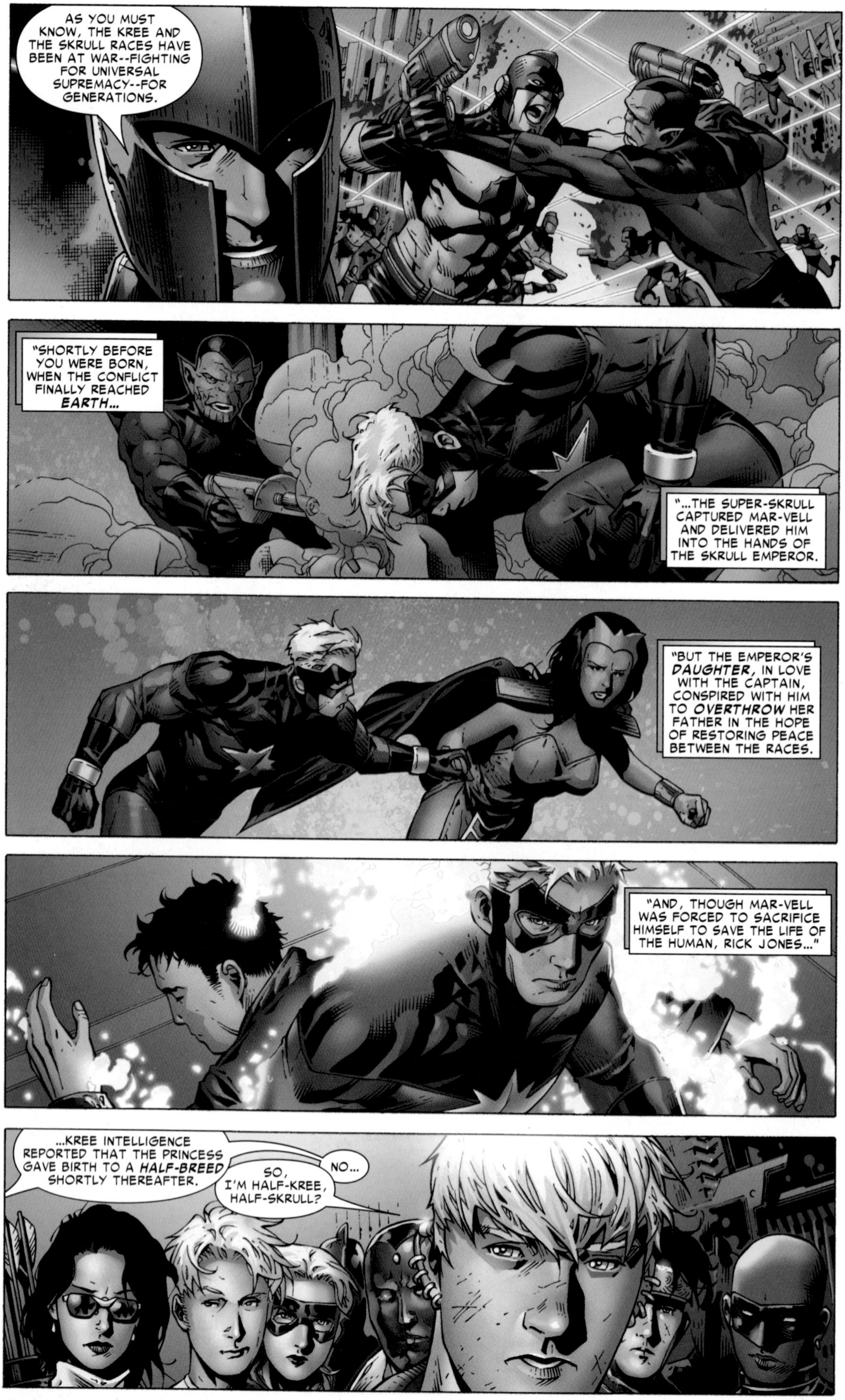
AS YOU MUST KNOW, THE KREE AND THE SKRULL RACES HAVE BEEN AT WAR--FIGHTING FOR UNIVERSAL SUPREMACY--FOR GENERATIONS.
"SHORTLY BEFORE YOU WERE BORN, WHEN THE CONFLICT FINALLY REACHED EARTH...
"...THE SUPER-SKRULL CAPTURED MAR-VELL AND DELIVERED HIM INTO THE HANDS OF THE SKRULL EMPEROR.
"BUT THE EMPEROR'S DAUGHTER, IN LOVE WITH THE CAPTAIN, CONSPIRED WITH HIM TO OVERTHROW HER FATHER IN THE HOPE OF RESTORING PEACE BETWEEN THE RACES.
"AND, THOUGH MAR-VELL WAS FORCED TO SACRIFICE HIMSELF TO SAVE THE LIFE OF THE HUMAN, RICK JONES..."
...KREE INTELLIGENCE REPORTED THAT THE PRINCESS GAVE BIRTH TO A HALF-BREED SHORTLY THEREAFTER.
SO, I'M HALF-KREE, HALF-SKRULL?
NO...

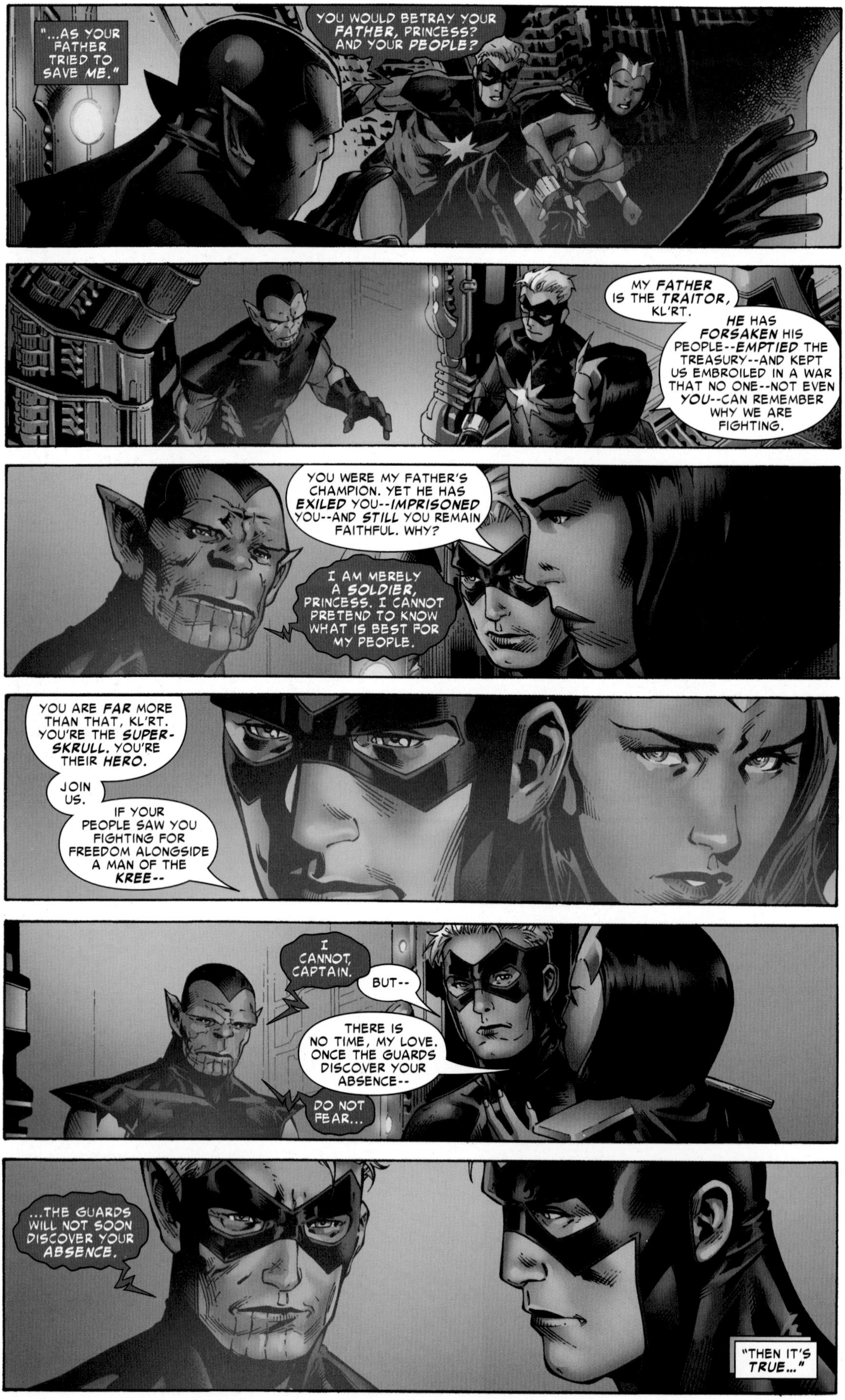
"...AS YOUR FATHER TRIED TO SAVE ME."
YOU WOULD BETRAY YOUR FATHER, PRINCESS? AND YOUR PEOPLE?
MY FATHER IS THE TRAITOR, KL'RT.
HE HAS FORSAKEN HIS PEOPLE--EMPTIED THE TREASURY--AND KEPT US EMBROILED IN A WAR THAT NO ONE--NOT EVEN YOU--CAN REMEMBER WHY WE ARE FIGHTING.
YOU WERE MY FATHER'S CHAMPION. YET HE HAS EXILED YOU--IMPRISONED YOU--AND STILL YOU REMAIN FAITHFUL. WHY?
I AM MERELY A SOLDIER, PRINCESS. I CANNOT PRETEND TO KNOW WHAT IS BEST FOR MY PEOPLE.
YOU ARE FAR MORE THAN THAT, KL'RT. YOU'RE THE SUPER-SKRULL. YOU'RE THEIR HERO.
JOIN US.
IF YOUR PEOPLE SAW YOU FIGHTING FOR FREEDOM ALONGSIDE A MAN OF THE KREE--
I CANNOT, CAPTAIN.
BUT--
THERE IS NO TIME, MY LOVE. ONCE THE GUARDS DISCOVER YOUR ABSENCE--
DO NOT FEAR...
...THE GUARDS WILL NOT SOON DISCOVER YOUR ABSENCE.
"THEN IT'S TRUE..."

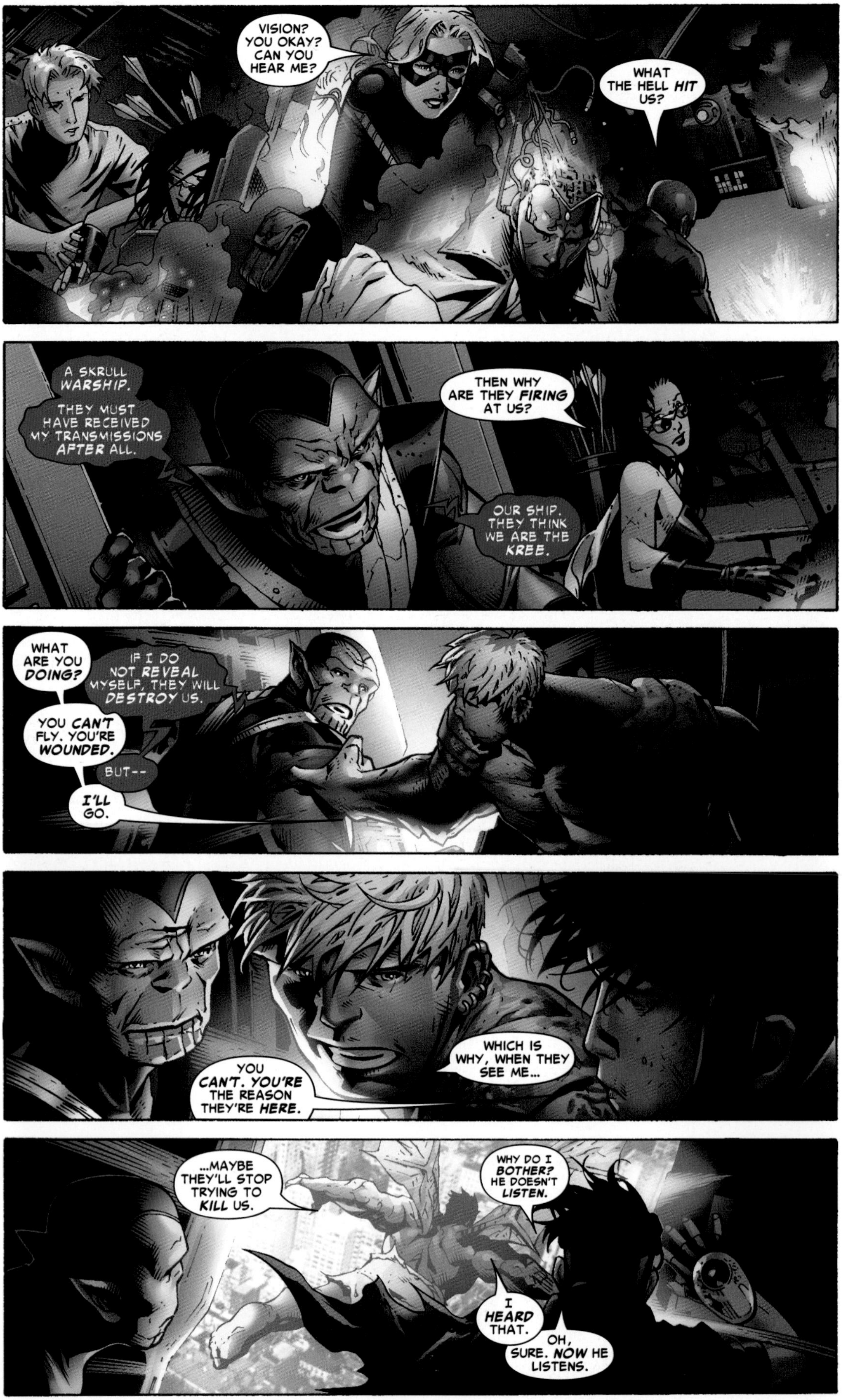
VISION? YOU OKAY? CAN YOU HEAR ME?
WHAT THE HELL HIT US?
A SKRULL WARSHIP.
THEY MUST HAVE RECEIVED MY TRANSMISSIONS AFTER ALL.
THEN WHY ARE THEY FIRING AT US?
OUR SHIP. THEY THINK WE ARE THE KREE.
WHAT ARE YOU DOING?
IF I DO NOT REVEAL MYSELF, THEY WILL DESTROY US.
YOU CAN'T FLY. YOU'RE WOUNDED.
BUT--
I'LL GO.
YOU CAN'T. YOU'RE THE REASON THEY'RE HERE.
WHICH IS WHY, WHEN THEY SEE ME...
...MAYBE THEY'LL STOP TRYING TO KILL US.
WHY DO I BOTHER? HE DOESN'T LISTEN.
I HEARD THAT.
OH, SURE. NOW HE LISTENS.

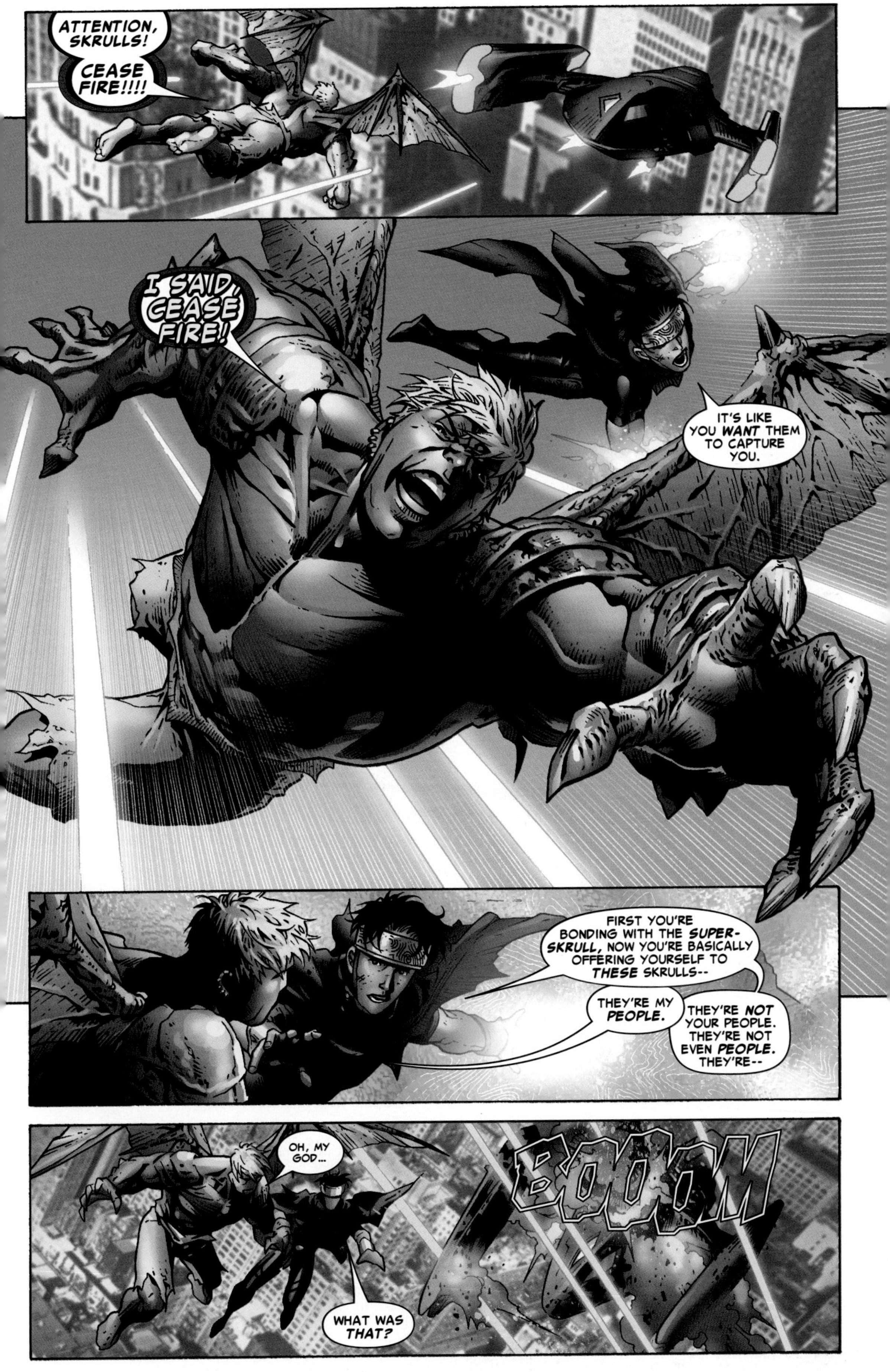
ATTENTION, SKRULLS!
CEASE FIRE!!!!
I SAID, CEASE FIRE!
IT'S LIKE YOU WANT THEM TO CAPTURE YOU.
FIRST YOU'RE BONDING WITH THE SUPER-SKRULL, NOW YOU'RE BASICALLY OFFERING YOURSELF TO THESE SKRULLS--
THEY'RE MY PEOPLE.
THEY'RE NOT YOUR PEOPLE. THEY'RE NOT EVEN PEOPLE. THEY'RE--
OH, MY GOD...
BOOOM
WHAT WAS THAT?

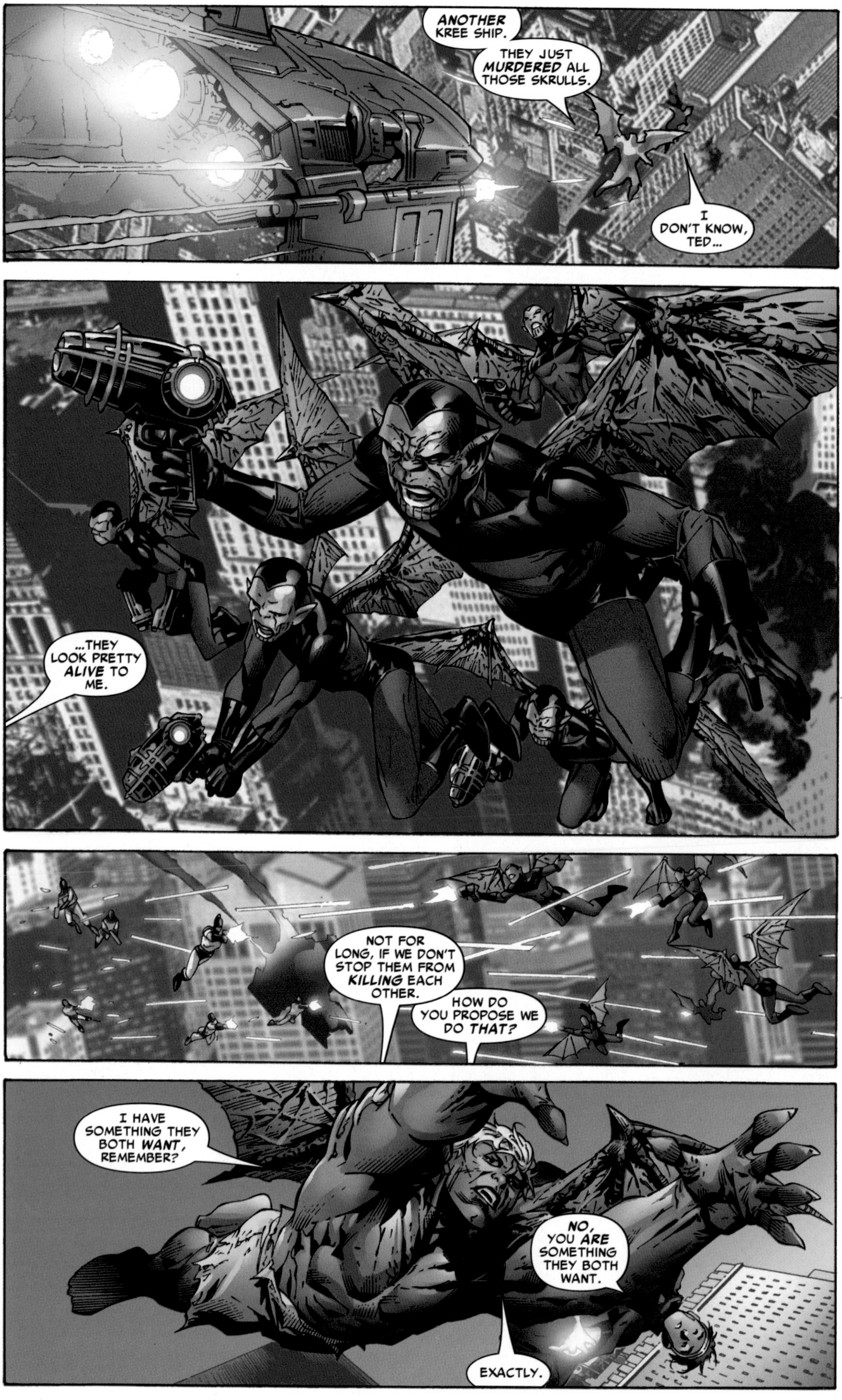
ANOTHER KREE SHIP.
THEY JUST MURDERED ALL THOSE SKRULLS.
I DON'T KNOW, TED...
...THEY LOOK PRETTY ALIVE TO ME.
NOT FOR LONG, IF WE DON'T STOP THEM FROM KILLING EACH OTHER.
HOW DO YOU PROPOSE WE DO THAT?
I HAVE SOMETHING THEY BOTH WANT, REMEMBER?
NO, YOU ARE SOMETHING THEY BOTH WANT.
EXACTLY.

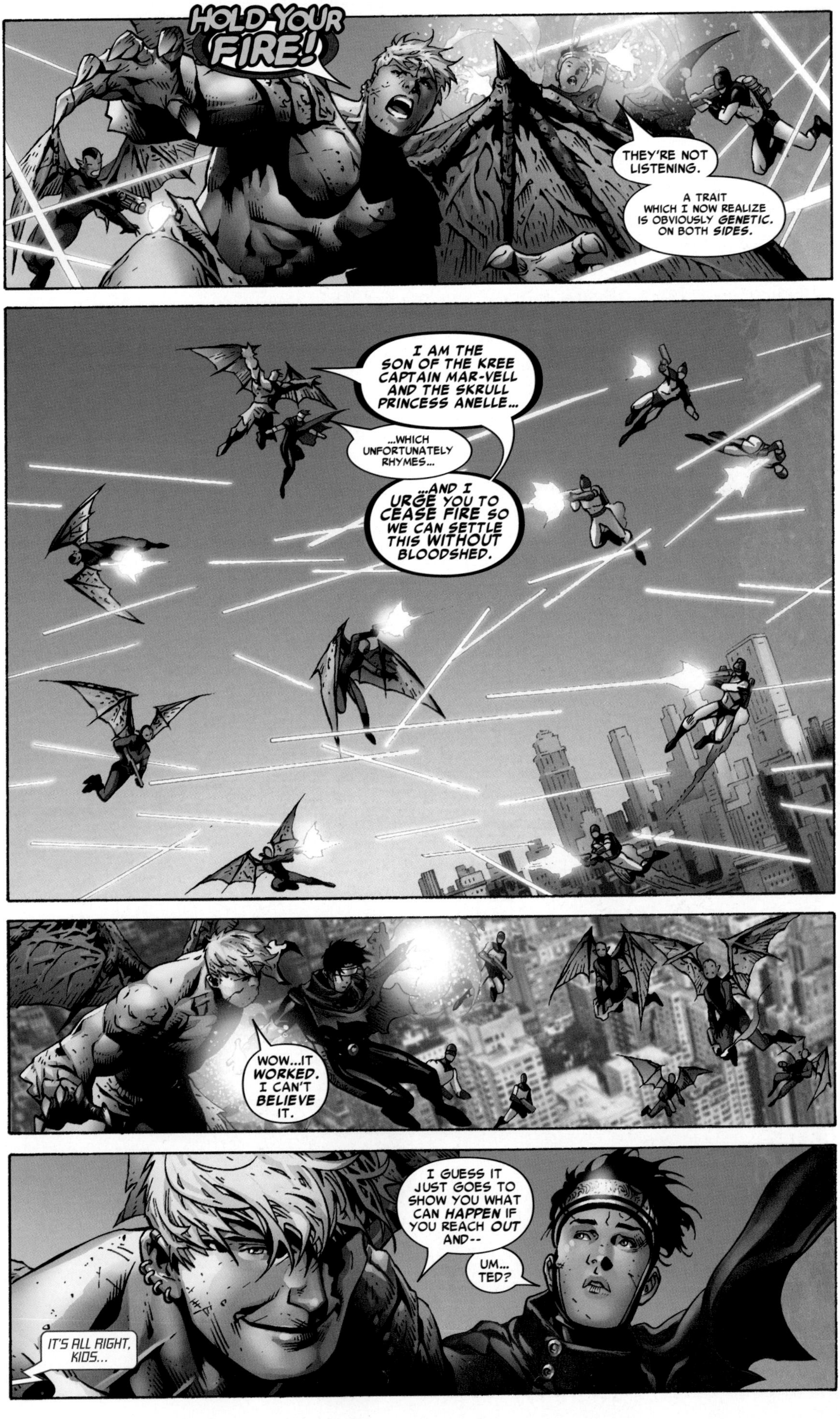
HOLD YOUR FIRE!
THEY'RE NOT LISTENING.
A TRAIT WHICH I NOW REALIZE IS OBVIOUSLY GENETIC. ON BOTH SIDES.
I AM THE SON OF THE KREE CAPTAIN MAR-VELL AND THE SKRULL PRINCESS ANELLE...
...WHICH UNFORTUNATELY RHYMES...
...AND I URGE YOU TO CEASE FIRE SO WE CAN SETTLE THIS WITHOUT BLOODSHED.
WOW...IT WORKED. I CAN'T BELIEVE IT.
I GUESS IT JUST GOES TO SHOW YOU WHAT CAN HAPPEN IF YOU REACH OUT AND--
UM... TED?
IT'S ALL RIGHT, KIDS...

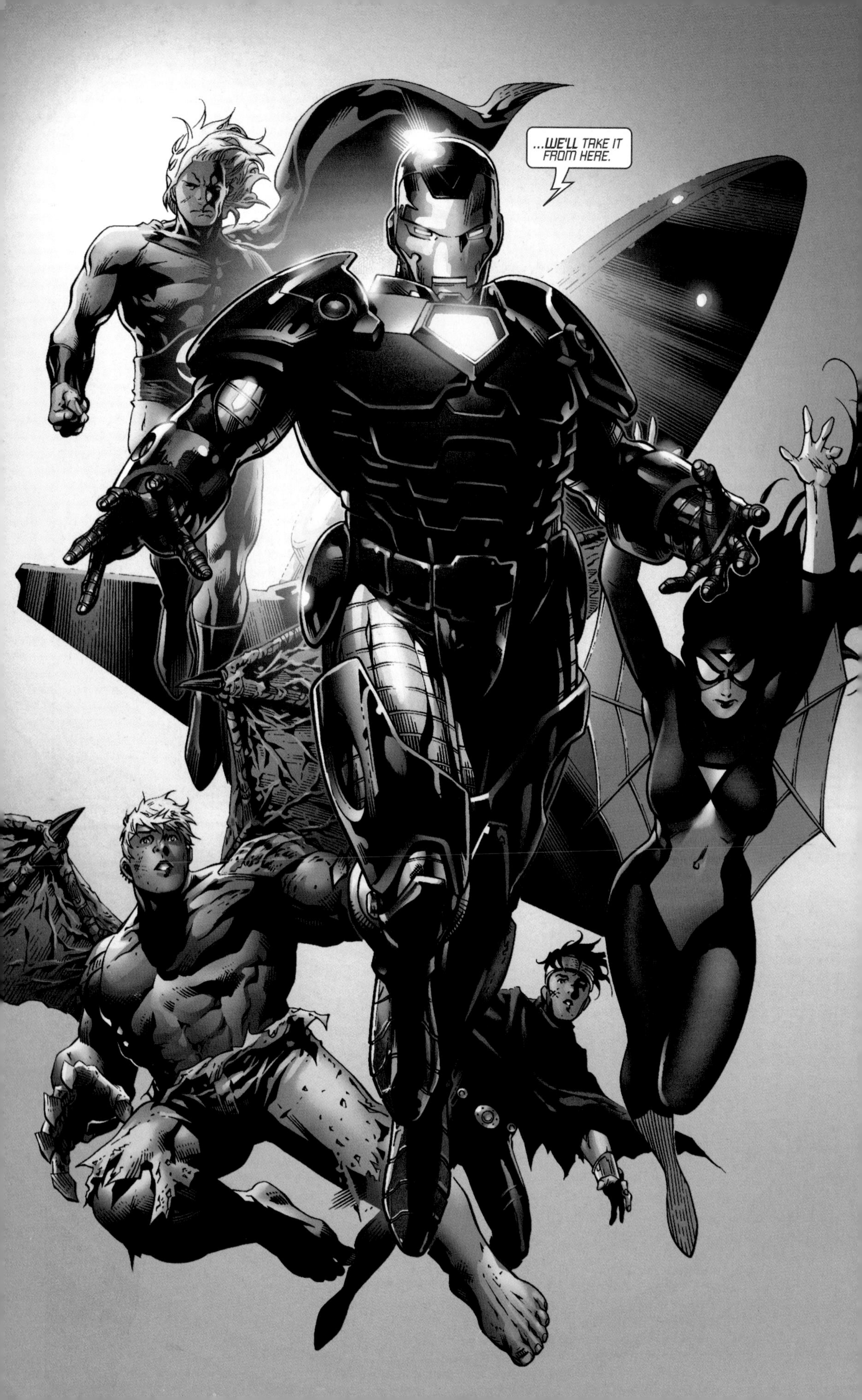
...WE'LL TAKE IT FROM HERE.

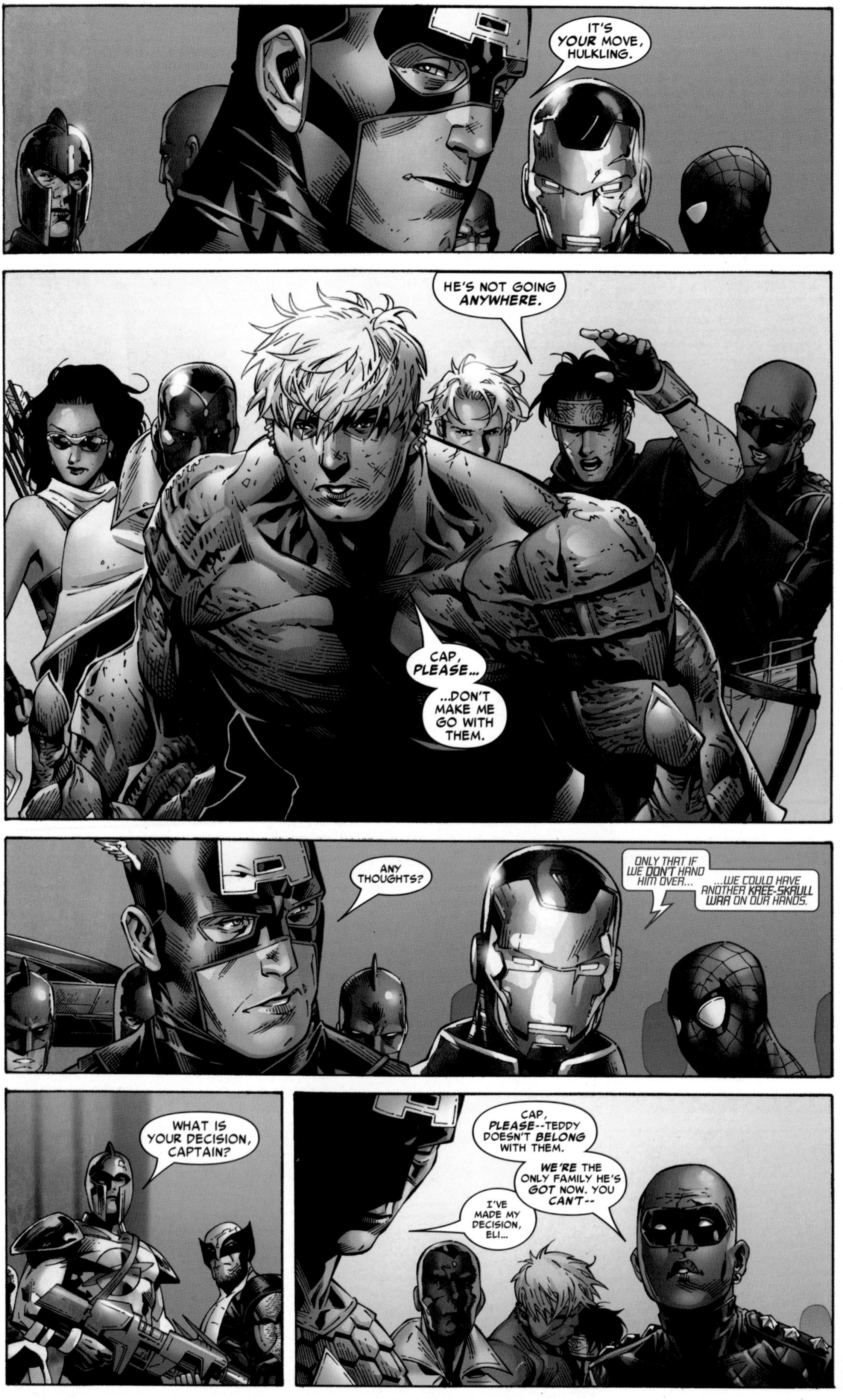
IT'S YOUR MOVE, HULKLING.
HE'S NOT GOING ANYWHERE.
CAP, PLEASE...
...DON'T MAKE ME GO WITH THEM.
ANY THOUGHTS?
ONLY THAT IF WE DON'T HAND HIM OVER...
...WE COULD HAVE ANOTHER KREE-SKRULL WAR ON OUR HANDS.
WHAT IS YOUR DECISION, CAPTAIN?
CAP, PLEASE--TEDDY DOESN'T BELONG WITH THEM.
WE'RE THE ONLY FAMILY HE'S GOT NOW. YOU CAN'T--
I'VE MADE MY DECISION, ELI...

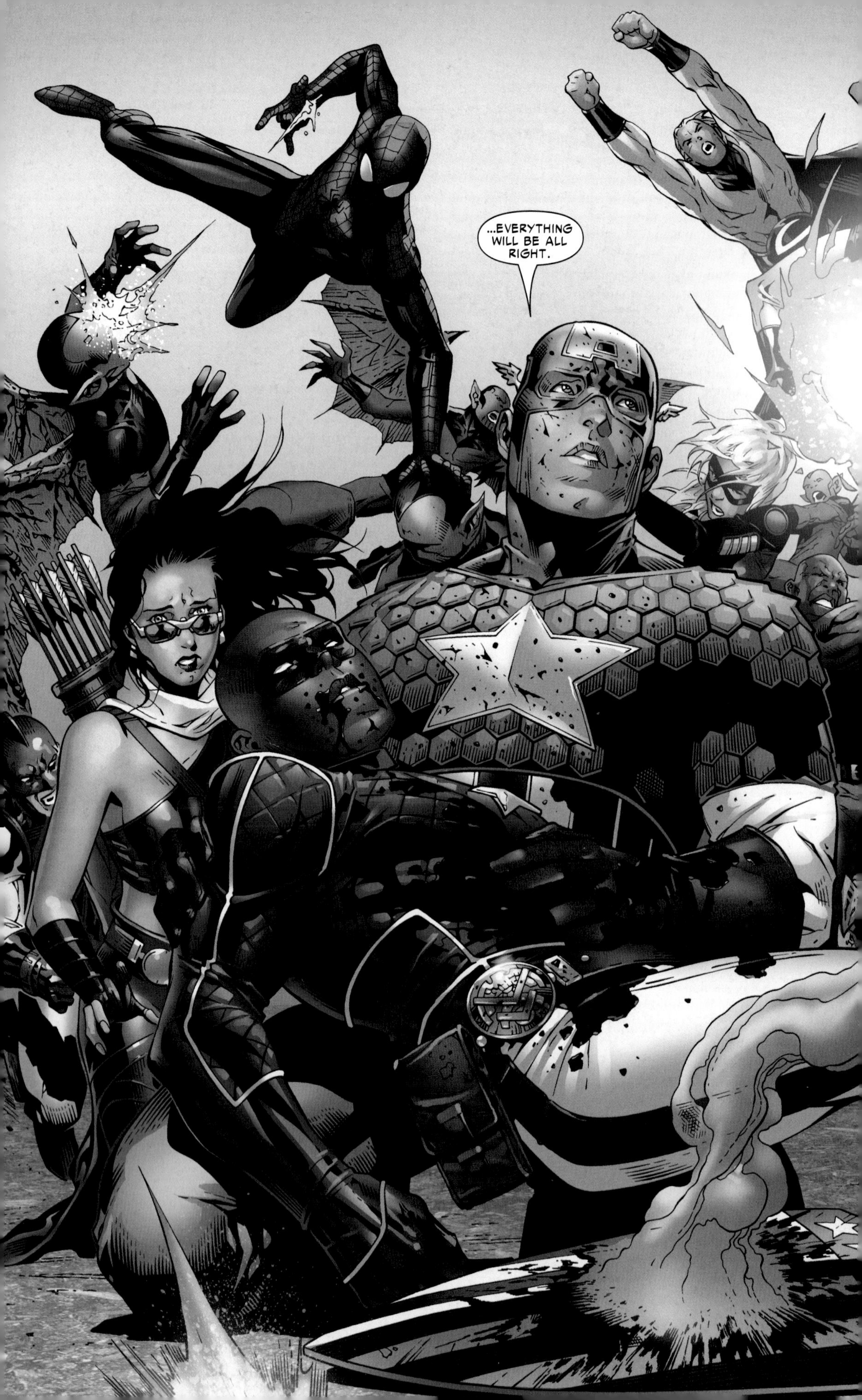
...EVERYTHING WILL BE ALL RIGHT.

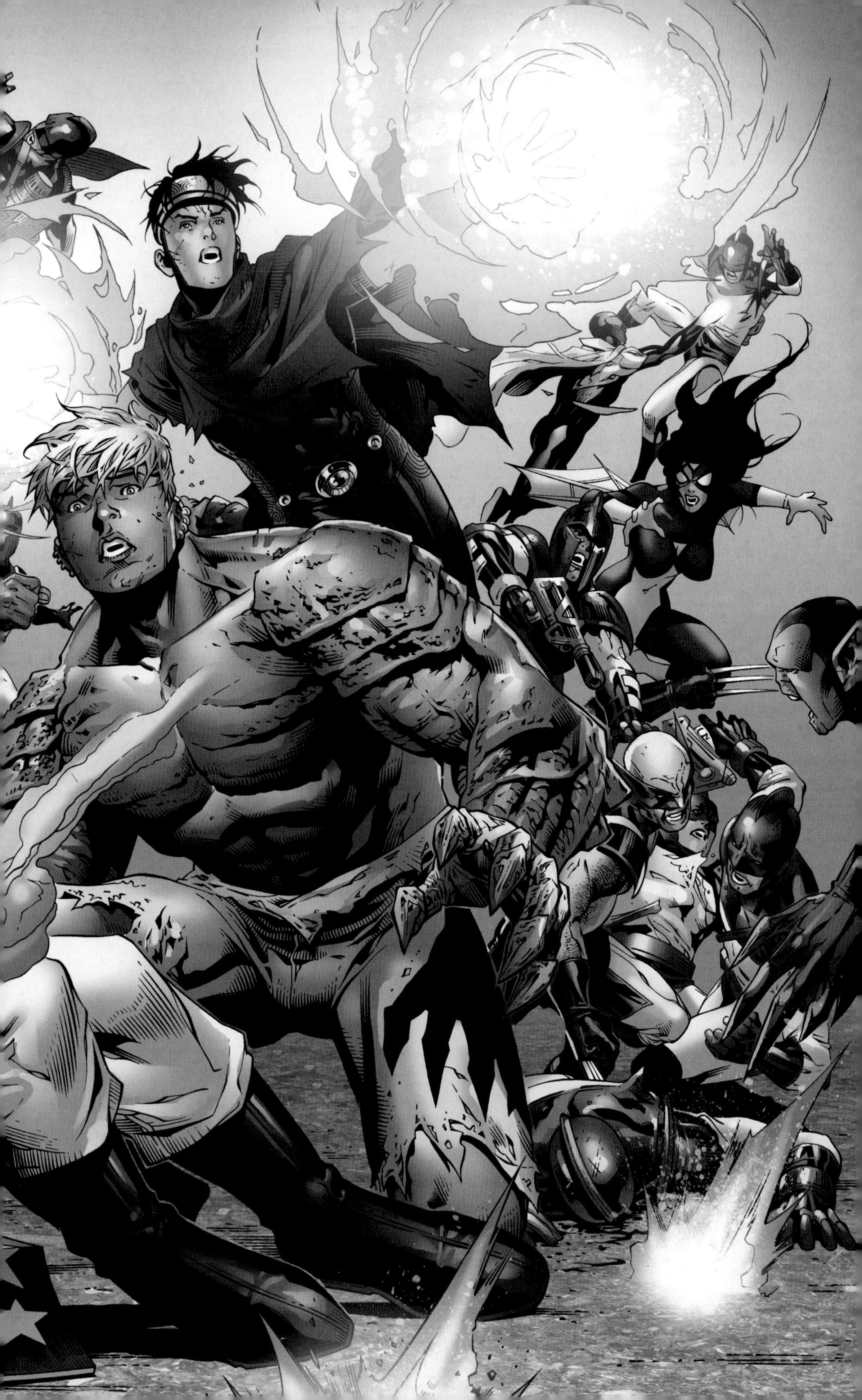

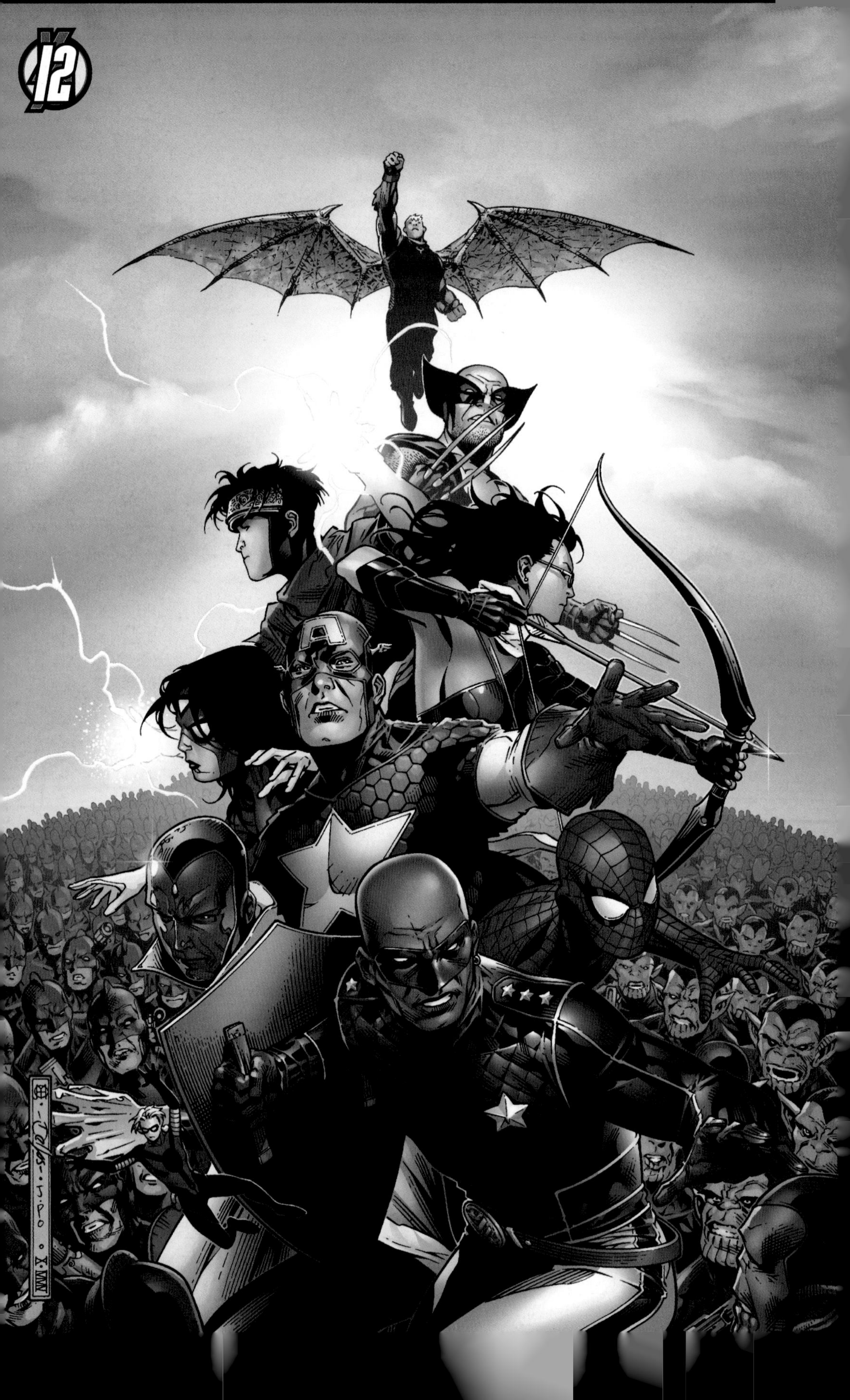

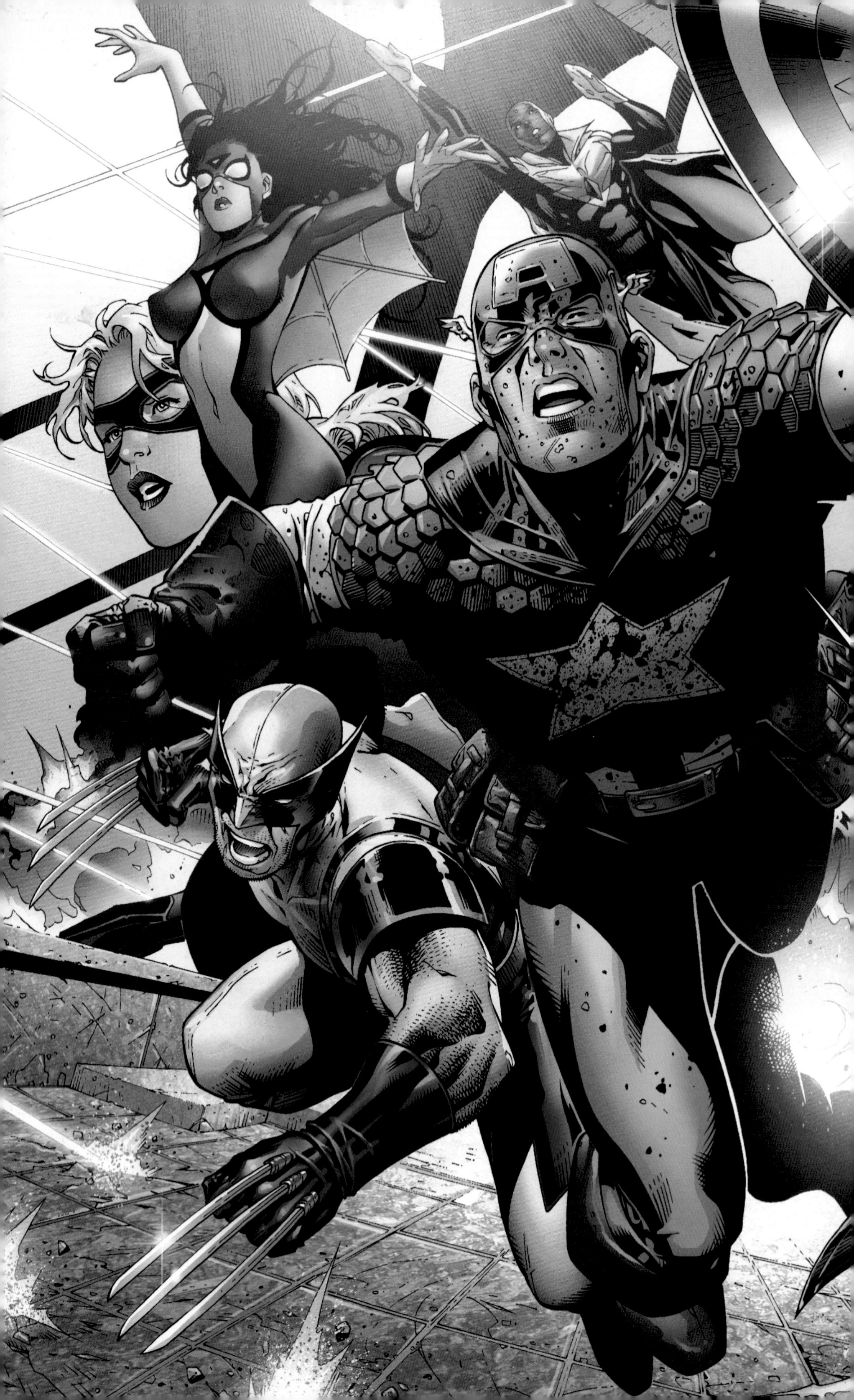

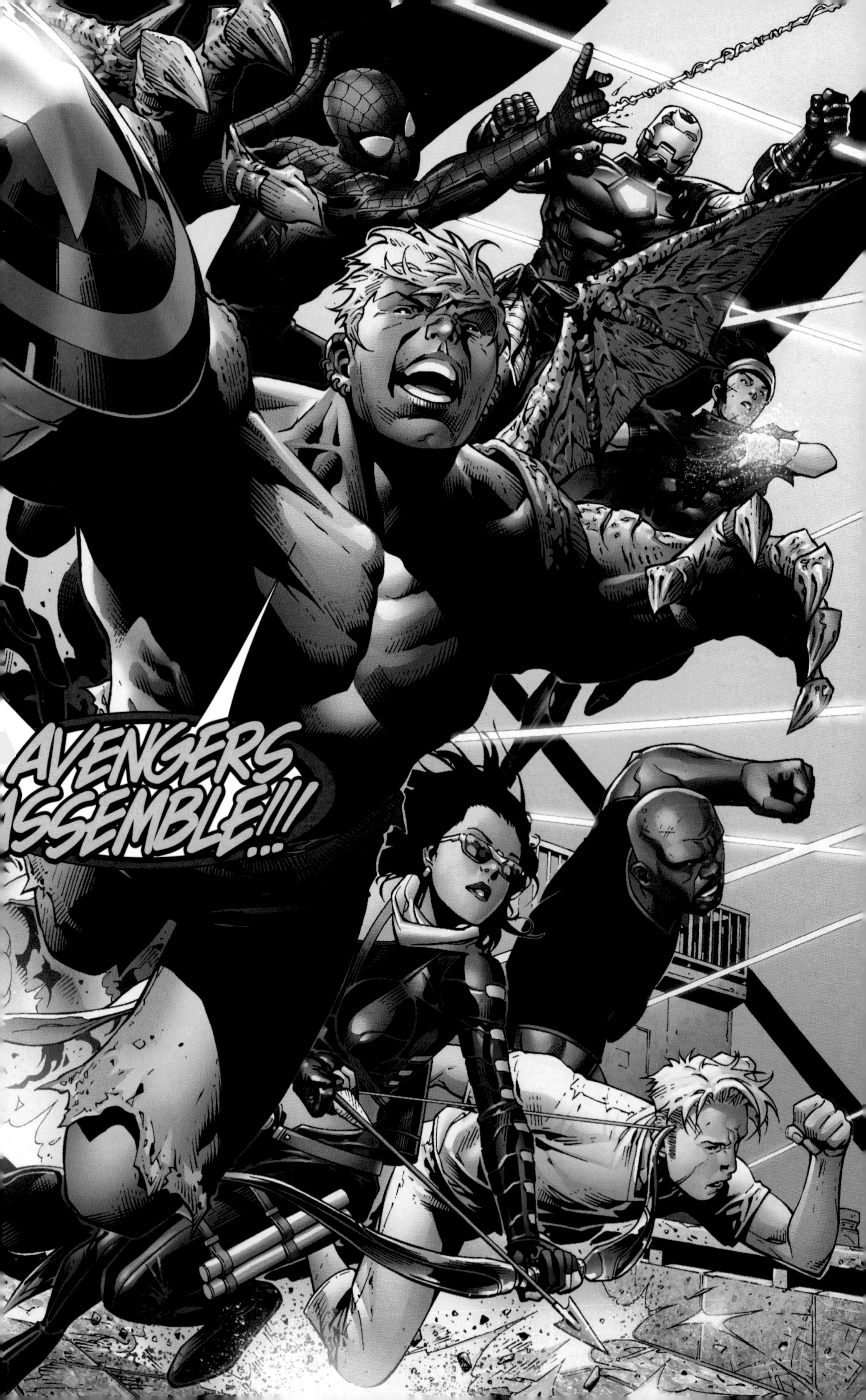
AVENGERS
ASSEMBLE!!!

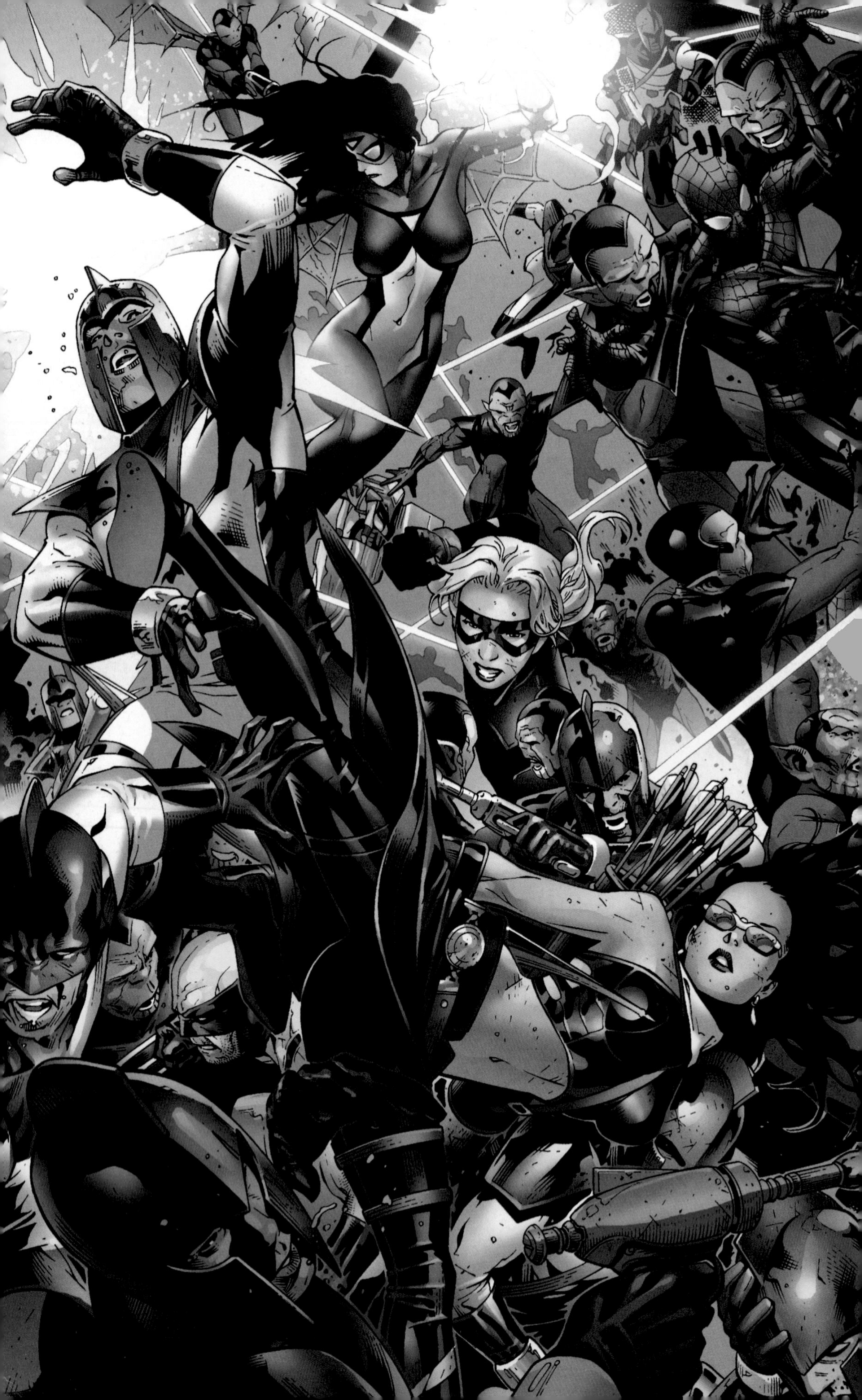

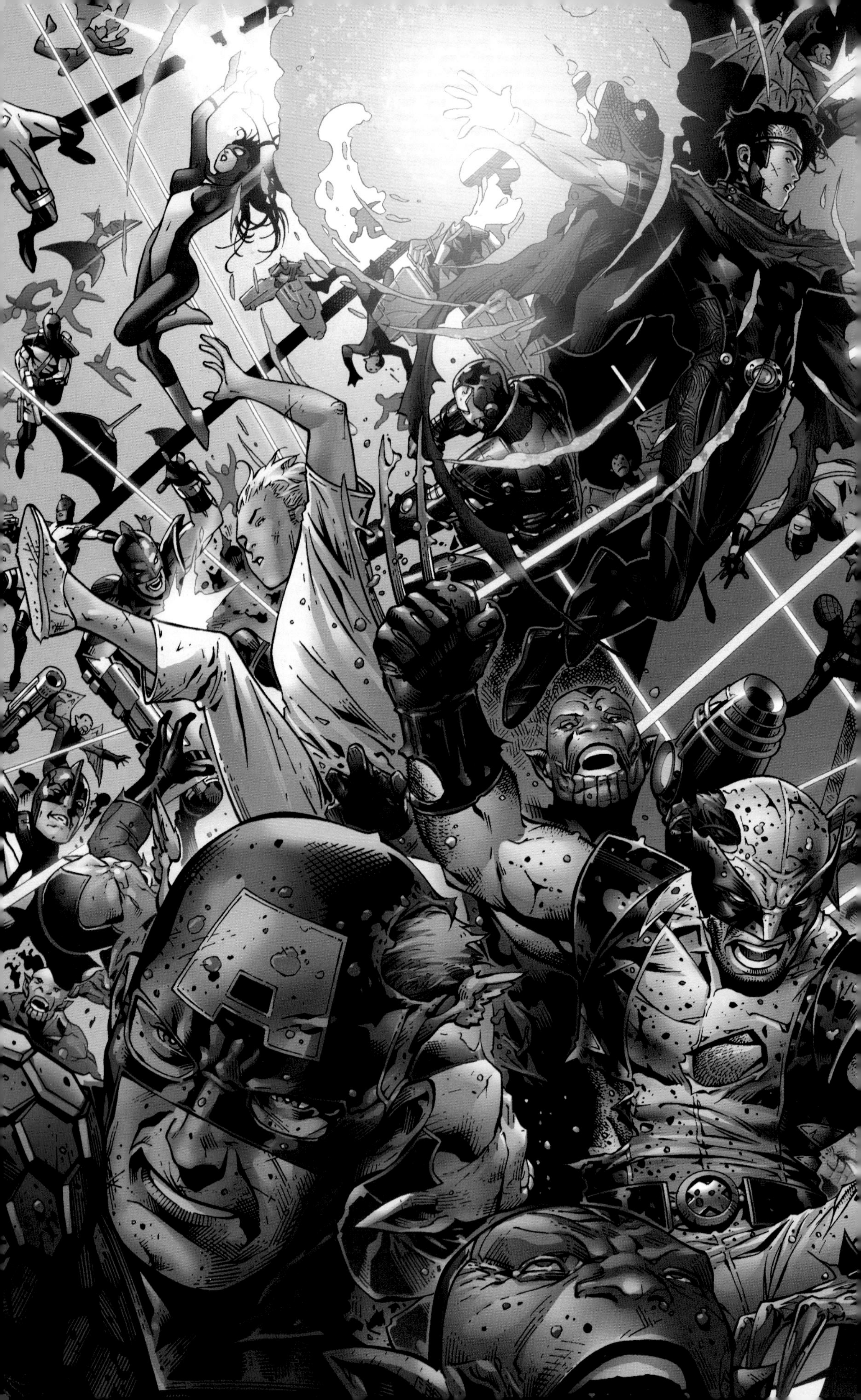

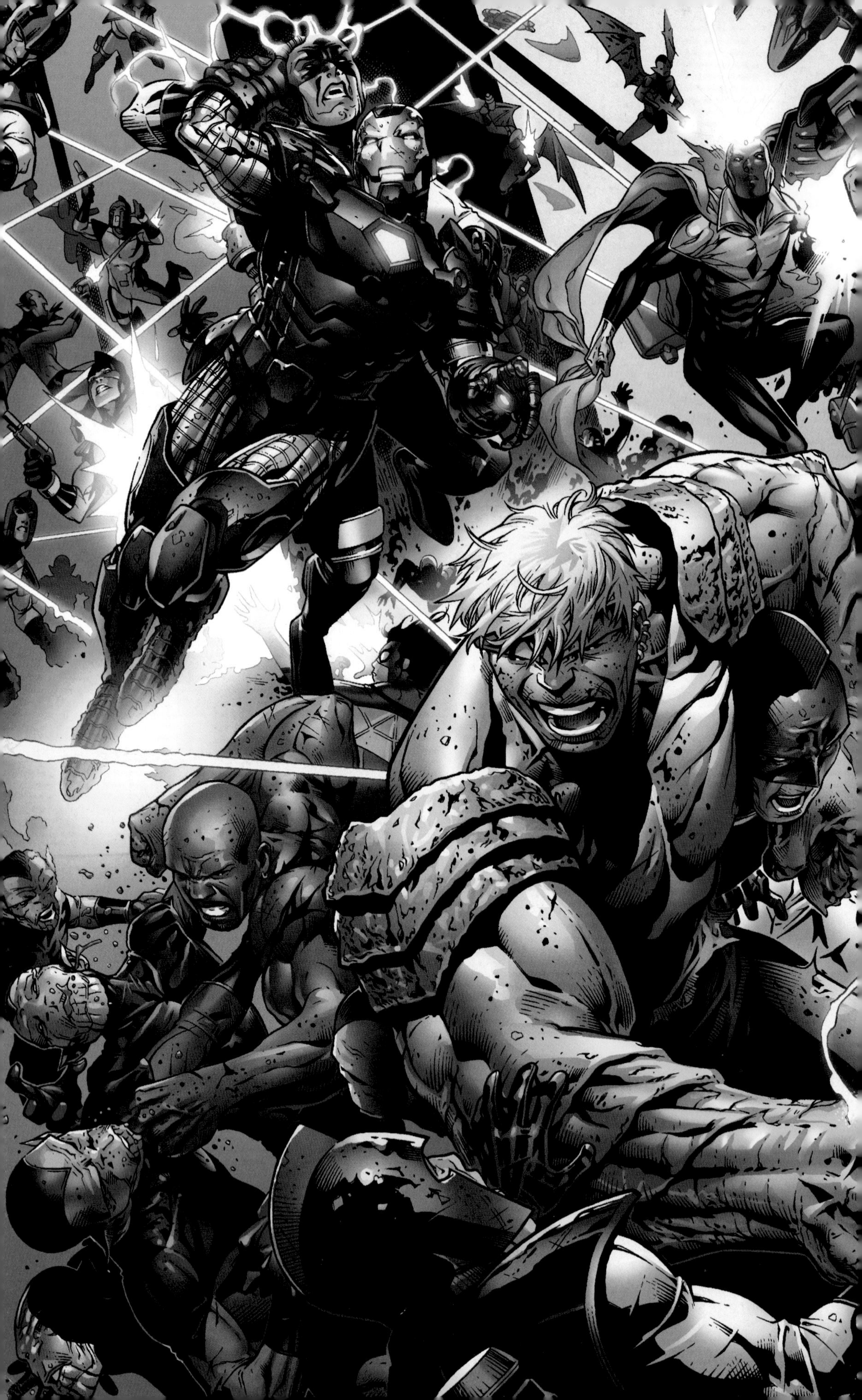

## SPEED DESIGNS BY JIM CHEUNG

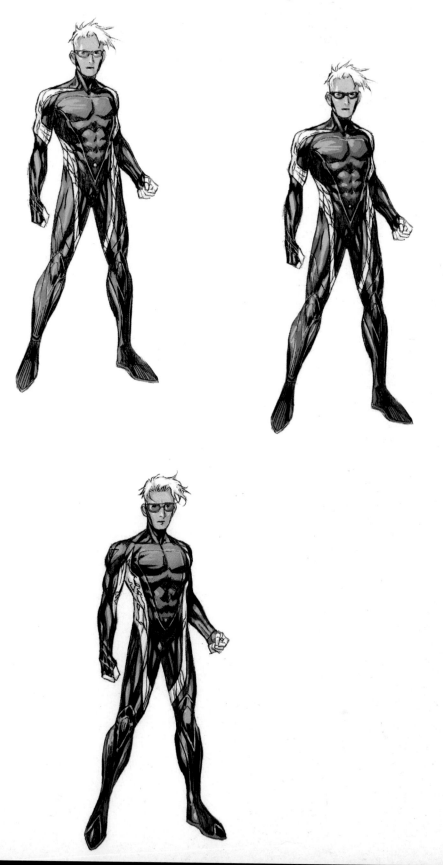